D1031639

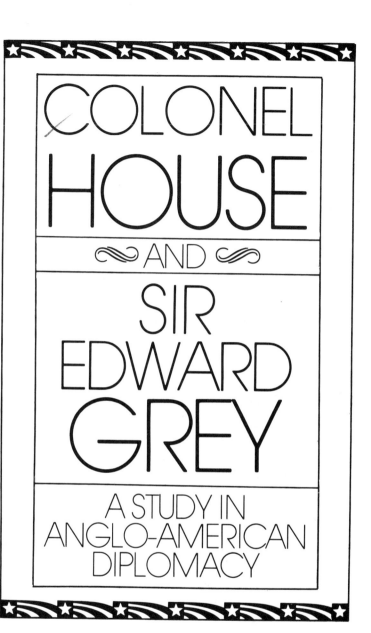

COLONEL HOUSE

∾ AND ∾

SIR EDWARD GREY

A STUDY IN ANGLO-AMERICAN DIPLOMACY

JOYCE GRIGSBY WILLIAMS

UNIVERSITY PRESS OF AMERICA,™ INC.

LANHAM • NEW YORK • LONDON

Library of Congress Cataloging in Publication Data

Williams, Joyce G.
 Colonel House and Sir Edward Grey.

 Bibliography: p.
 Includes index.
  1. World War, 1914-1918—Diplomatic history.
2. House, Edward Mandell, 1858-1938. 3. Grey of
Fallodon, Edward Grey, Viscount, 1862-1933.
4. United States—Foreign relations—1913-1921.
5. Great Britain—Foreign relations—1910-1936.
6. United States—Foreign relations—Great Britain.
7. Great Britain—Foreign relations—United States.
I. Title.

 D610.W44   1984   940.3'2   84-21002
 ISBN 0-8191-4356-1 (alk. paper)
 ISBN 0-8191-4357-X (pbk. : alk. paper)

To my parents
Mildred and Melborn Grigsby
In loving memory
and
To their grandchildren
Cynthia and Tommy

Acknowledgements

Many persons have helped me in various ways to tell the story of Colonel House and Sir Edward Grey. Some helped with the manuscript; others gave me support and encouragement.

For help in the beginning of the beginning, I would like to thank the following professors at Indiana University: Robert H. Ferrell gave me the first encouragement and the necessary inspiration; S. Y. Teng and Arthur R. Hogue provided moral support (more than they know) and Edward H. Buehrig, at all times, gave me the benefit of his knowledge and wisdom about Woodrow Wilson and his era.

Along the way, Professor Irene D. Neu, Professor Henry H. H. Remak, Paul W. Holtzman, M.D., Professor Donald J. Gray and Librarian Michael Parrish provided essential reinforcement through constructive comments about my research, as well as practical suggestions concerning publication.

During this period, I was also helped by the positive attitude of my husband, Edgar G. Williams, who accompanied me to Fallodon where we both felt the fascination of Grey.

I would like to acknowledge my secretary Fern Boruff, whose diligence and enthusiasm in preparation of the manuscript was unusual; William Bishel my research assistant, for his competent and dedicated work in the library, and Cynthia Mahigian for her intelligent assistance.

I wish to express my deepest gratitude to Christopher Graves, great-nephew of Sir Edward Grey, and to the Manuscript Division of the British Museum, for permission to use unpublished materials pertaining to Grey.

In addition, I would like to thank Peter Bridgeman, present owner of Fallodon, for permission to quote comments about Grey made by him and his mother, Joan Bridgeman and for their gracious hospitality extended to me while visiting Fallodon. Milton Gendel permitted me to quote from the letter by Edwin Montagu to Lord Asquith, March 18,

1916, located at the Bodleian Library, Oxford, while C. C. Haines of that institution deserves recognition for facilitating this permission. The Public Record Office in London kindly granted permission to use Crown copyright materials in their possession. This material is documented in the footnotes of the book. My thanks go to the Manuscript Division of the Library of Congress, Washington, D. C., for allowing me to use the unpublished papers of Woodrow Wilson. I also wish to acknowledge the National Archives, Washington, D. C., for use of their material about the House-Grey-Wilson relationship in 1919 and 1920. The Yale University Library allowed me to utilize materials from the Charles Seymour Papers, Edward M. House Papers, and George S. Viereck Papers. Speical mention must be made of Judith A. Schiff, Chief Research Archivist, who was most patient despite my repeated demands on her time. The Houghton Library, Harvard University, granted permission to quote from the David F. Houston manuscripts. Houghton Library also houses the Walter Hines Page Papers, a rich lode of information, and approval from that Library, together with permission graciously granted by Walter Hines Page, II, grandson of Ambassador Page enabled me to use the Page Papers.

I wish to thank Princeton University Press for granting permission to quote from Arthur S. Link, ed., *The Papers of Woodrow Wilson,* vol. 33: April 17-July 21, 1915, copyright 1980 by Princeton University Press, page 124; and vol. 37: May 9-August 7, 1916, copyright 1981 by Princeton University Press, pages 57-58, 113, and 221. Quotes from the *Intimate Papers of Colonel House,* edited by Charles Seymour, copyright 1928 and 1956 by Charles Seymour, were reprinted by permission of Houghton Mifflin Company. Judith W. MacDonald, granddaughter of Ray Stannard Baker, has kindly allowed me to quote from his multi-volume work, *Woodrow Wilson, Life and Letters,* vols, IV, V, and VI.

Contents

Chapter I

A Private Citizen and a Diplomat

The foreign relations of the United States in the twentieth century have been conducted by Presidents and Secretaries of State, and by diplomats in the Department of State, and on occasion they have been conducted by private individuals or, one might say, friends of the Presidents or friends of the Secretaries of State. Such was the case of Colonel Edward M. House, the friend of President Woodrow Wilson. Rarely, however, have the friends of the American Chief Executive developed a close friendship with an official in the foreign office of another country, paralleling in time and nature of interest that relationship with the President. The possibilities for development of a powerful, balanced partnership between the United States and a foreign country through such a concurrent pattern are apparent. So are the possibilities for an unequal partnership, where one of the countries, represented by a determined and manipulative person, could guide the relationship in such a way as to benefit his own nation. These are speculations. But a unique situation did exist during the administration of President Wilson, when Colonel House, the President's confidant and emissary, became the close friend of Sir Edward Grey, Foreign Secretary for Great Britain.

The friendship of House and Grey began in 1913 and continued until Grey's death in 1933, long after he had relinquished his official duties. Conjecture about the results for the history of the two countries because of this association is possible, but one fact requires no speculation. The rapprochement of Great Britain and the United States which had begun at the turn of the century when the growing American economy moved in the British direction was completed following the alliance of the two English-speaking countries during the First World War.[1] It was just prior to the beginning of the war that Sir Edward Grey and Colonel House developed their acquaintanceship into friendship.

House became Wilson's trusted adviser through a series of calculated political moves, beginning in a modest way in Texas and progressing to a point where he possessed the confidence of the President. It would not be unfair to say that the Colonel planned it that way and if this seemed unduly optimistic on the part of House, one has only to look at the lives of many ambitious men whose dreams come true. For in spite of the fact that the Colonel was called self-effacing many times, and was regarded as being totally without ambition (Wilson regarded House this way) he was tremendously ambitious. He chose to carry out his ambitions in a way different from most men because he recognized his limitations—the limits of a man whose personal appearance was not inspiring. House was a small man with an undistinguishable face (although one writer later who perhaps wanted to add to the mystique of the Colonel said that he possessed Mongolian cheekbones). He also lacked that weapon necessary for political popularity in his time—the gift of oratory. He chose to try to become the man behind men in power, the silent and unobtrusive behind-the-scenes adviser.

The background of House is interesting. He came from a moderately wealthy family in Texas; his father's success in banking provided the son with an independent income. This freedom from responsibilities allowed House "to pursue the bent of inclinations."[2] Although he attended several colleges he never graduated. House later said of himself that he was an indifferent student and that "the only thing that held my interest was politics."[3] House married in 1881, and he and his wife soon were entertaining extensively in Austin, bringing together the state's most important political leaders.[4] Cultivation of these individuals gained him the reputation for sagacity regarding political matters, and in 1892, Governor James Hogg, seeking reelection, asked House to become chairman of his campaign committee. Other men served on the committee but it was House who laid out the strategy, directed the forces, and suggested catch-words and tactical dispositions.[5] The victory which followed suggested that House had a winning pattern, and House guided other candidates for the governorship of Texas in the same way—among them Charles A. Culberson, Joseph D. Sayers, and W. H. Lanham. He became friend and adviser to all these governors.[6]

A memorandum in the Public Record Office in London describing Colonel House and his background (presumably for members of the Foreign Office) reported this of his early political record: "It was a peculiar characteristic of his attitude that he never approached any of the politicians, but that they seemed unavoidably forced to approach him and follow out his plans and act on his advice."[7] This statement may have frightened persons in the Foreign Office who at the time it was written—in early 1915—were having to handle the Colonel who was pushing for peace at an awkward time for England. The memo implied that House perhaps possessed magical qualities, and if not these, then a magnetic personality which made it difficult for individuals who worked with him to resist his propositions.

The memorandum overstated House's abilities, but in his early years of prominence in Texas politics, he did develop qualities which worked to his advantage. At a time when the science of psychology was in its academic childhood House liked to think of himself as a student of the psychology of the individual, particularly as men related to politics. What kind of man liked to run for office? Did such a person have the qualities which could ensure election? What kind of man is amenable to advice? How could advice be made acceptable to a strong-willed person? These are questions important to House.[8] And from his study (surely not from magical revelations), he evolved a style of behavior which was so agreeable that politicians did seek his company and advice.[9] He was unfailingly courteous to those political men he wished to impress; he appeared entirely unselfish (and it is true that he never accepted rewards of any kind for services to his patrons); he seemed in almost complete agreement with persons who talked with him. House's mannerisms were somewhat feminine. He made gentle fluttering movements with his hands as he talked. His soft Texas voice punctuated the sentences of his companions with "that's true, that's true." A characteristic pose while in conversation, captured in later years in a statuette by Jo Davidson, showed him sitting back, gazing upward with legs crossed. This somehow gave the listener the impression that the Colonel was absorbed in the subject discussed.[10] In this atmosphere of compatibility House could slip in words of advice. The Colonel was quietly but deliberately manipulative.

Arthur D. H. Smith, who wrote two books and many articles about House and who came to know him well, maintained that one of House's most useful qualities was patience. "[He can] outwait almost anyone in creation . . . and he never moves until he is convinced that to move is the best policy."[11] Such a quality was illustrated by the time the Colonel allowed to lapse between his political activity in Texas and his emergence into national politics. From 1902 until 1911—the era House referred to as his twilight years—he dropped out of the political scene in Texas, and devoted himself to business interests, largely the building of a railroad in his home state. Considering that House keenly wanted to become a leader in national politics, the nine years of waiting do seem the mark of an infinitely patient man. Afterward, in a conversation with George Sylvester Viereck, he explained his behavior. "Bryan kept me out of national politics," he told Viereck, "I could not support him with enthusiasm."[12]

William Jennings Bryan dominated the Democratic party during these years, running for president in 1900 and 1908. House, against free silver, aware that the popularity of Theodore Roosevelt made the likelihood of a Democratic presidency remote, stayed out of national politics until 1910 when it appeared that a split in Republican ranks between Roosevelt and Taft might make election of a Democrat possible in 1912.[13] In a supplement to his diary, written in 1921, House referred to his belief that a president "with the help of two or three men in the Senate and in the House could run the national government." In this interesting entry House intimated that his tremendous ambition could only have been satisfied when he had become adviser to the most powerful individual in the nation—the President of the United States.[14] In 1910 he had come to New York for the purpose of finding a candidate who could win for the Democratic party in 1912, and with whom he could establish the kind of relationship he desired. The person turned out to be Woodrow Wilson.[15]

The president of Princeton University, Dr. Woodrow Wilson, had been elected Governor of New Jersey in the autumn of 1910 after an arresting campaign. Wilson had had no political background; in his post at Princeton he had gained a reputation only as an educator. As Governor of New Jersey, however, he proceeded to sponsor liberal legislation and presented a forceful personality, acting independent of political machines. The cautious Colonel in his candidate-seeking had almost decided to back an established political personality, Mayor William J. Gaynor of New York City, but Gaynor—in the Colonel's words—"proved intractable."[16] House then had begun to study the speeches and writings of the Governor of New Jersey. He had always been aware of the effect of oratory on the public and it may have been that Wilson's truly remarkable ability as a speaker influenced him to pick Wilson.[17] For twelve months the Colonel conspired quietly for Governor Wilson, working through friends made during his Texas campaigns. During this period Wilson learned from associates that the well-to-do Texan was a "good politician" and could help him. House wrote Wilson several letters in 1911 adroitly suggesting ways. In response Wilson proposed that they meet, which they did on the afternoon of November 24, 1911, in the Gotham Hotel in New York City.

Years later House was asked, "How did your friendship with Wilson originate?" He made a terse reply: "I was looking for a candidate for the presidency. Wilson wanted to be president."[18] This over-simplifies the relation which developed between the two men. Wilson, in a much-quoted remark, stated that after their first meeting he felt as if they had known each other always.[19] It may have seemed so to Wilson, for in an amazing fashion their personalities and purposes complemented each other. In spite of his successful career at Princeton and as Governor of New Jersey, Wilson had such a thirst for accomplishment that it could never be assuaged. He needed friends who could reassure him. In the past such friends had appeared only to disappoint him in some way. In 1911 he needed someone to give him confidence, to talk to, someone to whom he could reveal his feelings without fear of censure.[20] House, whose career had been built on the development of intimate associations with political patrons he had sponsored, was looking for the kind of relationship Wilson needed.

If Wilson appeared to be truly naive about the reasons for the success of their friendship, House was not. It is true that after meeting with Wilson, he recorded: "The first hour we spent together proved to each of us that there was a sound basis for a fast friendship."[21] This should not be accepted at face value, for a more realistic attitude toward Wilson appeared in a letter to his brother-in-law, Sidney Mezes: "It is just such a chance as I have always wanted, for never before have I found both the man and the opportunity."[22]

One can imagine with what jubilation—after the conversation at the Gotham Hotel—House proceeded in his political maneuvering to help assure the success of Wilson in winning the Democratic nomination and ultimately the Presidency. The friendship developed rapidly. House became indispensable to Wilson, as a sampling of letters in 1912 indicates:

> On June 9, 1912, Wilson wrote House: "I shall be careful not to act independently in any matter in which I am not perfectly confident."

> On September 11 he wrote: "Your advice is as necessary as it is acceptable."

> On November 7: "I have depended upon your friendship throughout."[23]

After Wilson became President, House refused even to consider a Cabinet post, but chose to help Wilson in an independent capacity, advising him and consulting on matters of importance in every area of government. This political liaison was noted by members of the press, but House kept so quiet about the association that he was referred to as the Texas Sphinx.[24] A witty American once said that [until House] "I have often heard of a man talking himself into fame, and being talked into fame, but I have never heard of a man becoming famous through his silence."[25]

House closed his home in Austin and took an apartment in New York so he could be at hand when the President wished to see him. He did not intrude; it was Wilson who sought House, coming to New York whenever he felt the need for House's company or advice. The Colonel with his knowledge of political minutiae, which the new President professed not to understand, helped Wilson make appointments and develop a legislative program.[26] The Colonel's conduct toward Wilson was manipulative, as in the past with other individuals.

Colonel House surely owed part of his success to ability to remain silent and unobtrusive. This pleased Wilson; to persons outside the government, it also implied that House knew a great deal more than anyone else but preferred not to talk about it. There was indeed a sort of international style of taciturnity at this time. In Great Britain just before 1914 there was a vogue for those who spoke with reserve; statesmen might acquire a reputation for shrewdness and soundness if they moved quietly and said little.[27]

No one profited more from this vogue than Sir Edward Grey, who in Great Britain was His Majesty's Principal Secretary for Foreign Affairs from 1905 until 1916, the individual with whom House was to associate so closely during the World War. Grey's face, with its firm mouth and chiseled features, together with a certain retiring charm in his speech, gave the impression of a man who would show strength in an emergency.[28] Most people found Grey compelling. Unlike House, Grey had not sought political prominence, but he had worked diligently for his country and achieved high office.

Grey liked to refer to himself as country-bred because he had spent his childhood at the family estate of Fallodon in remote and rugged Northumberland.[29] There he developed what became a lifelong interest in fishing and bird watching. Later in life he would write a series of essays on these subjects which were collected in a book called *Fallodon Papers,* a volume whose praise of nature is reminiscent of the more lyrical parts of Thoreau's *Walden.* There can be no doubt that Grey had longed to spend his life as a country gentleman. Yet he spent twenty-five years serving the British Government in different capacities, eleven of them as head of the Foreign Office—a longer service than any other Foreign Secretary. Tradition and duty guided him into political prominence.

Perhaps more than most British families the Greys had stood for political reform, being collaterally related to Earl Grey, the prime minister who had carried the Reform Bill of 1832. Sir Edward's grandfather, Sir George Grey, had served forty years in Commons and was a colleague of Gladstone. His grandson, educated at Winchester and Balliol, had been brought up in a Liberal atmosphere, but displayed scant interest in politics until he found himself successor to his grandfather's estate and title in 1882.[30] Responsibility of an estate of two thousand acres with an honorable name and tradition seems to have changed Sir Edward from an indolent young man to an individual aware of an obligation to his government.[31] In the late nineteenth century the usual entry of a young man of birth and fortune into politics was through a private secretaryship. In the summer of 1884, Grey asked the First Lord of the Admiralty of Gladstone's Cabinet, Lord Northbrook, "for some serious and unpaid employment." With great good luck, or perhaps because of his connections, he first served as secretary to the future Lord Cromer, the Sir Evelyn Baring, British Agent to Egypt, and then became secretary to the Chancellor of the Exchequer, Childers. After a year in these employments, Sir Edward decided it was his duty to run for Parliament from his home region.[32] Elected as a Liberal, he thereafter made infrequent speeches in the House of Commons; he sometimes took an independent stand; but his speeches were always purposeful and showed signs of preparation. As one critic observed, "Sir Edward does not start on long fishing excursions for nothing."[33]

Grey at first had been concerned mostly with home affairs and social reform, but in 1892 the Foreign Secretary, Lord Rosebery, chose him as undersecretary. Rosebery may have made this choice because the two men had characteristics in common: both were idealistic, imaginative, and wealthy; both loved solitude. In the Foreign Office, they worked together in rare harmony.[34]

The Rosebery Government fell in June 1895, and the Unionists under Lord Salisbury and, later, Arthur Balfour, came to power, and Sir Edward and colleagues spent over ten years in the cold shade of the opposition. During this period the Government of Great Britain engaged in the Boer War, a conflict which divided the Liberal Party into two bitterly opposed factions. Grey associated with the so-called Liberal Imperialists led by Asquith and Richard B. Haldane. Because members of the Liberal Party tended to believe that the views of England must be wrong in any international controversy, the Liberal Imperialists ran considerable risks for their careers in alleging that England was right. When the Liberal Party returned to power under Sir Henry Campbell-Bannerman, in December, 1905, it could be said that Grey was out of step with many members of his party. He was to become almost an anomaly.[35]

Campbell-Bannerman in 1905 faced a problem in selecting his Foreign Secretary, and out of that problem came Grey's appointment. Tradition demanded an aristocrat in this position; development of the Party demanded a commoner. Grey, with Reform Bill blood in his veins, with his impeccable background of Winchester and Balliol, satisfied both requirements.[36] Grey had opposed Campbell-Bannerman and when the latter at first asked him to accept the post of Foreign Secretary he declined. The political world was thrown into a temporary confusion, and formation of the Ministry was held up. Asquith and Haldane finally convinced him to accept; Grey assumed office because of a feeling of duty. He wrote to his wife at Fallodon on January 1, 1906: "I am up to my eyes in work and have a settled sadness at being in office."[37]

Within a few weeks Grey suffered tragedy, for his wife, whom he had married in 1885 and who shared with him his love of nature, was killed in a carriage accident. One hesitates to say how much this accident affected his future decisions as Foreign Secretary. Grey's personality, already somber, turned melancholy.[38] Lord Rosebery recorded a pathetic meeting on June 11, 1906: "He lives entirely in the past, describes himself as 'waiting.' Waiting for the door that closed behind her to open for him, hoping it will be soon. His only ease is to immerse himself in the past. His present life is pure mechanical . . . ."[39] Was it perhaps mechanically, in those first months of 1906, that he assumed the foreign policy of his predecessor, Lord Lansdowne?

Whatever the reasoning, Grey as Foreign Secretary accepted his principal legacy from Lansdowne, the Entente with France. His autobiography, published in the mid-1920s, written after the Great War, reveals a rising loyalty to this partnership, an increasing concern lest England should be thought to have acted badly by its neighbor.[40] In 1907 he extended this system of ententes by reaching a similar agreement with Russia. Grey maintained that his European policy was not anti-German but that he wanted this policy to be "independent of Germany." He continued to make efforts to achieve more friendly relations with Germany. Later critics would point out that his efforts in European diplomacy did not avert war. Those who defended him would turn the accusation, to state that he averted war for more than eight years.

A just criticism of Grey in those critical prewar times might be that few people knew what course he was pursuing in the years between 1906 and 1914. This included high-ranking Liberals, for the Boer War cleavage in the party had persisted. Gey did not act without consent of the Prime Ministers (despite Grey's early doubts about Campbell-Bannerman, the two men proved congenial, and Asquith who followed in 1908 had always been in agreement with him), but some members of the

Cabinet did not know about the Anglo-French diplomatic and even military conversations concerning the defense of Europe against possible German aggression which were going on during the prewar years.[41] The British public certainly did not know of Grey's commitments. Members of Parliament could exercise some control over foreign policy by entering into debate with the Foreign Secretary over questionable issues. But Grey proved himself master of Parliament many times, by simply employing his personality to confront and confuse or parry awkward questions.[42]

A myth developed about Sir Edward, and it was the more effective because it was in part true. Here was a lonely, tragic man who devoted himself to his work. He had no ambition, therefore he had only the interest of his country at heart. When he confronted Parliament, which may have desired elucidation about some matter in foreign affairs, it was an uneven match. Picture an attractive man, made more attractive by his grave manner, who did not appear vain or arrogant, who did not seek applause, whose simple answers to questions implied that all possible avenues had been explored, and that the avenue open to the nation had been chosen only after the most serious and soul-searching consideration. Even individuals who opposed him perceived his integrity, and perceiving it often believed in his judgment.[43]

It would be naive to assume that Grey did not know of his effect on his listeners. Lloyd George, one of those Englishmen who least admired Grey, wrote of the effectiveness of his manner of speaking in this way: "He did not command the flaming phrase that illumines but sometimes scorches and leaves behind an irritating burn. On the other hand he possessed to perfection that correctitude of phrase and demeanor which passes for and sometimes is—diplomacy."[44] Another analysis of Grey by a contemporary suggested that the art in his presentations was not that of studied affectation, but of long hours of half-conscious cerebration while in the solitude of fishing.[45] An interesting theory, it seems doubtful in view of the number of instances that Grey practiced his persuasiveness not only upon Parliament and European diplomats but upon Americans who came to England. Grey believed Anglo-American friendship was essential to England, calling it one of the cardinal features of his policy.[46]

His desire to develop good will between the two countries, and his diplomacy toward that goal, was never more apparent than in 1913, the year when the United States moved from an era dedicated to preserving democratic principle in a changing society in the bonhomie Rooseveltian way, to the equally dedicated but more intense period typified by President Woodrow Wilson. This intensification may have indicated that the year 1913 rather than 1900 was for Americans the real beginning of the twentieth century. Problems which had arisen in the late nineteenth century as a result of a difficult New World blending of progress and morality had continued into the first decade of the century, but in 1913 the American people and their new President had a dramatic confrontation with these problems, resolving to meet them in a more positive way.

The United States in 1913 was ready for change, and yet in some ways it was not. A later generation would describe the national mood as ambivalent. From 1870 to 1910 the population had more than doubled, an increase that proved troublesome when accompanied by a dramatic shift in the character of gainful employment; large numbers of workers had been moving from farms into the new urban-industrial centers. The Populism of the 1890s, a kind of agrarian objection to industrial progress, had among its other elements a strong religious basis which implied that God was against material progress and wanted a return to rural virtues. Many gifted Populists harangued the public about the unwelcome change in the American way of life, and placed the devil where he obviously belonged—in the developing great cities.[47]

The new way of life—which many people acknowledged to be progress—brought problems to trouble the American conscience. The Muckrakers, writing with missionary zeal, had sharpened the line between good and evil. Around the turn of the century Americans discovered *How the Other Half Lives,* were outraged by *The Shame of the Cities,* became apprehensive of *The Greatest Trust in the World,* and were alarmed by the frightening aspects of *Wealth Against Commonwealth.* As one of the Eastern reformers who replaced the old leaders from the agrarian areas, Theodore Roosevelt deplored the evil depicted in these exposés—the slums in the cities, loss of competition through growth of trusts and monopolies, and unequal distribution of wealth—but he tempered his desire for reform by a realistic approach. As President he, and his successor William H. Taft, moralized about trusts and monopolies but believed that "regulation, not destruction" was the answer. Roosevelt saw regulation by the government as a way of curbing abuses within industry without losing the advantages of large-scale enterprise. But regulation sometimes seemed to make the trusts stonger, distribution of wealth more inequitable.

Toward the end of the Rooseveltian era there seemed a need for a new catalytic agent. The majority of the American people, who could be termed Progressives, custodians of democracy, culture and moralism, had done their best to make changes within the social structure. Democracy was sound, American institutions were sound, so they believed, but abuses had crept in because of the rapid change in the country; this needed only leadership to be straightened out. American literature, often a register of the national spirit, had been threatened by the novels of Stephen Crane, Frank Norris, and Theodore Dreiser, all of whom had been influenced by the Zola style of decadence and naturalism; but by holding on to the strategic centers of cultural war—the universities, the publishing houses, the influential magazines—Progressives had controlled American literary tastes. Novels of uplift and sentiment, Eleanor Porter's *Pollyanna* and Gene Stratton Porter's *Laddie* were best sellers in 1913. In these and other ways the reformers had tried to ensure morality and idealism in government and society. In the second decade of the twentieth century, as in the first, the Progressives, like their Puritan ancestors, had welcomed the struggle which would accompany the journey to their goal.[48]

With the election of Wilson in 1913 the Progressive Movement reached its zenith. The Populist era had faded into this Progressive Era with a kind of inevitability; the existence of the great cities and their industries had become a *fait accompli.* Wilson, people believed, now would harmonize everything, casting out the bad, ensuring the good. Wilson's public morality, developed through a rigid religious training imposed by his father, a Presbyterian minister, seemed to fit the needs of American society that year. He welcomed a struggle and he spoke the language appropriate to an expectation of a better future.[49] His inaugural address indicated his intent to combine progress with eternal moral values, "to cleanse, to reconsider, to restore." In a triumphant first year the new President's idealism and will appeared to force professional politicians into the tariff and banking reforms for which a generation of activists had been working.[50]

The forces which agitate domestic politics are bound to be reflected internationally; attuned to the attitude of the American public (democracy was, after all, the highest form of government and would some day be the rule of political life everywhere), Wilson prepared to make the American nation a moral arbiter leading more barbarous peoples toward the American light. The custodians of democracy and morality soon found to their delight that their ideals might extend beyond the borders of their country into foreign policy.[51]

Perhaps the nation most affected by this new approach to diplomacy during the Wilson Administration would be Great Britain. Wilson's policy of morality in international affairs was of paramount interest to leaders of the British Empire in those troubled years. The encounters between the two English-speaking nations in 1913 and succeeding years would be many and varied. Sir Edward Grey, whose avowed intention was to cultivate the United States, already had established friendly relations with Roosevelt, through correspondence and personal encounter (the two men took a bird walk when Roosevelt visited England in 1910).[52] He may have hoped to establish a similar friendship with Wilson. As events turned out, Wilson and Grey never became that close, but there did develop a remarkable association between Grey and Wilson's confidant, Colonel House, between His Majesty's Principal Secretary for Foreign Affairs and the closest friend of the President of the United States.[53]

Notes

1.   Bradford Perkins, *The Great Rapproachement: England and the United States, 1895-1914* (New York, 1968), p. 10.

2.   Charles Seymour, ed., *The Intimate Papers of Colonel House* (4 vols., Boston, 1926-1928), I, p. 18.

3.   Recorded conversation between House and George S. Viereck, Oct. 21, 1930, George S. Viereck Papers, Yale University Library.

4.   House's wife was apparently a political asset to him in a social sense, entertaining his friends often, and accompanying him many times on his diplomatic missions. Her opinion on any political matter is never mentioned in House's diary; perhaps she was accurately described by Edith Benham Helm, one of Mrs. Wilson's secretaries, who once said "Mrs. House is always so pretty, so well dressed, and such a bore!" Edith Benham Helm Papers, Library of Congress.

5.   Arthur D. H. Smith, *The Real Colonel House* (New York, 1918), p. 48.

6.   For an in-depth study of House's political friendships with these Texas governors, see Rupert Norval Richardson, *Colonel House: The Texas Years, 1858-1912* (Hardin-Simmons University, Texas, 1964).

7.   Great Britain, Public Record Office, Foreign Office Records, Series 371, 2505/ 1274, February 27, 1915. Hereafter citations from the Foreign Office will read, for example: F.O. 371/2505/1274.

8.   Alexander George and Juliette George, *Woodrow Wilson and Colonel House: A Personality Study* (New York, 1956), pp. 83-85.

9.   Richardson, *Colonel House: The Texas Years,* pp. 304-305. The men whom House aided politically did come to believe in the "magic" of his strategy and influence because of his unfailing success.

10.   Ray Stannard Baker, *Woodrow Wilson: Life and Letters* (8 vols., Graden City, N.Y., 1927-1940), III, p. 296. Hereafter cited as R. S. Baker, *Wilson;* also Douglas Church, "An Intimate Glimpse of Colonel House," March 5, 1933, Edward M. House Papers, Yale University Library.

     Davidson also did a highly acclaimed bust of Wilson in 1916. Davidson wrote to Wilson thanking him for the privilege of sculpting "one of the Great Statesmen that this country has produced." Davidson to Wilson, June 13, 1916, Arthur S. Link, ed., *The Papers of Woodrow Wilson,* (46 vols., Princeton, N. J., 1981), vol. 37: *May 9-August 7, 1916,* p. 221.

11.   A. D. H. Smith, *The Real Colonel House,* p. 68.

12. Recorded House conversations with Viereck, Oct. 21, 1930, George S. Viereck Papers, Yale University Library.

13. George and George, *Woodrow Wilson and Colonel House*, pp. 85-87.

14. Edward M. House Diary (Supplement), Dec. 21, 1921, Edward M. House Papers, Yale University Library.

15. George and George, *Woodrow Wilson and Colonel House*, p. 87; also recorded House conversation with Viereck, Oct. 21, 1930, George S. Viereck Papers, Yale University Library.

16. Recorded House conversation with Viereck, Oct. 21, 1930, George S. Viereck Papers, Yale University Library. Gaynor did not appear in Texas to make a speech as House had wanted him to. Thus, the Colonel regarded him as not suitable material for President.

17. House felt that Wilson's oratory was his primary asset. In a conversation with Charles Seymour on November 2, 1922, House made a list of Wilson's characteristics: "Power of expression" was at the top of the list. Conversations. Charles Seymour and Edward M. House. Nov. 2, 1922, Charles Seymour Papers, Yale University Library.

18. Recorded House conversation with George S. Viereck, Oct. 21, 1930, George S. Viereck Papers, Yale University Library.

19. R. S. Baker, *Wilson*, III, p. 300.

20. The termination of Wilson's friendship with John Grier Hibben at Princeton in 1908 after a difference of opinion in university policy had resulted in Wilson's temporary collapse. His recovery from the loss of this close friend had been slow; House appeared at a time when Wilson needed a new confidant. George and George, *Woodrow Wilson and Colonel House*, pp. 38-39, 128.

21. C. Seymour, *The Intimate Papers of Colonel House*, I, p. 45.

22. November 24, 1911, Edward M. House Papers, Yale University Library.

23. House enumerated these quotations from letters giving dates, in a conversation with Viereck, Oct. 13, 1930, George S. Viereck Papers, Yale University Library.

24. *The Saturday Review of Literature* on March 20, 1926 printed a poem which showed the impression House made:

> Always unquotable
> Wholly ungoatable
> Secretly notable
>
> Silence's Spouse.
>
> Darkly inscrutable
> Quite irrefutable
> Nobly immutable
>
> Edward M. House.

25. Quoted from Mrs. Belloc Lowndes, *A Passing World* (London, 1948), p. 215.

26. House was also adept at maintaining the President's image. For example, following the shooting of Theodore Roosevelt, House advised Wilson to cancel his speeches in order to appear generous and chivalrous. Edward Weinstein, *Woodrow Wilson: A Medical and Psychological Biography* (Princeton, N. J., 1982), p. 267.

27. David Lloyd George, *War Memoirs* (2 vols., London, 1938), I, p. 56; also Robert Rhodes James, *Churchill: A Study in Failure* (New York, 1970), p. 46. Winston

Churchill made many enemies during this period because he spoke flamboyantly and gave the impression he was impetuous.

28. Lloyd George, *War Memoirs*, I, p. 56.

29. Viscount Grey of Fallodon, *Twenty-Five Years: 1892-1916* (2 vols., London, 1925), I, p. xv.

30. George Macaulay Trevelyan, *Grey of Fallodon* (Boston, 1937), pp. 6-9, 25-26. Sir Edward's father died when he was twelve—hence the succession of the estate.

31. Anon., *Sir Edward Grey, K. G.* (London, c. 1915), p. 62. Neither the title page nor the Library of Congress catalog provide the name of the author of this interesting little book, although the latter source gave an approximate date of publication. One might suspect that a close friend of Grey's wrote it because it contains many perceptive observations about his personality.

32. *Sir Edward Grey, K. G.*, p. 78; also Trevelyan, *Grey of Fallodon*, pp. 26-28.

33. *Sir Edward Grey, K. G.*, p. 85.

34. Robert Rhodes James, *Rosebery* (London, 1963), p. 283. Rosebery became Prime Minister in 1894, Lord Kimberly succeding Roseberry as Foreign Secretary. Thus Grey served under two peers in succession.

35. The Earl of Birkenhead, *Contemporary Personalities* (London, 1924), p. 165; also Algernon Cecil, *British Foreign Secretaries, 1807-1916* (London, 1927), p. 320.

36. A. Cecil, *British Foreign Secretaries*, p. 322.

37. Trevelyan, *Grey of Fallodon*, pp. 110-111, 116.

38. For interesting comments about Sir Edward Grey's married life with Dorothy Widdrington see *A Passing World* by Mrs. Belloc Lowndes, an intimate friend of Grey's. According to this author, Edward and Dorothy Grey had what is called in France *un mariage blanc;* nevertheless, Mrs. Lowndes wrote they lived together in great amity and happiness for twenty years.

39. James, *Rosebery*, p. 461. See also Keith Robbins, *Sir Edward Grey* (London, 1971), pp. 152-154.

40. The Algeciras Conference which began in January, 1906 and ended in April made an immediate decision about France imperative. A. Cecil, *British Foreign Secretaries*, p. 322; also Grey, *Twenty-Five Years*, I, pp. 102-105.

41. Trevelyan, *Grey of Fallodon*, pp. 133-134.

42. Those in the Foreign Office felt that diplomacy was a specialist's craft and they were quick to resent interference from outside. Neither Grey nor his subordinates felt compelled to explain or defend their policies. Zara Steiner, "The Foreign Office, 1905-1914," in F. H. Hinsley, ed., *The Foreign Policy of Sir Edward Grey* (London, 1977), p. 66. Hereafter cited as Hinsley, ed., *Sir Edward Grey*.

43. A. Cecil, *British Foreign Secretaries*, p. 354.

44. Lloyd George, *War Memoirs*, I, p. 56.

45. Herbert Sidebotham, *Pillars of the State* (London, 1921), p. 34.

46. Trevelyan, *Grey of Fallodon*, p. 102.

47. Henry F. May, *The End of American Innocence: A Study of the First Years of Our Time, 1912-1917* (New York, 1959), pp. 123-126.

48. H. May, *The End of American Innocence*, pp. 20-22, 48-50.

49.   Edward H. Buehrig, "The Wilsonian Model in Retrospect," unpublished
       manuscript. See also Edward Weinstein, *Woodrow Wilson: A Medical and Psycho-*
       logical Biography. Weinstein writes that Wilson's command of the language
       enabled him to translate feelings of failure and guilt into ideas of moral and social
       uplift.

50.   H. May, *The End of American Innocence*, pp. 355-356.

51.   H. May, *The End of American Innocence*, pp. 356-357; also Buehrig, "The
       Wilsonian Model in Restrospect."

52.   Grey, *Twenty-Five Years*, II, pp. 87-92.

53.   In *Colonel House in Paris*, reprinted in 1980 by Princeton University Press, author
       Inga Floto, whose opinion of House's ability is not always positive, says that House
       was central in the Wilson administration's decisionmaking processes, and that his
       diary of over two thousand pages is one of the most important sources of infor-
       mation on the political history of the period, pp. 18-19.

Chapter II

Acquaintance

The destiny of Mexico would seem to have been an exotic cause for the first confrontation between Colonel House, political adviser to the President of the United States, and Sir Edward Grey, His Majesty's Principal Secretary for Foreign Affairs. It was on this issue, however, that President Wilson had chosen to make his first major effort in foreign policy. Like the early mystic St. Augustine ("with the flash of one glance, my mind arrived at that which is") the President assessed the complex Mexican situation in 1913 and decided to change the flow of events. Also like some mystics, he believed that if a measure or policy were right, it was bound to succeed.[1] The magic properties surrounding moral rightness failed to provide immediate success for Wilson in Mexico, and he looked about for the cause of failure. It soon appeared that the British Government's position was affecting the problem adversely, and so Mexico became the subject of conversation between Grey and House.

Before Wilson's Administration, the attitude of those in the Government of the United States toward the erratic progress of the Mexican nation's struggle for political and social unity had been one of expediency in the name of peace: a recognition of the *de facto* powers in Mexico even though the powers might have emanated from revolution and force. Porfirio Diaz, who had served as president for thirty years, had, extraordinary executive abilities, which partially obscured the fact that he had been one of a long line of strong men who had gained office through a revolutionary movement. In 1911, Diaz was overthrown by Francisco I. Madero, who became president; he in turn lost office when Indian General Victoriano Huerta seized power in 1913, just before Wilson's inauguration. Huerta promised amnesty to Madero, but allowed him to be shot. Since this violent political murder was not unprecedented in a Mexican *coup d'etat*, British Ambassador Stronge and his American counterpart Henry

17

Lane Wilson accepted Huerta's *coup* and Ambassador Wilson urged speedy recognition of Huerta's government by the State Department as the best way to obtain security for American citizens living in Mexico.

President Wilson, however, reacted differently to this political murder. He applied his Christian morality to foreign relations, and on March 13, 1913, announced his policy of withholding recognition of governments established by uncontitutional methods or contrary to the will of the people. He disregarded Ambassador Wilson's advice and looked for counsel from political and journalistic friends, some of whom knew little about Mexico. He sent one friend—ex-Governor Lind of Minnesota—to Mexico to urge a constitutional election. Lind sent back reports of Huerta's brutal character which fanned Wilson's anger. To those familiar with Mexican history, General Huerta might have been just one more in the procession of revolutionary leaders. But President Wilson turned him into an epochal figure—the symbol of unacceptable government.

The British Government had recognized Huerta's regime early in the game. Wilson and his Cabinet, sniffing the air, thought they smelled petroleum. Secretary of the Navy Josephus Daniels wrote in his diary that "it was largely due the English [Oil] Company that England was willing to recognize Mexico before we did." Lind also recorded: "The control and monopoly of the oil fields and oil business in Mexico is . . . the aim of the English Government. England's Mexican policy has been shaped . . . with this sole aim in view."[2] Wilson believed that Britain's materialistic interests were backing Huerta and that this placed an obstacle in the path of democracy in the New World. He also assumed that British recognition of Huerta meant they would fight his policy of nonrecognition. This was not Britain's position, but Wilson's handling of the diplomatic processes stifled understanding. Wilson did not ask for diplomatic advice from the Secretary of State or the State Department. Even if he had sought it, it might have been difficult to find. Because of the overturn in American politics, and accession to power of a party that had not held office for sixteen years, most of the men at the beginning of Wilson's Administration were novices.[3] The Secretary of State, William Jennings Bryan, chosen because of service to the party, had little knowledge of diplomacy. Bryan's critics laughed at the grape juice he served at banquets and receptions (he was following the advice of Wilson who had declared the White House dry five days after inauguration) and also at the Secretary's appearances on the Chautauqua lecture circuit.[4]

Wilson's attitude toward Bryan in the early days of his first term was friendly enough, but he simply did not use him to discover (by a normal diplomatic process) what the British stand in Mexico might have been.[5] Despite British recognition of Huerta, Foreign Secreatry Grey had no desire to suppport any faction in Mexico, and in *Twenty-Five Years* stated: "We had no intention of interfering attempting to influence the situation. All we could do was to wait for the Mexicans to settle their own Government; to appeal to the central authority when there was one in a position to protect long-established and legitimate commercial interests."[6] As for the rumor that these commercial interests were backing Huerta, Grey had professed ignorance and his attitude toward any action by the United States was that the British Government intended to look "passively on with acquiescence in whatever policy the United States thought fit to pursue about Mexico."[7]

There was a formidable issue between the two English-speaking nations which meanwhile became associated in the minds of the British with the Mexican problem—the question of the Panama Canal Tolls. The Clayton-Bulwer Treaty of 1850 between the United States and Great Britain had provided that the two countries would share in building and control of a canal across the Isthmus of Panama. This idea of joint ownership of a canal disturbed members of the State Department, especially in the last half of the nineteenth century. The war with Spain brought new doubts about joint ownership, and in 1901 the American Government persuaded Great Britain to abrogate the treaty of 1850 in favor of the Hay-Pauncefote Treaty which transferred the right of ownership and construction exclusively to the United States. It was stipulated that rules controlling the Canal should be the same for all nations. Despite this agreement, subscribed to by Secretary of State John Hay, Congress in 1912 passed the Panama Canal Act declaring American shipping exempt from tolls. The government of Great Britain protested the exemption as a violation of the treaty of 1901. Anything affecting British shipping touched Great Britain in a sensitive place.[8] Although the sensitivity may have been economic, Grey stated in his autobiography that it was primarily a question of honor.[9]

The American Ambassador in London, Walter Hines Page, perceived the importance of the Panama situation to the British Government. He wrote House a discourse entitled "The Panama Tolls Controversy."

> The English Government and the English people without regard to party—I hear it and feel it everywhere—are of one

mind about this: they think we have acted dishonorably. They
really think so—it isn't any mere political or diplomatic pretense.
We made a bargain, they say, and we have repudiated it. If it
were a mere bluff or game of party contention—that would be
one thing. We could "bull" it through or live it down. But they
look upon it as we look upon the repudiation of a debt by a state.
Whatever the arguments by which the state may excuse itself,
we never feel the same toward it—never quite so safe about it.
They say "You are a wonderful nation and a wonderful people.
We like you. But your Government is not a Government of honor.
Your honorable men do not seem to get control." You can't
measure the damage that this does us. Whatever the United States
may propose till this is fixed and forgotten will be regarded with
a certain hesitancy—they will not fully trust the honor of our
Government.[10]

To Page it seemed essential that in the interests of Anglo-American
friendship the Canal Act of 1912 should be repealed. To this purpose
he also wrote Wilson and the Secretary of State. Page did not know
if his advice was considered; he did not know if some of his letters
were read, for many remained unacknowledged due to Wilson's
indifferent attitude toward the correspondence of his ambassadors.[11]
Page, therefore, was in the dark most of the time as to plans and
opinions in Washington. One of his later letters to Colonel House
registered this complaint: "What in the devil do you suppose does
become of the letters and telegrams that I send from which and about
which I never hear a word . . . I've a great mind someday to send a
dispatch saying that an earthquake has swallowed up the Thames,
that a suffragette has kissed the King and the statue of Cromwell
has made an assualt on the House of Lords."[12]

Wilson and Bryan did not always read Page's letters, but House,
who had suggested Page for the Ambassadorship at the Court of St.
James's, did read those sent to him. And he did undertand the
importance of keeping faith with the British. As early as 1913 he
desired an American political companionship with Great Britain.
He believed that the day of isolation was past, and that when it became
necessary to form a plan for international cooperation America had
better have some kind of understanding with Great Britain.[13]

House in 1913 was entering the most satisfying period of his life—
his influence on Wilson was paramount.[14] Despite the overwhelming
majority in Congress that favored exemption for American shipping,
he persuaded Wilson that the American contention ought not to be
upheld because of the Treaty of 1901. House later recorded their
conversation on this problem: "We discussed the Panama Tolls

question. He expressed himself in favor of their abolition . . . He thought, however, that trouble would be encountered in the Senate, particularly in the opposition of Senator O'Gorman who constantly regards himself as an Irishman contending against England rather than a United States Senator upholding the dignity and welfare of this country."[15]

As minority President, Wilson could not act quickly for repeal because of this anti-British feeling in Congress, but did want to acquaint British officials with his honorable intentions, and to enlist their support for his campaign against the undemocratic Huerta regime. Since he did not use the normal channels of diplomacy, it seemed logical to send House as his executive agent to England to discuss the two current problems between the countries.[16]

Wilson's selection of House as his agent was no novelty in the annals of American foreign relations, not to mention domestic affairs. The use of private persons for confidential business in foreign affairs had begun with the first president, George Washington. Executive agents serving Presidents have gone to practically every country with which the United States has had diplomatic relations. Their tasks have varied; they have gone with much publicity and with every evidence of representing the nation; they have gone secretly and silently, performing duties sometimes known only to the President. In terms of length, variety, and importance of missions, Colonel House was the most important executive agent in American history.[17] This distinction came because Wilson assumed control of foreign relations.[18] Wilson believed that he understood the purposes of American foreign policy better than his subordinates. He chose House to represent him abroad, believing House an extension of himself.[19] Wilson's friend advised on domestic and foreign affairs and was, of course, dependent upon the President's favor for his authority. But House usually represented himself; so independent in thought was the Colonel, in fact, that he did not always feel bound to follow the President's instructions.

While it might be safe to say that Wilson's authority and altruism may have moved the successive missions on which House was sent, as each mission unfolded, House's purpose often became more apparent than the President's.[20] The 1913 mission illustrated this: Wilson sent House on what he considered a mission of honor; House's behavior on the mission was in no way dishonorable, but he did not perfectly represent the President.

Upon House's arrival in London in early July, Ambassador Page wrote a careful note to Sir Edward Grey to acquaint him with this new and influential person from America:

Coburg Hotel

Dear Sir Edward:

There is an American gentleman in London, the like of whom I do not know. Mr. Edward M. House is his name. He is "the silent partner of President Wilson"—that is to say, he is the most trusted political advisor and the nearest friend of the President. He is a private citizen, a man without personal political ambition, a modest, quiet, even shy fellow. He helps to make Cabinets, to shape policies, to select judges and ambassadors and suchlike merely for the pleasure of seeing that these tasks are well done.

He is suffering from over-indulgence in advising and he has come here to rest. I cannot get him far outside his hotel for he cares to see few people. But he is very eager to meet you.

I wonder if you would do me the honor to take luncheon at the Coburg Hotel with me, to meet him either on July 1 or 3, or 5—if you happen to be free. I shall have only you and Mr. House.

Very Sincerely Yours,

Walter Hines Page[21]

House thereupon met Grey for the first time at the small luncheon Page had planned on July 3, 1913—held at Sir Edward's house, 33 Eccleston Square, instead of Page's hotel because Grey said his house was more convenient to the House of Commons and he needed to be within easy reach. As it turned out, there was another guest—Lord Crewe, Secretary for India.

Grey did not mention this meeting in his memoirs, but House looked upon the luncheon of July, 1913, as an important event in his career, and although his diary is not usually chatty, in this instance it is very detailed:

> Our luncheon consisted of a course of lobster afterward mutton cutlets, green peas and potatoes, then ice cream with raspberry sauce, cheese, fruit and coffee. We were waited upon by two maids, no butler being present. The house is a simple one, but exceedingly comfortable and well arranged. He rents it from Winston Churchill . . . .[22]

The conversation, according to House, took up the two vexatious questions—Mexico and the tolls problem. He told the Foreign Secretary that Wilson felt the Panama Act violated the Hay-Pauncefote Treaty and intended to use all his influence to secure its repeal. The matter, House explained, was difficult since Congress must be persuaded to pass a law acknowledging its mistake. This would take time, but he assured the Britisher that it would be done. Grey agreed that the

President's position was difficult and that his government was willing at the moment to allow the matter to rest. Then "while Lord Crewe and Page were discussing the eradication of the hookworm in India and other countries [so recorded House] Sir Edward and I fell to talking of the Mexican situation."[23] House misconstrued Wilson's purposes at this point.[24] "I told him the President did not want to intervene and was giving the different factions every possible opportunity to get together. He wished to know whether the President opposed any particular faction. I thought it was immaterial as far as our government was concerned which faction was in power if order was maintained."[25] Anyone who had been close to Wilson knew of his animosity toward Huerta, but House seemed to have suppressed this aspect of American-Mexican relations, making it appear that the President's purpose was the same as that of the British Government—to see order in Mexico. Grey had no reason to doubt House's interpretation of Wilson's attitude; House was Wilson's representative. From July until October 1913, Grey worked under a misapprehension due to House's faulty reporting.[26]

Confused as to the President's attitude toward Mexico, the Foreign Secretary took a step which made as unpleasant an impression in Washington as had the recognition of Huerta. To succeed Stronge in Mexico he appointed Sir Lionel Carden. From the American viewpoint a more displeasing appointment could scarcely have been made. An economic imperialist, Carden doubtless was sent to protect British oil interests, but he was notoriously anti-American and not notably tactful. He soon made his opinions known. According to an article in the New York *Times* (October 22, 1913) he was reported as saying that President Wilson knew nothing about the Mexican situation, and that Mexico needed punitive and remedial methods of control—which was to say, a strong man like Huerta.[27] The President linked Carden, the British Government, and Huerta in an attempt to defy him. He composed a fiery circular letter which he intended to have sent to the foreign powers involved in Mexico. In it he declared the paramountcy of the United States in Mexico, accused the powers of giving aid to Huerta to keep him going, and said he would bring about Huerta's over-throw.[28] A draft of this circular found its way into the London press and struck British officials like a flash of lightning.[29] The President further alarmed the Foreign Office by having Page inform Grey that he considered the British to have special responsibility in maintaining the Huerta regime.[30] There was no longer doubt about the neutrality of Wilson's position. Despite what House had said, Wilson wanted Huerta out.

Page was rather in the middle of the negotiation. He had been given his first real diplomatic task—to persuade Great Britain to retrace its steps, to withdraw recognition of Huerta and help the United States bring about his downfall. He attempted to do this through a series of talks with Grey, the first of which occurred on October 28, 1913. Straightforward in approach, he told Grey that the United States resented the attitude of the British Government in Mexico.[31] He said that articles in the press criticizing Wilson's views as idealistic were bound to give offense in the United States. He said the whole country backed the President's desire for a democratic government in Mexico, and that the American Government might have to intervene (as it had in Cuba) to get the desired result. This, of course, might prove detrimental to British oil holdings, and in addition there would be "a very critical mood [toward Britain]."[32] Grey formally declared his reaction to the American Ambassador's statements in his *Twenty-Five Years:* "Page saw an ideal in the Mexican policy of President Wilson. I was ready to sympathize with the ideal, and to believe in the moral purpose of the policy; but I did not believe that morally there was much to choose between Huerta and his opponents."[33] A more informal reaction could be obtained from a letter to Spring Rice in which Grey related his interview with Page. Grey wrote that Page seemed to think that if the British withdrew recognition of Huerta, it would result either in his being displaced in Mexico by someone better or else chaos would result, and that either alternative seemed to the Ambassador to be better than the existing state of things. Grey's wry comment was that "it was hardly reasonable that we should take a step to promote chaos."[34]

Despite House's intervention of July, 1913, despite Page's sharp diplomacy, everything then turned out all right. However impractical Grey might have believed Page and Wilson to have been, he did not want "a critical mood" from the United States regarding the Panama Tolls. Free tolls through the canal (which Wilson had promised to sponsor) meant more to British commercial interests than influence with a tottering regime in Mexico. Grey moved quickly to seal off any controversy between the two countries, persuading the Prime Minister to announce in a speech at Guildhall that Britain would neither intervene in Mexico nor do anything else to frustrate American policy. He procured a statement from Carden intimating that he, Carden, had been misquoted in the New York *Times*. He sent his personal secretary, Sir William Tyrrell, to Washington, ostensibly to visit Spring Rice, in reality to sound Wilson's position concerning Mexico and the Panama Tolls.[35] The visit was similar in motive to that of House to England in July. Page, who felt that his effort to change the British attitude had been successful, wrote expansively to House about Sir William's mission:

> He's a good fellow, a thoroughly good fellow, in spite of his monocle; and he's an important man. He, of course, has Sir Edward's complete confidence, but he's also a man on his own account . . . The Lord knows you have far too much to do, but in this juncture I should count it worth your while to pay him some attention. I want him to get the President's ideas about Mexico, good and firm and hard . . . His going gives you and the President and everybody a capital chance to keep our good American-English understanding. I think the chief thing in the way here is their slow density. Sir William will bring straight back to Sir Edward all that he hears and sees—perhaps (I know you will pardon me) you'll have him fall into the right hands in New York and Washington.[36]

House by this time may have felt chagrin at being left out of the maneuvering concerning Mexico, and needed little encouragement from Page to take over this important visitor. With the docking of Tyrrell's ship, the *Imperator,* on November 3, 1913, House wrote in his diary: "He desired to see me before the President."[37] Next day he recorded: "I have gotten in touch with him and he is to dine with us on Thursday and go to the play. Mrs. Wilson is also to be with us. I arranged it in this way in order to bring him in touch with the White House."[38] During the social evening House had a "great deal of quiet conversation with Mrs. Wilson. She was much disturbed over the Mexican situation and urged me to come to Washington at once to better advise the President."[39]

This was the invitation House needed to secure an interview with the President for Sir William. The two men went to Washington and apparently spent the next few days discussing the situation between their two countries. House's diary reveals some of the conversation:

> We talked of the Panama tolls question. Sir William said Sir Edward Grey's idea was that no possible good came to nations if either the letter or the spirit of a treaty was broken. He said that the English people felt deeply upon this subject and no one more so than Sir Edward himself, and the only reason he held office was his desire to promote the peace of Nations.[40]

Following this altruistic talk House arranged for the President to meet Tyrrell:

> "[Wilson] insisted upon my remaining the night at the
> White House. After we had finished our talk about Mexico, he
> read aloud out of Chesterton's "Little Father Brown" detective
> stories. We talked until nearly eleven . . . He went to bed and
> I telephoned Sir William Tyrrell at the British Embassy to come
> to the White House at half-past nine tomorrow . . . . I then went
> to bed in the yellow room."[41]

Grey's secretary and the President met on November 13 for
informal talk. House evidently felt in charge. He saw the meeting
this way: "From half-past nine until half-past ten the President and
Sir William repeated to each other what they said separately to me
and which I had given to each."[42]

Tyrrell sent his version of the encounter in a long dispatch to
Grey marked Private and Personal:

> At the suggestion of Mr. House, who is an intimate friend of
> the President and whom you met last summer, I was sent for
> to the White House where the President gave me his views on
> Mexico for communication to you.
>
> With the opening of the Panama Canal it is becoming in-
> creasingly important that the government of the Central American
> Republics should improve, as they will become more and more
> a field for European and American enterprise: bad government
> may lead to friction and to such incidents as the Venezuelan
> affair under Castro. The President is very anxious to provide
> against such contingencies by insisting that those republics
> should have fairly decent rulers, and that men like Castro and
> Huerta should be barred. With this object in view the President
> made up his mind to teach those countries a lesson by insisting
> on the removal of Huerta . . . he does not propose to examine
> with a microscope what happens in Mexico, as he is under no
> illusion with regard to the capacity of Mexicans for maladmin-
> istration. Huerta however exceeded the limit of what was
> permissible. The President is confident that the Mexican Congress
> could and would elect a President capable of maintaining law
> and order. The President did not seem to realize that his policy
> will lead to a *de facto* American protectorate over the Central
> American Republics . . . It seems to me that we have neither
> the intention nor the power to oppose this policy . . . The Prime
> Minister's speech . . . has created an excellent impression on
> the Administration and the public, and done much to dispel
> the suspicions aroused by the attitude attributed to H. M.
> Minister at Mexico . . . .[43]

Tyrrell suggested "with all diffidence" that Carden's bias for

Huerta should be controlled, and that such action "would be highly appreciated by the President." He followed this by stating:

> As regards Panama Tolls the President volunteered the statement for your personal and confidential information that he is in entire agreement with your view on the subject and that his is determined to overcome the opposition of the Senate which, as he told me, is partly due to the vanity of certain Senators, and partly to the Hibernianism of others. With this object in view he is even prepared to invoke the assistance of Republican Senators.

He closed by saying that the President seemed to like this informal channel of communication and hoped Grey would make use of it if he had any personal views to communicate, "as he apparently did not wish to use the Secretary of State for the purpose."[44]

With this direct information concerning Wilson's policy toward Mexico, Grey set about smoothing the diplomatic path between the two countries. Carden, described by Page as a slowminded, unimaginative, heavy-footed commercial Briton, appeared to be (to change the figure of speech) the fly in the ointment in Mexico, and Tyrrell showed House dispatches from the Foreign Secretary indicating that Carden had been told to reverse policy toward Huerta.[45] Tyrrell underscored Grey's control of the situation when he told John Bassett Moore on November 28 that relations between the two English-speaking countries had improved "in the last two weeks" and the man in charge of the foreign policy of Great Britain was Grey.[46] In December a report came through the Associated Press from London that Carden was to be transferred to Brazil.[47] In the succeeding months Wilson, with advice from House, attempted to persuade the Senate to repeal the Panama Act of 1912 since it was a violation of the Hay-Pauncefote Treaty.[48]

Wilson on March 5, 1914, made good his implicit promise to Tyrrell by going before Congress and asking support. He hinted at a mysterious catastrophe if Congress did not grant the toll-free privilege to Great Britain and, indeed, all countries. "I ask this of you," he said, "in support of the foreign policy of the Administration; I shall not know how to deal with other matters of even greater delicacy and nearer consequence if you do not grant it to me in ungrudging measure."[49]

Congress in June, 1914, repealed the special American exemption from canal tolls. Without British support Huerta fled Mexico in the following month. The golden age of Mexico did not thereafter arrive, and solution of the Mexican problem continued to elude

Wilson for many years, but the tremendous explosion in Europe in August, 1914, temporarily turned his mind from this question.[50]

Reciprocity—though there may have been no formal bargain between the English-speaking nations—marked Wilson's diplomatic ventures in the first year of his Presidency.[51] It is interesting that neither Grey nor Wilson admitted to this. Wilson told correspondents on March 26, 1914, that his phrase about matters of nearer consequence and great delicacy, "a phrase that seems to have puzzled many people," simply referred to Latin American relations in general, and to the fact that the United States meant to honor new treaties entered into with South American republics.[52] To those who suggested that Grey had bargained with the United States Government, the Foreign Secretary replied obliquely by praising Wilson in a speech in the House of Commons on June 29: "The really great satisfactory feature of the view and action taken by the President . . . is that he has not done it to please us specially even in the interests of good relations between the United States and Britain . . . but with the much greater motive and feeling that any government must never when the occasion arises flinch or quail from interpreting treaty rights . . . in a strictly fair spirit."[53]

Grey's biographer of twenty years later, George Macaulay Trevelyan would ignore this talk of idealism and purity of motives. He wrote that Wilson's inexperienced altruism placed the Foreign Secretary in an embarassing position because the British commercial interests in Mexico required a working agreement with the current Mexican dictator. Grey, however, "in recognition of the Monroe Doctrine and in order to keep friends with America" did accede to Wilson's wishes and withdrew English support of Huerta. Trevelyan concluded that because of Grey's actions, the Panama Tolls Bill was repealed. But on the subject of Mexico, Trevelyan's last statement may have been the most telling and important of all:

> The Panama and Mexican affairs had brought Grey, Tyrrell and the British Foreign Office into close and friendly relation with Wilson, House and Page, and had taught them much about America on the very eve of war.[54]

Trevelyan put his finger on the importance of the diplomatic exchanges between America and England in the first year of the Wilson Administration. In so doing he illuminated the importance of the House Mission of 1913. Was this mission successful? Did it clarify the American position toward Mexico? Declaring Wilson's impartiality toward the Mexican factions, House had spoken for himself; his statement that "I thought it was immaterial . . . which faction was in power if order was maintained" meant that *he* thought it immaterial. Grey could not have known this, and the confusion may have prolonged misunderstanding and resulted in the appointment of Carden. It was Page the Ambassador, not House the special agent, who set the record straight about Huerta. The importance of the mission was, as Trevelyan stated, what Grey learned about America on the eve of the war. And in this case America, of course, meant the President and his friend.

From House's visit Grey learned that Wilson was friendly toward England. He learned that House's relation to the President was close. It took Tyrrell's visit to America to clarify House's role. During this visit House changed from an adviser primarily on domestic issues to an adviser on foreign affairs.[55] Tyrrell no doubt was impressed with the Colonel's efficiency in getting him to see the President, and dutifully reported that the President liked informal diplomacy performed by House. It was then that Tyrrell suggested (one can assume he was prompted by Grey) that he and House should continue to work together privately if "anything discloses itself on either side which was important for Grey or the President to know."[56] Grey may well have decided at this point that he and House could have a working arrangement with a goal—strengthening the Anglo-American bond. Where House's sympathy lay, could Wilson's be far behind?

The process of getting acquainted during 1913 operated on both sides. Charmed by Grey at his home in London, later flattered by Tyrrell who told him how grateful Grey was that House arranged the meeting with the President, House felt that Grey approached his ideal of a statesman.[57] Acceptance of House as a diplomat on the same level as himself beguiled the Colonel. Grey's artlessness in discussion of state matters, and evident desire to maintain a friendship with the United States, made other European diplomats appear gauche. On the eve of the war House, impressed by the treatment accorded him through the Foreign Office, unknowingly had pledged Grey his allegiance.

Notes

1. Conversations. Charles Seymour and Edward M. House. January 11, 1924, Charles Seymour Papers, Yale University Library.

2. Reprinted in Perkins, *The Great Rapproachement*, pp. 198-200.

3. R. S. Baker, *Wilson*, IV, p. 25. See also Rachel West, *The Department of State on the Eve of the First World War* (Athens, Georgia, 1978), pp. 38-43.

4. H. May, *The End of American Innocence*, p. 358. Bryan said he needed the money. His talks on such subjects as "The Value of an Ideal" sometimes earned him as much as one thousand dollars for an appearance.

5. William Jennings Bryan Papers, General Correspondence, 1913, Library of Congress. In this collection there are many warm notes to Bryan from the President praising him in general terms.

6. Grey, *Tweny-Five Years*, II, p. 93.

7. F. O. 800/241/1775, Grey to Spring Rice, Oct. 28, 1913.

8. Burton J. Henderick, *The Life and Letters of Walter Hines Page* (3 vols., Garden City, N. Y., 1924-1926), I, p. 241-244. Hereafter cited as Henderick, *Page*.

9. Grey, *Twenty-Five Years*, II, pp. 94-95.

10. Walter Hines Page to E. M. House, undated, 1913 file Walter Hines Page Papers, Houghton Library, Harvard University.

11. House once said that except on rare occasions Wilson did not take his ambassadors seriously. He simply did not think that it mattered what they thought. Recorded conversation between House and George S. Viereck, Oct. 13, 1930, George S. Viereck Papers, Yale University Library.

12. Henderick, *Page*, I, pp. 239-240.

13. C. Seymour, *The Intimate Papers of Colonel House*, I, p. 194.

14. House told Wilson during this year that he enjoyed what he was doing so thoroughly that he was in better health than he had been in twenty years. House Diary, Nov. 29, 1913, Edward M. House Papers, Yale University Library.

15. House Diary, Oct. 16, 1913, Edward M. House Papers, Yale University Library; also C. Seymour, *The Intimate Papers of Colonel House*, I, p. 193.

16. C. Seymour, *The Intimate Papers of Colonel House*, I, pp. 193-194.

17. Henry M. Wriston, *Executive Agents in American Foreign Relations* (Baltimore, 1929), pp. 807, 823-824.

18. Arthur S. Link, *Wilson the Diplomatist: A Look at His Major Foreign Policies* (Baltimore, 1957), p. 22.

19. The President told Dudly Malone: "Mr. House is my second personality. He is my independent self. His thoughts and mine are one." House Diary, Aug. 16, 1913, Edward M. House Papers, Yale University Library.

20. R. S. Baker, *Wilson*, IV, p. 358.

21. Hendrick, *Page*, I, p. 245.

22. House Diary, June 29, 1913 and July 3, 1913, Edward M. House Papers, Yale University Library.

23. C. Seymour, *The Intimate Papers of Colonel House*, I, pp. 194-195; also Hendrick, *Page*, I, p. 246.

24. R. S. Baker, *Wilson*, IV, p. 259.

25. C. Seymour, *The Intimate Papers of Colonel House*, I, p. 195.

26. R. S. Baker, *Wilson*, IV, pp. 258-259.

27. Hendrick, *Page*, I, pp. 196-197; also Perkins, *The Great Rapprochement*, p. 202.

28. A draft of this note is in the William Jennings Bryan Papers, General Correspondence for Sept.-Oct., 1913, Library of Congress. Bryan apparently had more to do with this proposed action of the President than did House, although House certainly knew of Wilson's vehement stand. House to Page, Oct. 22, 1913, Walter Hines Page Papers, Houghton Library, Harvard University. Also Perkins, *The Great Rapproachement,* p. 202.

29. The circular itself was never sent because Counsellor John Bassett Moore of the State Department told Wilson it would be diplomatically unwise. In the Moore Papers, Library of Congress, listed under "Mexican Crisis" several memoranda can be found of conversations on this subject between the President and the Counselor. Moore seemed to be appalled at Wilson's belligerent attitude toward Huerta. For example, Moore recorded incredulously on Oct. 31, 1913, that ". . . the President said he supposed if we declared war, foreign bankers would be prevented from furnishing money to Huerta . . . ."

30. Hendrick, *Page,* I, pp. 183-185.

31. Hendrick, *Page,* I, pp. 183-185. Page used a different approach in his social conversation with other British officials. He told the Prime Minister at a reception that "it was hazardous to prematurely recognize a bandit." Page to W. J. Bryan, Nov. 14, 1913, Walter Hines Page Papers, Houghton Library, Harvard University.

32. F. O. 800/241/1775, Grey to Spring Rice, Oct. 28, 1913.

33. Grey, *Twenty-Five Years,* II, pp. 96-97.

34. F. O. 800/241/1775, Grey to Spring Rice, Oct. 28, 1913. This letter had been sent after Page's talk with Grey on approximately Oct. 24, 1913. The British Ambassador in America, Spring Rice, received a summary from Grey of every conversation the Foreign Secretary had with the American Ambassador. Page once wrote Wilson "if I could be informed correspondingly, I should be greatly helped." Page to Wilson, July 12, 1914, Walter Hines Page Papers, Houghton Library, Harvard University.

35. R. S. Baker, *Wilson,* IV, pp. 287-288; also Perkins, *The Great Rapproachment,* p. 203.

36. Page to House, Oct. 26, 1913, Walter Hines Page Papers, Houghton Library, Harvard University.

37. House Diary, Nov. 3, 1913, Edward M. House Papers, Yale University Library.

38. House Diary, Nov. 4, 1913, Edward M. House Papers, Yale University Library.

39. House Diary, Nov. 6, 1913, Edward M. House Papers, Yale University Library. This is typical of the first Mrs. Wilson's attitude toward House. She encouraged the friendship and believed that the Colonel's advice was very helpful to her husband.

40. House Diary, Nov. 12, 1913, Edward M. House Papers, Yale University Library.

41. Ibid.

42. House Diary, Nov. 14, 1913, Edward M. House Papers, Yale University Library.

43. F. O. 800/241/1775, Sir William Tyrrell to Grey, Nov. 14, 1913.

44. Ibid.

45. House Diary, Nov. 26, 1913, Edward M. House Papers, Yale University Library.

46. John Bassett Moore Papers, "Mexican Crisis," memorandum of conversation with Sir William Tyrrell, Nov. 28, 1913, Library of Congress. See also Zara S. Steiner, *Britain and the Origins of the First World War* (London, 1977), pp. 185-189. Steiner emphasizes that Grey was "all powerful" in the Foreign Office at this time, giving his attention even to matters of secondary concern.

47. Carden's transfer was also announced by Page in a communique to the State Department on Jan. 6, 1914. This communique was published almost verbatim in *The Daily Mail* on Jan. 8, causing a minor diplomatic crisis because Page accused the State Department of releasing information prematurely since the British Government had not yet declared publicly that Carden was being transferred. Page predicted that this would postpone the transfer in order to save face for those involved. As a matter of fact, Carden's transfer to Brazil was held up until April although he returned to London temporarily. State Department files, 701/4112/13, National Archives, Washington, D. C.

48. R. S. Baker, *Wilson*, IV, p. 405.

49. Hendrick, *Page*, I, p. 253; also C. Seymour, *The Intimate Papers of Colonel House*, I, p. 205.

50. Trevelyan, *Grey of Fallodon*, p. 237; also R. S. Baker, *Wilson*, IV, p. 351.

51. This theory is repudiated by William S. Coker in an article entitled "The Panama Canal Tolls Controversy: A Different Perspective," published in the *Journal of American History*, vol. 55, no. 3 (Dec. 1968), pp. 555-564. Coker states: "The argument that President Wilson traded repeal of the objectionable tolls clause in the Panama Canal Act of 1912 for British support of his Mexican policy has been discredited . . . . It is fallacious to assume that the British gave in to Woodrow Wilson's Mexican policy because of his promise to repeal the objectionable tolls or because they were convinced of the merits of his moral crusade there . . . . The evidence indicates that Grey did not agree with Wilson about Mexico, but did not actively oppose him there because the British were more concerned with Europe . . . . After December 1913 the merely adopted a 'hands off' attitude."
It is true that Grey did not agree with Wilson about the need to replace Huerta, but after Tyrrell's report on November 14, Grey asked Carden to reverse his policy toward Huerta, and he later brought Carden home. This was a positive action against Huerta—not a "hands off" policy. Page recorded in his diary on January 5 that the rumored transfer of Carden meant that the British Government had done everything the U.S. had asked for in regard to Mexico (this was one area on which Page was well informed) and that it was then the United States' turn regarding the tolls. Certainly Tyrrell's wording in his dispatch—"the President will be most appreciative if we can do anything to help"—can be interpreted as a promise of reciprocal action.

52. R. S. Baker, *Wilson*, IV, p. 410.

53. Ibid., pp. 420-421.

54. Trevelyan, *Grey of Fallodon*, pp. 236-237. Trevelyan's analysis of Grey's actions and motives certainly have to be taken seriously since he had a long friendship with Grey before writing his biography.

55. Conversations. Charles Seymour and Edward M. House. Dec. 16, 1921, Charles Seymour Papers, Yale University Library. Tyrrell's importance was also clarified: he was more than a private secretary to Sir Edward. Grey discussed questions of

policy with him, and used him as an informal ambassador. Steiner, *Britain and the Origins of the First World War,* p. 185.

56. House Diary, Nov. 26, 1913, Edward M. House Papers, Yale University Library. House commented that he hoped Mr. Bryan did not find out this arrangement— "I am afraid he might be hurt."

57. Ibid.

Chapter III
A Second Mission: 1914

Colonel House of Texas had lunch with the Kaiser at the Imperial Palace in Potsdam on June 1, 1914. The Colonel and Ambassador James J. Gerard were the only nonmilitary guests present. Dressed in somber evening clothes, they looked, so the Kaiser said (perhaps piqued because he had wanted them to wear some sort of court dress), like two black crows against the colorful background. The other guests wore dress uniforms glittering with medals. The palace walls were made of seashells encrusted in the plaster, and glistened—behind the two black crows. [1] House sat next to the Chief of the Imperial General Staff, General von Falkenhayn, who directed the conversation toward military strategy. The luncheon celebrated an ancient military festival, the *Schrippenfest.* As President Wilson's confidential emissary, on his second mission to Europe, the Colonel had been invited to this function because of his military standing—the Kaiser did not understand that the title of Colonel had been bestowed by Governor Hogg of Texas for political, not military favors—this dispite House's explanation, freely offered during the luncheon. The German Ambassador in Washington, Count Johann von Bernstorff, had used the title when he cabled that House wished to visit Berlin on a mission to promote better understanding between Great Britain and Germany. [2] To German officials a mission of such importance had to be handled by a soldier or a diplomat. [3] They presumed that House was a military man.

The idea behind President Wilson's policy toward Europe in June, 1914, was, like many of House's future diplomatic projects, beautiful in its simplicity, magnificent in proportions, but perhaps naive. [4] House intended to meet with the Foreign Ministers of Britain and France, and with the Kaiser, and through discussion persuade them that it was to their best interests to restrict armaments, pledge nonaggression, and direct their energies toward helping second- or third-rate powers. [5] Unlike some of his plans which seemed to have been conceived quickly,

35

often as a result of a chance conversation, this plan developed over a considerable time; it had unfolded throughout 1913 and in the early months of 1914 as House began to discover opportunities to explore his diplomatic ambitions.

Before Wilson had entered the White House—as early as January, 1913, while the Balkan crisis was at its height—House had lunched with Edward S. Martin, the editor of *Life,* and confessed that he was interested in European politics and that it "would be my endeavor to bring about a better understanding between England and Germany."[6] He had spent most of his life in American politics working with the governors of Texas. This had led to his connection with the national Democratic party and friendship with Wilson. But, as he later confided to his biographer, Charles Seymour, his true interest lay in foreign politics.[7] As confidant of the new President the Colonel believed he might be able to indulge this ambition. Like most other individuals in Wilson's entourage, he had no diplomatic experience, but this did not deter him in his pursuit.

The recurrent crises in Europe during the period before the Great War had challenged House's imagination. He had made the visit to England in 1913 to discuss the Mexican problem. His meeting with Grey may have given the impression that foreign ministers were susceptible to persuasion and very reasonable (and Grey *was* reasonable at that time).[8] The Colonel's confidence, based upon his past successes in handling projects on which he had embarked, led him toward the assumption that a situation did not exist which he could not control; he had a plan for every contingency. In the prewar months, bored with Wilson's domestic program, he had turned to the problems in Europe. "The Great Adventure" followed: the 1914 mission, which "grew like a green bay tree" from his thoughts on an understanding between England and Germany.[9]

House had corresponded regularly with the American Ambassador in London, Page; in 1913, their ideas coincided—both men believed in Anglo-American friendship. It was Page's favorite topic in letters and conversation. Page, typically, wrote House that "whatever the United States and Great Britain agree on, the world must do." A compact between the two countries for peace and general disarmament, strengthened by a visit from the President to England, might forestall a European war. "Then we can go about our business for a hundred years . . . ."[10] The proposed visit by the President was not seriously considered by Wilson, but House had become intrigued with an earlier suggestion by Page: "There is a way if we can be so fortunate to find it, to do a great piece of constructive work in the right adjustment of world-forces by using just right this English admiration of our greatness and strength, using it positively, without boast or formal alliances with no artifical force at work, with perfect naturalness." Page had based this idea of an entente between the two countries, whose influence would avert conflicts with other powers, on the old balance of power theory of international politics.[11] One of Page's phrases, used while expounding the theory, may have captured House's imagination: "Work on a world plan. Nothing but blue chips, you know."[12] Probably taking the idea from Page, perhaps thinking it up himself—whatever the inspiration—the Colonel decided to include Germany in a power pact. He believed that Germany and England were unrealistically frightened of each other, and that American influence could help alleviate this fear and channel the energies of all three countries into developing the waste areas of the world.[13] House proposed to advance this scheme through a personal mission to Europe.

What might be described as the Page-House plan had developed through the correspondence of the two men in the latter half of 1913. In November, House believed he had found another enthusiast for the idea, Grey's private secretary, Tyrrell. The latter was engaging and sympathetic, and on the several occasions when House entertained him had managed to promote a feeling of utmost cordiality. He told House that Page's best work had been to bring together House and Grey "for it had been of incalculable service to both our countries."[14] When House approached Tyrrell about a sort of sympathetic alliance between the United States and England, the Britisher was delighted. House said to him that "the next thing I wished to do was to bring about an understanding between France, Germany, England and the United States regarding a reduction of armaments, both military and naval. I said it was an ambitious undertaking, but so worthwhile I intended to try it." House asked Tyrrell's advice on procedure. Tyrrell's suggestions were subtle. The Britisher agreed that House should include Germany. and suggested that if the Colonel intended a mission to Europe he could proceed "quietly and secretly," first to Berlin and there representing himself as "the power behind the throne."[15] These suggestions corresponded with House's idea of himself, and the Colonel agreed with the rest of Tyrrell's ideas: the Kaiser must be informed that England and the United States had "buried the hatchet" and in view of this fact it would be wise for Germany to stop building an extravagant navy and curtail militarism. Tyrrell promised to show House the memoranda that had passed between Britain and Germany on the question of disarmament, to indicate "how entirely right Great Britain had been in her position."[16] During this little talk House appeared to have dropped his altruistic inclusion of the second- and third-class powers, and to have inferred that the United States might join Britain in a stand against German

militarism.[17] Tyrrell could not have represented the position of
Grey and the British Empire more perfectly.

Ten days after this talk, House approached the President with
the details of his mission. Apparently he dwelt on the aspect of checking
armaments through friendly advice to the European governments
on behalf of the President.[18] House recorded: "I was pleased to obtain
his warm approval and cooperation."[19] There is no other documentary
expression of Wilson's attitude, but it is probable that the President
had no intention of committing the United States to any intervention
in European politics—certainly no kind of entente.[20] Wilson had
always repudiated the balance of power theory, and his interests lay
closer to home. His leadership rested on a gift for oratorical persuasion.
He was prepared to take interest in foreign affairs when his voice
could be heard, such as in the Mexican situation when an inspirational
speech to Congress could be effective. House had done his best to
convince the President to be a world figure by taking in the politics
of Europe. This manipulative process added to Wilson's conviction
of the efficacy of informal diplomacy no doubt caused the President
to agree to House's new mission.[21] Wilson nevertheless appeared
reluctant to part with his friend's company for he told the Colonel:
"I am afraid your health will not permit you to go abroad before
spring." The Colonel agreed to postpone the trip until early summer.[22]

House's plans matured during the late winter and early spring.
In January, 1914, he asked Gerard in Berlin to make an appointment
with Kaiser Wilhelm. Gerard advised that the best time would be
early June after the royal family's annual spring holiday in Corfu.
Meanwhile House decided to undertake a study of German psychology,
especially the character of the Kaiser.[23] He interviewed a close friend
of the Imperial family, Benjamin Ide Wheeler, recently returned to
America. Wheeler told him that Theodore Roosevelt and the Kaiser
were much alike in regard to memory and impulsiveness. House then
elaborated this interview in a letter to Page: "I know now the different
Cabinet officials who have his confidence and I know his attitude
toward England, naval armaments, war and world politics in general."[24]
Later he checked the political line-up in Germany with the Counsellor
of the Embassy in London, Irwin Laughlin, formerly of the Embassy
in Berlin. Laughlin secretly deplored House's mission and felt that
the "only thing to do with an Amateur Diplomat is to pass him on to
some other fellow." He passed him to Prince Munster.[25] But several
interviews later the Colonel felt ready to take on the Kaiser. He explained
to the President his preparation for the journey, and Wilson replied,
"The object you have in mind is too important to neglect."[26]

It was not much of a mandate but it was adequate, and so House told Bernstorff he was going to Berlin. Bernstorff meanwhile had done homework and had sent one or possibly two reports to Berlin on the "power behind the throne" and the approaching visit.[27] At last the great day came and on May 16, 1914, the Colonel sailed on the *Imperator* for Germany.

House had kept Page informed, and although Page said he approved the Berlin visit he was thinking more narrowly, in terms of "the tightest sort of alliance, offensive and defensive between all Britain, colonies and all, and the United States."[28] Page already was adopting the British attitude toward Germany which would drive him apart from House and Wilson after the war began. He believed the German Government had embarked on a naval building plan that nothing could stop. He wrote to House that he hoped he was mistaken, but "I do not expect you to produce any visible or immediate results." House, however, had been encouraged by the President and he wanted Page to know that. In a letter to Page, he quoted Wilson in this manner: "Our friend in Washington thinks it is worthwhile for me to go to Germany, and that determines the matter."[29]

The friend may or may not have cared whether House went to Berlin. He was far more interested in House's friendship than in ideas and plans for the mission. House carried a letter from the President acknowledging him as Wilson's spokesman, but the letter was interesting for its omissions:

> My dear friend:
> It is hard to say good-bye, but knowing what I do it is delightful to think of what awaits you on the other side, and it is particularly heartening to me to know that I have such a friend and spokesman.
> Mrs. Wilson and my daughters join with me in most affectionate messages and in the hope that you will find your trip refreshing and stimulating in every way.
>
> Your affectionate and grateful friend,
> Woodrow Wilson[30]

Mr. E. M. House
New York City

The Colonel arrived in Berlin the last week in May, 1914. Gerard and Bernstorff had laid groundwork, and he had long talks with Tirpitz, Falkenhayn, and Jagow, the Minister for Foreign Affairs.[31] Bethmann Hollweg's wife and died, and it was impossible to see the Chancellor, who might have been responsive to his plans. House explained the mission to the other German leaders—first to help ease tension between England and Germany, then to encourage the two European countries to work with the United States for disarmament. The German officials were courteous but cynical. Tirpitz was hostile, but House did not seem to mind. "I was advised to avoid Tirpitz as being very unsympathetic, however, I went directly at hi;m and had a most interesting talk." During this talk Tirpitz denounced England, and "reeking with belligerency" said the English were not to be trusted. He found House's proposal for disarmaments distasteful. He brought up the walled-in condition of Germany, and talked about the vigilant enemies against whom it was necessary to prepare. He disclaimed any desire for conquest and insisted that Germany wanted peace and the way to maintain it was to put fear in the hearts of enemies.[32]

The atmosphere in Berlin impressed House as "militarism run stark mad." He wrote the President that "unless someone acting for you can bring about a different understanding, there is some day to be an awful cataclysm. No one in Europe can do it. There is too much hate, too many jealousies."[33] House felt confident, however, that once he had talked to the Kaiser all would be well. He had insisted on a private conversation with Kaiser Wilhelm—believing that through such discussion he could accomplish more than through diplomatic intermediaries or in the presence of others. He had his opportunity on the day of *Schrippenfest,* for after the luncheon the Kaiser took him to the terrace and the two talked intimately, in sight but out of earshot of the rest of the company.[34]

The Kaiser seemed animated and emphatic, bringing his face close to House's, sometimes using a forefinger to press a point. House found him difficult to interrupt, but willing to listen once the flow of words stopped. House carefully recorded the conversation:

> At first I thought I would never get his Majesty past his hobbies, but finally I drew him to the subject I had come to discuss . . . I found him much less prejudiced and much less belligerent than Tirpitz. He declared he wanted peace because it seemed to be to Germany's interest. Germany had been poor, she was now growing rich, and a few more years of peace would make her so. "She was menaced on every side. The bayonets of Europe were directed at her," and much more of this he gave me. Of England he spoke admiringly, England, and America and Germany were kindered peoples and should draw closer together . . . He spoke of the impossibility of Great Britain being able to make a permanent and satisfactory alliance with either Russia or France. I told him the English were very much concerned over her ever-growing navy, which taken together with his enormous

army constituted a menace . . . I spoke of the community of interests between England, Germany and the United States, and thought if they stood together the peace of the world could be maintained . . . He replied that he must have a large navy in order to protect Germany's commerce in an adequate way . . . He also said it was necessary to have a navy large enough to be able to defend themselves against the combined efforts of Russia and France.

I told him that the President and I thought perhaps an American might be able to better compose the difficulties here and bring about an understanding with a view for peace than any European, because of their dislike and distrust for one another. He agreed to this suggestion. I had undertaken the work and that was my reason for coming to Germany, as I wanted to see him first. After leaving Germany it was my purpose to go directly to England where I should take the matter up with that Government as I had done with him.

I explained that I expected to feel my way cautiously and see what could be accomplished, and if he wished it, I would keep him informed. He asked me to do this and said letters would reach him through our friend Zimmermann here in the Foreign Office."[35]

House then left the terrace and got in the car with Gerard, who remained in the dark about the meeting he had arranged. To his diary House excused the lack of communication: "I was very tired and in no humor to discuss with him what I had done so I touched it lightly and gave him no more than a vague idea of my purpose."[36]

The Colonel seemed to feel that the interview had gone satisfactorily, and that although the Kaiser made no promises he gave sufficient encouragement for House to take up the plan with the British. House wrote Page on June 3:

> I had a satisfactory talk with the Kaiser on Monday, I have now seen everyone worthwhile in Germany except the Chancellor. I am ready now for London. Perhaps you had better prepare the way. The Kaiser knows I am to see them, and I have arranged to keep him in touch with results—if there are any. We must work quickly after I arrive, for it may be advisable for me to return to Germany, and I am counting on sailing for home July 15th or 28th . . . I am eager to see you and tell you what I know.[37]

House was in Paris when he wrote this letter, having left Germany the evening after his interview with the Kaiser.

In Paris he had no opportunity to pursue his plan for international cooperation. There had been three ministries in two weeks, and the public was obsessed with the Caillaux trial, a *crime passionnel* with political implications. The heroine, the wife of former Finance Minister Joseph Caillaux, had shot the editor of *Figaro*, Gaston Calmette, to prevent him from publishing *lettres intimes* by her husband to his mistress. The affair monopolized the nation's curiosity. The British Ambassador, Lord Bertie, wrote that "everybody [is] very nervous," which seems to have been a curious observation. Whatever the state of mind in France, no one wanted to talk foreign policy. House left, feeling there was no government stable enough—or, he might have thought, serious enough—to make a diplomatic conversation worthwhile.[38]

He took the boat train to London, confident of a warm reception in a city where such an affair as Caillaux's *lettres intimes* would have been unthinkable. He had followed Tyrrell's advice in conversation with German officials, and Tyrrell and Page presumably had prepared Sir Edward Grey for a visit. But he found distractions in England too, a civil war threatening over the question of home rule for Ireland, disorderly ladies agitating for suffrage, a struggle between Liberals and Conservatives.[39] The social season was at its height—garden parties and Ascot. Years later House's biographer Charles Seymour would intimate that Grey was unable to see House until a full week after arrival because Grey was caught in the social swing.[40] In truth Grey was not socially minded (he once told House he had dodged Ascot for fifty-two years); a more plausible reason for delay was the domestic and diplomatic problems of June, 1914, too pressing to enable him to see immediately an amateur diplomat with a plan for solving Europe's ills.

Grey had his hands full. England's difficulties and those of countries on the Continent had been accumulating for decades and there was no easy solution. In the latter half of the nineteenth century Britain had continued its traditional detachment from Europe while the new German nation, supported by alliances with Austria-Hungary and Italy, held the center of the stage. Chancellor Otto von Bismarck had declared Germany a satisfied power. For a while he maintained the *status quo* in Central Europe by reassuring Russia that Germany had no territorial ambitions and by isolating France from other continental powers. As the years passed, Bismarck's power weakened and in 1890 Kaiser Wilhelm dismissed him and thereafter the equilibrium among European nations began to change.

Grey had become Foreign Secretary in 1905, accepting the reorientation of foreign policy arranged by his predecessor Lansdowne—the dropping of splendid isolation, an alliance with Japan in 1902 together with the entente with France in 1904. To this policy Grey had brought two special beliefs: England could not afford to lose control of the seas; and the diplomatic independence of France must be maintained to avoid a German hegemony on the Continent. Grey's policy was no mere jealous antagonism to German expansion; he attempted to negotiate an agreement for more German colonies in Africa. But he did hope to gain a diplomatic preponderance for Britain which would help him establish a detente between the two European camps or, better, a restoration of the nineteenth-century European concert.[41]

A revived European concert might have saved Europe. The grand device of general conferences attended by representatives of the major powers which had worked for the welfare of Europe in the first years after Napoleon's defeat had been invoked occasionally after the time of Metternich. The Berlin Conference of 1884-1885 had solved problems of the Congo. The Conference of Algeciras in 1906 had laid the basis for a settlement of the dispute in Morocco. Grey had been responsible for conferences held in London in 1913, attended by ambassadors of six powers, summoned to settle politics in the Balkans. As he later described the conferences of 1913: "When we ceased to meet, the present danger to the peace of Europe was over; the things that we did not settle were not threatening peace; the things that had threatened the relations between the Great Powers in 1912-13 we had deprived of their dangerous features."[42]

At the time of House's arrival in England in 1914, Grey does not seem to have anticipated a European war in the immediate future. Along with Asquith and Lloyd George he had confidence in the German Ambassador in London, Prince Lichnowsky, and in Chancellor von Bethmann Hollweg. These men—personable and peaceful—were regarded as guarantees against a German attack.[43] Other individuals in Britain did feel that war could come at any moment because of what they termed the German Menace. Sir Arthur Nicolson, who assisted Grey in the Foreign Office, thought the German Army and the growing German Navy too large for mere defense, and that a small minority of men in Germany would use these forces to impose the will of their nation.[44] Winston Churchill, as First Lord of the Admiralty, feared that the Triple Entente was not strong enough to discourage the Germans and declared that the Entente entailed "the obligation of an alliance without its advantages, and above all, without its precise definitions."[45] Grey did not want a precise division of power. He wanted the Entente and, at the same time, wanted to preserve relations with the German Chancellor, which might counteract the army and navy clique in Germany. In June, 1914, he was working to reconcile the opposing groups of European powers, engaged in the difficult task of reconciling loyalty to France and Russia with impartiality toward Germany.[46]

A month earlier, as a gesture of friendship within the Entente, officals of the Foreign Office and the Russian government had discussed defensive naval arrangements in the Baltic Sea. Similar conversations had been held with France concerning operations in the Mediterranean. Since these conversations might seem incompatible with the cordiality Grey continued to express toward Germany, he concealed their existence from the German and British publics.[47] During this same period he and his associates proposed that British war ships make a courtesy visit to Kiel.[48] The Germans, however, learned of the Anglo-Russian discussions through an article in the *Tageblatt* headed "A Russian Proposal for Anglo-Russian Naval Understanding." The British Ambassador in Berlin, Edward Goschen, wrote Nicolson that if the article had appeared in the *Post* it might have been propaganda for a "Naval Novelle" but since the *Tageblatt* was usually against naval expenditures it was considered true—and that a visit of a British Squadron to Kiel would be a "passing pageant," poor consolation for advocates of good Anglo-German relations.[49] The article caused a furor in Germany and consternation in England; Parliament asked Grey to explain. His answer on June 11, 1914 was evasive. He did not confess or deny that there had been naval conversations but said there were no engagements with Russia to hamper the freedom of the government and that no such negotiations were in progress.[50]

Although Jagow professed to Goschen, who passed this information to Nicolson, that he was relieved by Grey's statement in the House, the *Tageblatt* reiterated its story, and Lichnowsky asked the Foreign Secretary for clarification on the naval talks.[51] Grey assured him that he did not intend to allow the entente between Britain and Russia to assume an anti-German direction. According to Grey, "the Ambassador cordially endorsed this."[52] The amicable Ambassador departed that same day for the Continent, and left Grey in a diplomatic dilemma—he could hardly explain his foreign policy and, anyway, the British public's attention was on domestic problems, notably the Irish question.[53] During the month of June, Grey had fallen into half-truths and day-to-day expedients.[54]

Small wonder that the American visitor had to wait a week for a luncheon engagement. During House's first meeting with Grey, a great deal of the time passed with the Colonel's description of the interview with the Kaiser. "I suggested that the Kaiser, he and I meet at Kiel in some way; but this was not gone into further . . . . I explained the part we desired to play as pacificators and why I felt we could do this better than they could do it themselves . . . ." At this point House's diary reveals his euphoric feeling: "I have seen the Kaiser, and now the British seem eager to carry on the discussion . . . . Every government in the world may be more or less affected by the moves we are making . . . It is difficult for me to realize that the dream I had last year is beginning to come true."[55]

In his letters to the President at this time House gave only a general idea of his activities, but Wilson did not trouble to ask what was going on. The President wrote the Colonel on June 26, 1914, two days before the assassination of Archduke Franz Ferdinand at Sarajevo: "I hope you are getting a lot of fun and pleasure out of these things, and all my little circle here join me in the warmest messages to both of you. Take care of yourself, and think of me always as your devoted friend."[56]

In a second meeting with Grey, House had been more definite about how to remove the factors that threatened war in Europe: it was the plan which he and Page had worked on—international cooperation with a constructive purpose. He pushed the idea of the three men—Grey, the Kaiser, and himself—getting together at Kiel to discuss the plan. He told Grey: "I thought it essential that the principals should get together." House reported Grey in "a delightful mood," but the Foreign Secretary feared the proposed visit to Kiel would disturb France and Russia; as for the plan, his response was that it should be discussed at a future date, but "a frank and open policy should be pursued between all parties at interest . . . ."[57]

House now had discussed this plan with Page, Bernstorff, Jagow, the Kaiser, and Grey. He decided to let the President know about it. On June 26 he wrote:

> Dear Governor,
>   There is another matter I have taken up, which I hope may have your approval. I have suggested that America, England, France, Germany and the other money-lending and developing nations, have some sort of tentative understanding among themselves for the purpose of establishing some plan by which investors on the one hand may be encouraged to lend money at reasonable rates and to develop, upon favorable terms the waste places of the earth, and on the other hand to bring about conditions by which such loans may be reasonably safe . . . If this can be brought about, it will not only do away with much of the international friction which such things cause, but it will be a step towards bringing about a stable and healthful condition in those countries which are now misgoverned and exploited both at home and abroad.[58]

> Your faithful and devoted,
> E. M. House

No dissenting cable from Wilson reached House in the next few days, and since the latter usually took Wilson's silence to mean consent, he proceeded.[59] By this time Tyrrell, instead of the Foreign Secretary, had begun meeting with House. The two—Tyrrell and House—worked on an elaboration of the plan. Tyrrell kept assuring House of Grey's interest in the project, and conveyed messages from Grey. One message suggested that House write the Kaiser of England's peaceful sentiments since Grey could not write for fear of hurting the sensibilities of France.[60] Page, who felt he had a co-author's interest in House's mission, wrote the President: "I am keeping House's ball rolling (slowly) . . . Haldane and I are to lunch together in a few days. Then a few days later, the Prime Minister is to dine with me—all designed for talk about House's big plan. You can't talk with them except at luncheon or dinner—food with talk everywhere . . . ."[61]

It did appear that British officials were finding ways to slow the discussions. House chafed but could not get a commitment from the British Government. He could not return to Germany without it.[62]

The plan was shattered in the making. House's thoughts on international cooperation took on a futile aspect when the shot at Sarajevo began to reverberate through Europe.

House's Great Adventure had contained many interesting facets. The Colonel had touched the fringes of the European alliances and ententes, of which he was apparently quite uninformed. He was left uninformed by British leaders. In a letter to the President on June 26th, House wrote that he had been told by the British that there was no written agreement between England, France, and Russia, that they were attempting merely to conserve the interests of one another. Anglo-Russian naval negotiations were being discussed by the press, as well as Grey's disingenuous explanation in Parliament on June 11. Although House had arrived in London on June 9 he apparently did not ask enlightenment on this topic. In any event Grey would not have been apt to reveal all to the American when he had been less than frank with Parliament.[63]

House did write the Kaiser, as Grey—through Tyrrell—suggested. He asked that the Kaiser use his influence in behalf of peace, and wrote that "while this communication is, as Your Majesty knows, quite unofficial, yet it is written in sympathy with the wellknown views of the President, and I am given to understand, with the hope from His Britannic Majesty's Government that it may bring a response from Your Majesty which will permit another step forward."[64] The Kaiser did not receive the letter until, far too late for House's appeal, he returned hastily from a Norwegian cruise, late in July, to lend the royal touch to the mobilization precipitated by the Austro-Hungarian note to Serbia. House must not have seen Grey during these crucial days, for he and Page both recorded in their diaries that it was Page who told Grey that House had written the Kaiser. To Wilson and House, Page reported Grey's terse comment concerning House's letter: "Good as far as it goes, and I don't see how he could have gone farther." This somewhat dubious comment evidently pleased the Colonel because Page observed: "House is happy, having sent his letter to the Kaiser and he is now enjoying himself."[65]

Still, it was obvious that House could not go back to Germany; it seemed that he must return to America to report to the President. He left quietly for the United States on July 21. On the eve of his departure Tyrrell brought another message from Grey: "He was sorry he had not seen more of me and it was only on account of the Irish question that kept him from it."[66] That Grey remembered to send a message to House showed him the well-mannered Englishman, for during the last days of July the future of Europe was in the balance. Grey was trying for a conference of the four Great Powers to conciliate the repercussions of the assassination in Bosnia. The conference never materialized; the sullen sequence unfolded. As Grey had feared, each country acted within its alliance.

House did not go home to face perfect understanding from the President, for Wilson, while sympathizing with the general object for peace, had never identified himself with the mission. Until the end of the journey House kept him from knowing the specific objectives. After Wilson was informed there is no record that the President discussed House's proposals with any member of the Cabinet, or party leaders, or officials in the Department of State. The President did not seem to take these proposals, so foreign to American tradition, seriously. His inexperience with diplomacy perhaps kept him from realizing that House as his spokesman had wrongly represented the policy of the President and of the United States Government while he was in Europe. House realized that he was regarded as the articulator of the President's policies, and had used his position for his own purpose—a second demonstration of the unclear relation between the two men, a second beclouding of American foreign policy. It was a relationship of faith without understanding on the part of Wilson. House used the ambiguities in this friendship to carry out his plan for world peace.[67]

When the Colonel reached America he went directly to the North Shore in Massachusetts, and a month passed before he saw the president. Mrs. Wilson died on August 6, and the President was grief-stricken and withdrawn.[68] At the end of August, Wilson went to a summer house in Cornish, and there the Colonel visited him:

> August 30, 1914: I was glad to find the President situated so delightfully. The House reminds one of an English place. The view is superb, and the arrangement and furnishings are comfortable and artistic. The President showed me my room himself. It was the one Mrs. Wilson used to occupy and was next to his, with a common bath between. We are in one wing of the house and quite to ourselves. A small stairway leads down to his study, and it was there that we sat and discussed matters until after one o'clock when lunch was announced. I told him of my experiences in Europe and gave him more of the details of my mission . . . He said it made him heartsick to think how near we had come to averting this great disaster . . I expressed regret that the war did not begin before I left England, as there was a bare possibility I might have done something to have held it up long enough to have brought about a conference.[69]

But what was Grey thinking at this time—if indeed he was thinking about the House Mission? It is now clear that Grey did not have the confidence possessed by House, of believing that one man's action could have averted the World War. Grey possessed a kind of fatalism. In his *Twenty-Five Years* he put his philosophy delicately: "There is in great affairs so much more, as a rule, in the mind of events (if such an expression may be used) than in the minds of the chief actors . . . ."[70] Just prior to the German invasion of Belgium, Grey had told Page that it looked as if Europe were in the clutch of blind forces.[71] With tragedy unfolding before him, he made his moves during the period of House's stay in London in 1914. He made them in a way which he felt would serve Britain's best interests. First things first. If war came he wished England to have allies.[72] He refused to endanger the Entente with France and Russia through such cooperation with Germany as House was seeking. At the same time, he wanted to strengthen the Anglo-American friendship. Thus in the midst of domestic and foreign crisis he gave House what attention he could. When this became impossible he sent his secretary. It is worth noting that no description of House's 1914 visit appears in Grey's memoirs, although House regarded the mission to Europe as a Great Adventure. The Foreign Secretary's finesse was such, however, that although House once complained about the slowness of British officials he did not receive the impression they were uninterested in him or his mission.

What was the effect of the House mission in general? After the Colonel's return, Sir Cecil Spring Rice produced an ingenious theory, that House had come near to making a general war possible, and that this effort alarmed the war party in Berlin and Vienna:

> They probably knew why you were in Berlin, and what you said to the Kaiser. They also knew why you went to England and they undoubtedly knew the contents of your letter to the Kaiser. That, together with Sir Edward Grey's conversations with the German Ambassador in London, alarmed the war party and they took advantage of the Archduke's murder and the Kaiser's absence to precipitate matters . . . believing that it was now or never.[73]

It is arguable, contrariwise, that such a mission at such a moment by a man of the Colonel's temperament could have sparked the very catastrophe he sought to prevent.[74] House's diplomacy in June of 1914 was at best a dangerous business.

Notes

1. "Memoir on Trip to Germany," 1914 file, House Diary, Edward M. House Papers, Yale University Library.

2. Ibid.

3. George Sylvester Veireck, *The Strangest Friendship in History: Woodrow Wilson and Colonel House* (New York, 1932), p. 57.

4. L. J. Maxse, "The Intimacies and Some Indiscretions of Colonel House," *National Review*, 87, (April 1926), p. 26.

5. C. Seymour, *The Intimate Papers of Colonel House*, I, p. 240; also R. S. Baker, *Wilson*, V, p. 28.

6. House Diary, Jan. 22, 1913, Edward M. House Papers, Yale University Library.

7. Conversations. Charles Seymour and Edward M. House. Dec. 16, 1921, Charles Seymour Papers, Yale University Library.

8. House Diary, Nov. 6, 1913, Edward M. House Papers, Yale University Library. House's opinion of government officials was thus expressed: "Before I came in close touch with the head of governments I imagined them made of superior clay. But they are very like the rest of us, neither better nor worse."

9. House was later to refer to this mission as the Great Adventure. House to Page, May 21, 1914, Walter Hines Page Papers, Houghton Library, Harvard University; also R. S. Baker, *Wilson*, V, p. 35.

10. Page to House, Jan. 8, 1914, Walter Hines Page Papers, Houghton Library, Harvard University.

11. R. S. Baker, *Wilson*, V, pp. 30-31.

12. Page to House, Aug. 28, 1913, Walter Hines Page Papers, Houghton Library, Harvard University.

13. C. Seymour, *The Intimate Papers of Colonel House*, I, p. 242; also Perkins, *The Great Rapproachement*, p. 293.

14. House Diary, Dec. 2, 1913, Edward M. House Papers, Yale University Library.

15. House Diary, Dec. 2, 1913, Edward M. House Papers, Yale University Library; also House to Page, Dec. 13, 1913, Walter Hines Page Papers, Houghton Library, Harvard University. Tyrrell may have borrowed this idea from the press, who sometimes referred to the Colonel this way and also as "the man who pulled the strings"; somewhat later he was called "the pleasant and altogether gentlemanly Rasputin of Washington." Press clippings, Edward M. House Papers, Yale University Library.

16. C. Seymour, *The Intimate Papers of Colonel House*, I, pp. 242-243; Hendrick, *Page*, I, pp. 277-278.

17. R. S. Baker, *Wilson*, V, p. 33.

18. Ibid.

19. House Diary, Dec. 12, 1913, Edward M. House Papers, Yale University Library.

20. R. S. Baker, *Wilson*, V, p. 33.

21. George and George, *Woodrow Wilson and Colonel House*, pp. 161-162; also Harley Notter, *The Origins of the Foreign Policy of Woodrow Wilson* (Baltimore, 1937), p. 297.

22. House Diary, Dec. 12, 1913, Edward M. House Papers, Yale University Library.

23. C. Seymour, *The Intimate Papers of Colonel House*, I, p. 244.

24. House to Page, Jan. 4, 1914, Walter Hines Page Papers, Houghton Library, Harvard University.

25. Maxse, "The Intimacies and Some Indiscretions of Colonel House," p. 296.

26. House Diary, April 28, 1914, Edward M. House Papers, Yale University Library.

27. C. Seymour, *The Intimate Papers of Colonel House*, I, p. 247. House wrote Page as early as January 19, 1914 that Bernstorff had been tipped off "that it would be well to cultivate me . . . . I am lunching with [him] Saturday." Walter Hines Page Papers, Houghton Library, Harvard University.

28. Page to House, Jan. 2, 1914, Walter Hines Page Papers, Houghton Library, Harvard University.

29. Hendrick, *Page*, I, pp. 286-287; House to Page, April 20, 1914, Walter Hines Page Papers, Houghton Library, Harvard University.

30. R. S. Baker, *Wilson*, V, p. 37.

31. House complained to Wilson that Gerard had arranged for him to see more than he wanted to. C. Seymour, *The Intimate Papers of Colonel House*, I, p. 249. Gerard, however, was working in the dark since he did not know the purpose of House's visit. House to Page, Feb. 26, 1914, Walter Hines Page Papers, Houghton Library, Harvard University.

32. "Memoir on Trip to Germany," 1914 file, House Diary, Edward M. House Papers, Yale University Library; also House to Page, May 28, 1914, Walter Hines Page Papers, Houghton Library, Harvard University.

33. C. Seymour, *The Intimate Papers of Colonel House*, I, p. 249.

34. Ibid., p. 257.

35. "Memoir on Trip to Germany," 1914 file, House Diary, Edward M. House Papers, Yale University Library.

36. House Diary, June 1, 1914, Edward M. House Papers, Yale University Library.

37. House to Page, June 3, 1914, Walter Hines Page Papers, Houghton Library, Harvard University.

38. Lady Algernon Gordon Lennox, ed., *The Diary of Lord Bertie of Thame, 1914-1918* (2 vols., London, 1924), I, pp. 1-2; also Hendrick, *Page,* I, p. 297.

39. Hendrick, *Page,* I, pp. 297-299.

40. C. Seymour, *The Intimate Papers of Colonel House,* I, p. 259.

41. Trevelyan, *Grey of Fallodon,* pp. 251-253, 269-272. According to Prince Lichnowsky, German Ambassador to Great Britain, Grey may have wished to divert German strength from Western Europe to Africa, but, in general, Lichnowsky considered Grey's action as a gesture of goodwill toward Germany.

42. Grey, *Twenty-Five Years,* I, p. 272.

43. Hendrick, *Page,* I, p. 298.

44. Harold Nicolson, *Sir Arthur Nicolson, Bart., First Lord Carnock: A Study in the Old Diplomacy* (London, 1930), p. 330.

45. Trevelyan, *Grey of Fallodon,* p. 247.

46. Lord William Strang, *Britain in World Affairs; The Fluctuations in Power and Influence from Henry VIII to Elizabeth II* (New York, 1961), p. 266.

47. A. Cecil, *British Foreign Secretaries,* p. 333.

48. F. O. 800/374/1803, Sir Arthur Nicolson, miscellaneous correspondence, 1914, Nicolson to E. Goschen, May 25, 1914.

49. F. O. 800/374/1803, E. Goschen to Nicolson, May 23, 1914. The *Tageblatt* reportedly picked up the story in Paris when the King of England visited the French capital in April. Grey, on one of his rare visits to the continent had accompanied King George.

50. Trevelyan, *Grey of Fallodon,* p. 274.

51. F. O. 800/374/1803, Goschen to Nicolson, June 20, 1914.

52. Grey, *Twenty-Five Years,* I, pp. 303-304.

53. Nicolson wrote Lord Hardinge on June 11, 1914, that the country was split into armed camps primarily over the Irish question, and the Government had to stand by "watching the clouds gathering." F. O. 800/374/1803.

54. H. Nicolson, *Sir Arthur Nicolson, Bart.,* p. 332.

55. House Diary, June 17, 1914, Edward M. House Papers, Yale University Library. The last two sentences are transposed.

56. R. S. Baker, *Wilson,* V, p. 42.

57. House Diary, June 24, 1914, Edward M. House Papers, Yale University Library; also C. Seymour, *The Intimate Papers of Colonel House,* I, p. 263.

58. For complete text of letter see C. Seymour, *The Intimate Papers of Colonel House,* I, pp. 264-265.

59. Ray Stannard Baker, Wilson's biographer, has concluded from a later letter sent to the President from House that the one dated June 26 was not sent for several days, therefore, Baker explained, "if the President knew nothing of the plan, how can he have approved it by silence or otherwise." R. S. Baker, *Wilson,* V, p. 44.

60. House Diary, July 3, 1914, Edward M. House Papers, Yale University Library.

61.   Page to Wilson, July 5, 1914, Walter Hines Page Papers, Houghton Library, Harvard University.

62.   C. Seymour, *The Intimate Papers of Colonel House*, I, pp. 267-271. House did want quick action on his plan, but in the meantime he was enjoying himself thoroughly. He "felt very much at home in London now," and he filled his days with social engagements.

63.   R. S. Baker, *Wilson*, V, pp. 46-47.

64.   C. Seymour, *The Intimate Papers of Colonel House*, I, pp. 273-274.

65.   House Diary, July 11, 1914, Edward M. House Papers, Yale University Library; Page to Wilson, July 12, 1914, Walter Hines Page Papers, Houghton Library, Harvard University.

66.   House Diary, July 20, 1914, Edward M. House Papers, Yale University Library. This decision to suspend House's talks with British officials was made by his confreres in London. One gets the feeling that Grey gracefully eased him out of the country.

67.   R. S. Baker, *Wilson*, V, pp. 42, 49-50. Wilson wrote to House in June when he was in England" [Your letters] sustain the energies in me." Wilson to House, June 26, 1914, Edward M. House Papers, Yale University Library.

68.   Wilson felt the need to see House, but simply could not get away from family and official business. A poignant letter from Wilson to his friend written on August 18 read: "I simply must see you soon and am thinking every day how to manage it." Ray Stannard Baker Papers, Letters of Wilson to House, Series I, 1911-1920, Library of Congress.

69.   House Diary, Aug. 30, 1914, Edward M. House Papers, Yale University Library.

70.   Grey, *Twenty-Five Years*, I, p. 51.

71.   Page to Bryan, July 31, 1914, Walter Hines Page Papers, Houghton Library, Harvard University.

72.   Trevelyan, *Grey of Fallodon*, p. 229.

73.   C. Seymour, *The Intimate Papers of Colonel House*, I, pp. 280-281.

74.   Maxse, "The Intimacies and Some Indiscretions of Colonel House," p. 297.

Chapter IV

The 1915 Mission

The *Lusitania,* queen of the Atlantic, approached the Irish coast on February 5, 1915, on the last leg of her trip home. As she did so, the Captain ran up the American flag. Only a few hours earlier the German Admiralty had announced its intention to begin unrestricted submarine warfare within waters surrounding the British Isles, and the *Lusitania's* captain was taking all precautions.[1] This *ruse de guerre*—displaying a neutral's flag—was a legitimate maneuver, but its use showed questionable judgment at a time when Great Britain had no desire to provoke the United States. One of the passengers on board was President Wilson's personal envoy, Colonel House, about to begin a diplomatic mission with a two-fold purpose: to have conversations with Sir Edward Grey concerning Anglo-American issues of neutral rights, and to discuss with representatives of the major belligerents the possibility of mediation of the European War.[2]

Since the beginning of the war in August of the preceding year, Wilson's major activity in foreign policy had been to promote peace and safeguard American trade rights.[3] The German Government had announced adherence to the Declaration of London in its maritime warfare, and had kept that promise until February, 1915, so the Administration's early trade problems had been with Great Britain. The British Government had refused to accept the Declaration in entirety and in an Order of Council of August 20, 1914, made some major modifications which enabled the Royal Navy to retain some control over neutral shipping.[4] Grey explained later that distrust of German promises made it necessary for Britain to take a modified stand toward the Declaration: "to bind ourselves by rules we intend to keep and others intend to break is unreasonable so long as those who can break them can do so with impunity."[5] The strength of the British Navy made possible this position. The Government began an intensive campaign to keep any material which could have been converted to war use from entering Germany. According to international law, a blockade would have meant an armed encirclement of the approaches to German harbors. Since this was not feasible the British Navy treated the whole North Sea as a blockaded area, seizing and searching for German harbors. However, instead of searching at the point of interception, neutral vessels were taken to Allied-controlled ports for a time-consuming search. For the neutral shipper this caused hardship. The chief neutral shipper was the United States and most of its cargoes went to the British Isles, but ships with cargoes for the Central Powers soon found themseles under control of the British Navy. During the autumn and winter of 1914-15 Secretary of State Bryan and Counselor of the State Department Robert Lansing kept up a running protest against this British control. This diplomacy was conducted, of course, through Ambassador Page, whose British sympathies caused him to resist the protests and at times to suppress them.[6] He revealed his attitude in a letter to House in November in which he wrote that "Sir Edward Grey values American friendship more than anything else that kind . . . he is not going to endanger it . . . . To this day he hasn't confiscated a single American cargo."[7] The Navy did not need to confiscate; the British used delay, which served to keep material out of Germany. For the most part the American protests were cordial and Grey was anxious to keep the situation that way. He sometimes sent secret messages to the President through Spring Rice assuring Wilson that "we wish in all our conduct of the war to do nothing which will be a cause of complaint or dispute as regards the United States Government." On one such occasion Wilson asked Spring Rice to express to Grey, also secretly, his most sincere sympathy for the British cause.[8] At this time the President did not want to make a serious issue over Britain's maritime warfare because economic and political aspects of American policy overlapped. And at the base of this policy was a preference for the Allied cause.[9]

British supremacy on the seas with all its implications of controlling a vast non-European area was the premise of Germany's quarrel with Great Britain. The United States saw no threat to its interests in Britain's predominant position; the prospect of Germany supplanting British power on the seas did, in fact, appear more of a threat. Fortunately, the bulk of American trade was with Britain and the economic and political factors reinforced each other. Wartime trade could be indulged without running counter to the Administration's underlying judgment regarding political consequences of the war.[10] Wilson did not have to make a change in policy. He could proclaim neutrality with all sincerity, for he perceived neutrality as a way of getting along with the belligerents and as being ready to help both sides when the struggle was over. His request to his countrymen to "act and speak in the true spirit of neutrality which is the spirit of impartiality and fairness and friendliness to all concerned" could be made comfortably in 1914 because there was no serious damage to American interests in British control of the seas.[11]

In the autumn of 1914 the Germans had made the world aware of the submarine, and this novel weapon eventually would undo Wilson's hope for a legal neutrality. The first sinking of British cruisers by this silent deliverer of death was reported September 23; thereafter engagements took place frequently. The British were no longer to enjoy undisputed naval supremacy; the war was spreading upon the sea. Neutrality did not remain the simple ideal Wilson wanted. It became difficult for the United States to give even acquiescence to the British system without impairing relations with Germany.[12] To the President, it appeared that only a speedy end to the conflict afforded an escape from a steadily increasing American entanglement in the controversies of Europe. This solution satisfied his hope for America, and in his annual message in December, 1914, Wilson spoke of this hope: "The great tasks and duties of peace are the chief challenge to our best powers demanding the finest gifts of constructive wisdom we possess."[13]

Wilson shared his desire for peace with Secretary Bryan and in the first months of the war the President let Bryan have a free hand in pursuit of peace. Bryan's most notable effort was the "Straus move." The former ambassador to Turkey, Oscar Straus, had relayed to Bryan a statement by Ambassador Bernstorff in Washington that his government stood ready to consider a peace proposal. With Wilson's permission, Bryan communicated with American representatives in Berlin, London, and Paris to check out the feeling toward mediation. The effort failed because it started from a false premise; Bernstorff had made his statement independently, without instructions from Berlin. The curt denials abroad made Bryan look ridiculous.[14] Colonel House told the President that Bryan had mismanaged that situation—direct and open proposals would not work. Perhaps, the Colonel said, he could accomplish something himself by a private negotiation.[15]

House probably convinced Wilson that Bryan's actions had been unwise, for the President sent a telegram to House on September 19: "Think there can be no harm in your going on."[16] At this pint Wilson's dependence on Bryan as a negotiator ceased, and Colonel House became director of America's mediation effort.[17]

House already had begun a series of secret conversations with the Ambassadors of the belligerents—lunching with one, dining with another. He had confided to his diary on September 5, 1914: "I am dining tonight to meet Ambassador Dumba. I am laying plans to make myself persona grata to all the nations involved in this European war so that my services may be utilized to advantage and without objection in the event a proper opportunity arrives. I have been assiduously working to this end ever since the war broke out. I do not believe in leaving things to chance."[18] These conversations he duly reported to the President, but concealed them from Bryan "for fear they would offend him." House also feared Bryan's influence upon the President, and unconsciously revealed his feeling toward the Secretary in a letter to Page: "I have counselled the President to remain quiet for the moment and [referring to his talks with the Ambassadors] let matters unfold themselves further . . . . I do not think there is any danger of anyone on the outside injecting himself into it unless Mr. Bryan does something on his own initiative."[19] Clearly he considered the Secretary of State an outsider.

The content of the American mediation proposal changed when the President began to rely on House rather than Bryan. The latter, truly neutral, believed in direct and open communication with the belligerents; his hope was that the American government could bring moderation into such proceedings.[20] House, however, believed that a German victory would be a threat to the United States, and mediation should not occur until Germany was sufficiently beaten to consent to a change in military policy. It is difficult to know if Wilson accepted House's views. The President was moved by an ambition to mediate which may have been without precise form. He relied on House to advance and make explicit this vague desire for peace. And so at this time—the late months of 1914—House's policies became, at least for the time being, the policies of the United States.[21]

In the private conversations between House and the ambassadors, House had proposed the he take a trip to Europe to discuss peace with belligerent statesmen. He had great confidence, and despite the failure of the 1914 mission believed that through a series of conferences he still could shape Europe's destiny. Bernstorff told him privately that the German government would encourage mediation. On one occasion House talked about his peace mission with the ambassadors of all three major Allies—Russian Ambassador Boris Bakhmetieff, French Ambassador Jules Jusserand, and the British Ambassador Sir Cecil Spring Rice. The Russian Ambassador, Bakhmetieff, described this discussion in a dispatch to Petersburg, and since this is one of the few documents paralleling House's diary it is interesting to compare the two records of the same meeting.[22] Bakhmetieff wrote:

> We remarked to him [House] that a proposal to end the war through a restoration of the "status quo ante" with no reparation or guarantee, could hardly be taken under consideration, for it would only give Germany a breathing spell in which to recover from the unsuccessful war and prepare for a new one. Thereupon House replied very naively, he hopes to obtain a promise from the Chancellor that Germany will give up her militarism, and thus the danger of a new conflict with her will be entirely removed. Here we reminded him, if Bethmann-Hollweg has called treaties scraps of paper—how much trust can be put in his words, if he conveys them through a third and unofficial and personally unanswerable individual? He appeared embarrassed and assented to all we said; finally he explained it to be his mission at the desire of the President to become acquainted with "the true feeling of Germany" . . . . I finally declared to him that if Germany really wants peace, she knows the way by which she can attain it—through a direct approach to the allied powers, and not through private talks and empty promises."[23]

This was blunt and discouraging talk, but House did not become dismayed. He recorded:

> It was rather awkward at first. Both Jusserand and Bakhmetieff were violent in their denunciation of the Germans and evinced a total lack of belief in their sincerity. They thought my mission would be entirely fruitless.
>
> Later, I brought them around to the view that at least it would be well worth while to find how utterly unreliable and treacherous the Germans were, by exposing their false pretense of peace to the world. That suited them better and it was not a great while before we were all making merry and they were offering me every facility to meet the heads of their Governments . . . [Jusserand and Bahkmetieff were] somewhat sensitive about my going to London and Berlin, each thought Petrograd and Paris should also be visited. I agreed to this, but made a mental reservation that it would be late in the spring before I got as far as Russia.[24]

A possible interpretation of the discrepancy between the two recollections would be that House was not always trustworthy as an interpreter of the moods and thoughts of other people. The words "I brought them around" appear frequently in the House diaries and must be judiciously appraised as his hopeful opinion.

Sir Edward Grey had first been informed of House's intent to mediate in a letter of September 22, 1914, from Spring Rice, who wrote that House had informed him he had consulted the President and that they "fully understood and admired our policy." House intimated that a move toward peace by the Allies would solidify this sympathy for the British.[25] Thereafter, the Ambassador's communications to Grey contained not only references to American objections to the British blockade, but references to the desire of "the President's friend" (both Spring Rice and Grey began to refer to House in this way) to visit Europe for the purpose of mediation.[26] Probably Grey thought a visit from House would put more pressure on the British to alleviate the blockade. He made no definite answer to House's proposal. In his letters to Page, House complained about the lack of British action in the matter of peace parleys. Page ambiguously wrote back that he saw "no sign that anybody in Washington understands the war . . . . Come over and find out."[27]

The Colonel had made up his mind to do that. Through Spring Rice he ascertained that "the Belgian point" (evacuation and compensation) was the minimum requirement for peace as far as Grey was concerned, and after a conversation with Bernstorff, he sent a message to Grey through Spring Rice that the German Ambassador had told him in clear terms that his Government would agree to evacuation and compensation.[28] One evening in late December, 1914, the British Ambassador sent word that he would like to see House in the morning "about a matter of importance." House did not wait until morning (a trip in the middle of the night was one of House's favorite maneuvers) and he was rewarded with some encouragement from Spring Rice who said that, concerning peace proposals, Grey did not think it would be a good thing for the Allies to stand out against a proposal which embraced indemnity to Belgium.[29] With this tenuous British approval, House went to the White House to tell the President that he had encouraging news. House recorded the President as "much elated . . . . He said he needed me on two continents."[30]

The two friends conferred again at the White House on January 12, 1915. House's diary is explicit about this meeting:

> I went into the President's study and in a few minutes he came in. We had exactly twelve minutes before dinner, and during those twelve minutes it was decided that I should go to Europe on January 30. I had practically decided before I came in that this was necessary . . . I was certain when I gave my thoughts to the President he would agree that it was the best thing to do . . . I thought we had done all we could do with the ambassadors at Washington, and that we were travelling in a circle. It was now time to deal directly with the principals . . . .[31]

An air of secrecy surrounded this mission of 1915 which House encouraged. It was so secret that Wilson himself did not know on what basis House proposed to mediate; the President did have a list of code words for messages between the Colonel and himself. House was to be known as "Beverly," Page as "Yucca," Sir Edward Grey as "White," and the Kaiser as "Dante." To compound the mystery, House took two personal letters as credentials from the President. An excerpt from one reveals the mission as Wilson saw it: "It gives me peculiar pleasure to give you my commission to go as my personal representative, on the mission you are now so generously undertaking, a mission fraught with so many great possibilities, and which may, in the kind Providence of God, prove the means of opening a way to peace." In the second letter—to be shown to those individuals who had to be told something, but not the truth—Wilson authorized House to make a study of opportunities for relief of suffering in Europe with a view to coordinating America's humanitarian efforts.[32]

There was a leave-taking between House and the President full of affection. The President's eyes were moist as they parted. On January 30, 1915, House sailed away on the fated *Lusitania* surrounded by the aura of mystery he had created.[33]

Sir Edward Grey, wearied by the war (Page thought he had aged a year each month, and had a "Lincoln look"), had rightly feared House's mission as a threat to Anglo-American relations.[34] Earlier he had welcomed mediation talks, and not been offended by Bryan's proposal as had the French foreign minister and the Tsar. He had told Page in September, 1914, that he hoped the United States could devise some way of ending the war. But Britain's situation changed. Peace terms had grown more complex. The Allies were talking of dividing up German and Austrian possessions, of sharing Germany's colonies, of the size of reparation payments. It seemed essential to have Rumania and Greece on the Allied side; Italy's help was needed; to attain the support of these countries there had to be promises of spoils. Grey could no longer state that his country's terms were simply reparations for Belgium and disarmament.[35]

There was also friction between London and Paris. The reported jest in France that Germany would fight to the last German, and England to the last Frenchman, revealed that the French Government felt Britain was not carrying its share of responsibility. Any encouragement to the United States might make it seem as if England were deserting the Allies.[36]

One increasingly difficult problem existed—the blockade, the taking of ships into harbor for search. Grey felt that any talk of peace would be complicated by the hostile American attitude toward British infractions of neutral law. He had analyzed the situation correctly as far as it concerned the American President's feelings. Wilson had approved House's mission because he wanted some solution to the controversy with the Allies over neutral rights. This was as important to him as was the desire to bring mediation. He hoped that somehow his two purposes could be accomplished at the same time.[37]

House's proposed visit had thus caused Grey much anguish. Two letters to Spring Rice on January 2, 1915, and January 18 reveal how complicated he felt the British predicament to be. While he said he would "gladly see the President's friend and talk freely to him" he knew he had to convince the American government of British interest in peace while maintaining an unswerving attitude toward the necessity of a blockade; he had to assure England's Allies of opposition to an unsatisfactory and premature peace; he had to convince Germany that a reasonable offer would be considered.[38] This meant that talks with House would have to be artful, and certainly would not be free.

House's visit was entirely different from the anticipations of Grey. The two men had met before, and proved compatible, but Grey took nothing for granted. They were meeting for the first time since the war began, and a situation of stress existed between their countries. Grey had worried unnecessarily. House soon revealed that his attitude toward wartime problems was not necessarily that of the State Department or the President; instead of finding him an antagonist in a bout over mediation, Grey found him resolved to preserve Anglo-American friendship.[39] As for House's reaction to their first meeting on February 7, 1915 (it lasted three and one-half hours), his diary showed his enthusiastic response: "Grey answered questions with the utmost candor telling me the whole story as he would to a member of his own Government. It was an extraordinary conversation and I feel complimented beyond measure that he has such confidence in my discretion and integrity."[40]

It was Grey's custom to put in a long day at the Foreign Office, arriving at seven in the morning, and returning home to 33 Eccleston Square about seven in the evening. He rested for an hour before dinner, and it was at this time that House came whenever he, the Colonel, wanted to talk. House wrote of these conversations: "We talked of nature, solitude, Wordsworth . . . we sat by the fire in the library facing each other, discussing every phase of the situation with a single mind and purpose."[41] Grey was at his best in fireside

chats. No one could appear more charmingly confidential. He explained
the bars to mediation—the need for luring Greece, Rumania and Italy
into the Allied camp; he explained the necessity of the blockade.
One can imagine him deploring some British actions, but since this
was the way the world worked, it had to be done. Grey could talk
engagingly about sin without taint of sin himself, yet give the suggestion
that human weakness was not alien to him.[42] He fortified House's
pro-Ally feelings.

Soon Grey was able to notify the Allies that there was no danger
of mediation. He relayed this information to the French Foreign
Minister in person, and telegraphed Petersburg: "Colonel House
does not intend to mediate, but wishes merely to obtain information
about the prospects for peace."[43]

House had arrived in London on February 6, 1915, and there
seemed at that time a desire on the part of the German Government
to discuss peace. In early February, Gerard had written the President
that there was a disposition to accept a reasonable peace.[44] He advised
peace terms be sent to the Embassy in Berlin "verbally and secretly."
It was necessary to do this immediately for "this peace matter was
a question almost of hours." If the government decided to use the
submarine in retaliation to the British blockade, as it threatened to do,
"once begun, a feeling will arise which may make it [peace] impossible
until after another phase of war."[45] A note from Undersecretary
Zimmermann of the Foreign Office to Colonel House in London
on February 12 stated that House's visit to Berlin would be welcome
and that the German Government was ready to do its share to bring
the desired termination of the war.[46]

House showed Zimmermann's letter to Grey, who spoke seriously
of a rumored German attempt to envelop Russian armies in the East;
Grey said "he did not think it was wise for him to undertake a peace
mission to Germany until after this enveloping movement had either
succeeded or failed."[47] House agreed to this peculiar reasoning (why
wait until Germany succeeded?) and wrote Wilson of his desire to delay
the visit to Berlin.

In Washington the President was not feeling the Grey magic,
and convinced by Gerard's messages he sent House a code telegram
urging an immediate trip. "Success is dependent upon immediate
action."[48] House replied that although Gerard also had expressed
urgency, "Asquith and Grey thought it would be footless for me
to go to Berlin until the present German enveloping movement
in the east is determined . . . . It looks bad for the Russians; and they
do not want me to be in Berlin at such a time."[49] This strangely worded

communication invoked a tart response from Wilson on February 20: "It will, of course, occur to you that you cannot go too far in allowing the English Government to determine when it is best to go to Germany because they naturally desire to await some time when they have the advantage because of events in the field or elsewhere."[50] This statement did not appeal to the President's envoy caught up as he was in a leisurely discussion with Grey about how to guarantee world peace after the war.[51] House knew of the President's interest in permanent peace and may have thought he was accomplishing much by staying in England.

The Colonel had discovered Grey's intense interest in postwar international security through a league of nations, and began to fill in the President about this interesting subject. Grey may have been dreaming of a substitute for the Concert of Europe, with the addition of a powerful ally across the sea.[52] At the onset of the talk about a postwar organization House avoided an American commitment by suggesting two peace conferences: the first among the belligerents, to discuss peace terms, and the second including all nations for discussion of the principles of conduct of civilized welfare if a similar war occurred in the future. Wilson had been informed of these House-Grey discussions and encouraged them as "the right foundation . . . and spirit of your mission."[53] House had replied to Wilson's caustic comment on undue British influence by directing attention to this area about which he knew there was agreement. He appealed to Wilson's ambition: "The one, sane, big figure here is Sir Edward Grey; and the chances are all in favor of his being the dominant personality when the final settlement comes . . . He speaks of that second convention which the President may call. He has come to look upon it as one of the hopes for the future and, if we accomplish nothing else, you will be able to do the most important world's work within sight."[54]

At this point, the President, influenced by this letter but over-burdened with problems at home, seems to have turned his mind from House's activities. His cables were approving. His immediate answer was: ". . . I am, of course, content to be guided by your judgement as to each step."[55]

House continued to stay in England, meeting frequently with Grey. His diary contains a lyrical description of one session: "We dropped all discussion of politics and war and went into dream land. We talked of the country and of the wildness of the Northerland Shore, of beautiful sunsets and of the delicious quiet that comes at dusk. I told him how I missed being in Texas this winter, of the long rides

I took in the hills, where oftentimes I cooked my evening meal at a campfire returning home in the starlight . . . I think it must have been a long while since either of us had laid bare his inmost thoughts freely."[56]

Following one conference which apparently was about politics (by this time House had been in England a month) the Colonel wrote the President: "We both think the time has come for me to go to Germany."[57] The preceding day House had received a letter from Gerard different from those received in February. The letter of early March stated: "I see no prospect of peace now . . . The Chancellor is not boss . . . Von Tirpitz and Falkenhayn (Chief of Staff) have more influence . . . I hope you are coming soon or if you are going to Italy, I will run down to report to you there . . . ."[58] Grey had seen House's correspondence from Gerard and Zimmermann, and no doubt saw this letter, too. It must have been clear that there was little danger of the German Government agreeing to mediation. He encouraged House to go; he also gave House advice on how to talk to M. Delcassé, the Minister of Foreign Affairs, since House would be going to Germany via France. Delcassé, Grey told him, was decidedly of the opinion that it was no time for peace parleys. House should be "guarded in what he said." House assured Grey that "he need have to fear of his being indiscreet."[59]

Grey also attempted to control the situation from the French side, and cabled Bertie in Paris that House's visit was imminent—that it would be wise for Delcassé to see House since he is "a close friend of the President of the United States," and "in view of the delicate situation with the United States respecting Anglo-French reprisals on German commerce in neutral vessels." Grey assured Bertie that Delcassé would not find the interview embarrassing since House "does not suggest mediation or press any proposal."[60]

With more instruction from Grey than from Wilson, the peace emissary prepared to leave for the Continent in the second week of March, 1915. Referring to this portion of House's mission, Wilson had written on March 8: "This is just a message of personal greeting and to express the hope that the journey you are about to undertake may be accomplished without untoward adventure and in perfect health. You may manage all the rest. I have no anxiety about it."[61] There was not much help here, but the Colonel did not need much. His answer to Wilson was, "Just a last word to say that I leave everything here in admirable shape. It could not be better."[62] Presumably things would go as well in Germany, and on this note House left England.

The Colonel's first stop was Paris, and he had a discouraging conversation with Delcassé whose briefing by Grey through Bertie did not make him agreeable. The Foreign Minister did not speak of the noble peace terms House had discussed with Grey. There was talk of territorial acquisitions. House's attitude appeared to be that the French did not understand the purpose of his visit, and he went on to Berlin, arriving on March 19, in the middle of a snowstorm, several weeks after Gerard had said that "peace was a matter of hours."[63]

The situation in Germany indeed had seemed to change from month to month, and in March 1915 the prospects for peace seemed distant. Bethmann had been compelled to make speeches encouraging the annexationists; the Kaiser, restlessly parading from front to front, was passing under the influence of the Army and Navy staffs. Most important, the submarine campaign had opened, and relations between Germany and the United States were bound to worsen.[64] The Chancellor and officials in the Foreign Office received House cordially enough, but neither Bethmann nor Jagow offered encouragement to talk of peace. House saw himself getting nowhere, and like the magician he was, pulled out of his bag a proposal he called "the Freedom of the Seas." He was searching, as he wrote Wilson, "for a thread to throw across the chasm separating the Allied and the Central Powers."[65]

The doctrine of Freedom of the Seas was dear to Americans, who like to link morals with wars. The United States government had upheld neutral rights in a war with Great Britain, a hundred years earlier. House's proposal—to restrict contraband to implements of warfare, allowing belligerents and neutrals to carry goods between all countries in time of war—had behind it the force of American tradition. Even Grey had worked for a limited version of this principle at the Second Hague Conference in 1907. In talks with House in February, 1915, Grey had said that he approved the principle of the belligerent shipping in time of war.[66] His approval lay at the bottom of House's suggestion to the Germans. Ostensibly a boon to Germany, the plan would eliminate wartime complications between America and the belligerents, but it would in fact—or so House thought—benefit Great Britain the most. It would offset the disadvantages of an island position, greatly increasing British defensive strength. The Germans fell upon the suggestion with an enthusiasm which surprised House. He presented an impartial attitude to the Chancellor, however, and said that "The United States would be justified in bringing pressure upon England in this direction, for our people had a common interest with Germany in that question." Zimmermann remarked that he felt freedom of the seas could be the beginning of peace parleys.[67] House naively felt he had found the magic formula, and left after nine days to take it back to England.[68]

In Paris, en route to London, the Colonel interviewed Delcassé and President Raymond Poincaré. He was prepared for the coldness characteristic of the French President, and told an American diplomat that "his coldness and silence would not embarrass me if it did not embarrass him, and I could be as quiet, and for as long, as anybody."[69] He wrote Sir Edward from Paris that the German visit had had value and that he had awakened enthusiasm in Germany over Freedom of the Seas; he added that this new direction would make the future for England "more secure and splendid."[70]

Grey did not think so, finding it difficult to believe that his friend could imagine England giving up the indispensable offensive weapon— the blockade of Germany by the British Navy.[71] Here was an example of Grey's diplomacy backfiring, for House had taken him literally when he had agreed to immunity for neutral shipping.[72] He soon set House straight in a letter to Paris: "As to Freedom of the Seas," if Germany meant that German commerce was to go free upon the sea in time of war, while she remains free to make war upon other nations at will, it is not a fair proposition." He allowed himself a comment on the idea that Germany was interested in peace talk at all: "Fudge!" wrote the Foreign Secretary.[73]

Wilson had been kept informed of House's progress by coded letters, but his amiable replies carried no instructions. On April 1 he wrote: "I warmly admire the way you are conducting your conferences at each stage." On April 15: "It is fine how you establish just the right relations and just the right understanding at each capital."[74] House was finding it sticky going to establish the right understanding in his favorite capital with his good friend Grey. Back in London, Grey told him regarding freedom of the seas, that if Great Britain accepted this doctrine it should ask freedom of the land, so that Germany or other nations could not make aggressive war. He said that public opinion would have to be educated in the direction of freedom of the seas.[75]

The undefatigable Colonel met with British leaders of variety of opinion the rest of April and the first week of May. On May 7 he had a pleasant and busy schedule, including an appointment in the morning with Grey to visit the Gardens at Kew—the trees and flowers were lovely in the spring. He saw the King in the afternoon; that evening there was a dinner for himself and Mrs. House at the American Embassy.[76] At four o'clock in the afternoon preparations were under way for the dinner when news came that a German submarine had sunk the *Lusitania.* The first announcement declared that only the ship had been destroyed, and all passengers and the crew had been saved. There seemed no reason to abandon the dinner.[77]

Page that evening had the shocking news that the first announcement was a mistake. More than a thousand men, women, and children had been lost, and more than a hundred of them were American citizens. The dinner went on, but the affair was one of the most tragic in the social history of London. Throughout the evening bulletins were brought in on little yellow slips. In the gleam of the elegant gowns, the jewelry, the white ties and shirts, moved the dark shadow of war. Everyone was convinced that the United States would enter the conflict immediately. None was more outspoken than Colonel House. "We shall be at war with Germany within a month." he declared.[78]

The Colonel's words did not mean he had given up his plans of Freedom of the Seas. The *Lusitania* tragedy merely caused him to push a substitute: Germany should abandon submarine warfare against commerce in return for a British concession admitting foodstuffs through the blockade.[79] He remained in England through the month of May, sending messages to Gerard to approach the German Government on this substitute plan. He lunched with Grey frequently, discussing a series of reciprocal concessions.[80] These were futile gestures because the intense hatred between Germany and Great Britain after the *Lusitania* precluded any compromise. Grey must have displayed infinite patience with House during this time because House's diary still indicates Grey's responses as warm and cordial, but vague.[81] One can imagine Grey saying, "I am personally in favor of your plan, but the British public, you know . . ."

Gerard's responses indicated that Germany had no intention of compromising and on May 30 House decided to return home. He wrote Grey, who was temporarily at Fallodon: "I have concluded to sail for home on the *St. Paul* on Saturday . . . My reason for going is that, for the moment I believe I can be of more service there than here. It seems as though we would evitably drift into war and before long. If this occurs, I do not want it to be a milk and water affair, and I would like to be near the President so as to urge him to give the world an example of American efficiency."[82] The Colonel left England on June 5.

For four months House had been traveling, discussing peace conventions, writing optimistically to the President, talking of a freedom of the seas which Ray Stannard Baker later was to call a chimera. The impression from his letters and diaries is that he was enjoying the meetings, conversations, luncheons with celebrities. His intentions were undebatable; he had no responsibility, and the mission was so secret it was beyond criticism.[83] As for the purpose of the mission—peace—Page may have written its epitaph on April 30, 1915, when House returned from the Continent: "Peace-talk, therefore is yet mere moonshine—House has been to Berlin, from London, thence to Paris, thence back to London again—from Nowhere (as far as peace is concerned) to Nowhere again."[84]

Meanwhile, the bond between the two English-speaking countries had grown so strong through the developing friendship of Grey and House that a British navel escort accompanied House's ship, the *St. Paul*, through the treacherous submarine-infested waters. House wrote Page complacently that "the papers have made much of it, particularly, the *World*."[85] Grey perhaps could afford a convoy; his diplomacy with House had paid off. The Colonel had lingered long enough in England to discourage those individuals in Germany who might have wanted to make peace—and the peace suitable for them at that time would have been most unsuitable for Grey and Allies of Great Britain.

Notes

1. Arthur S. Link, *The Struggle for Neutrality* (Princeton, N.J., 1960), p. 218. It was also of questionable value since the substitution of one flag for another did not change the Lusitania's distinctive appearance. *The Manchester Guardian* put it: "A goddess is known by her gait, not her garment." Armin Rappaport, *The British Press and Wilsonian Neutrality* (Stanford, California, 1951), p. 29.

2. Kent Forster, *The Failures of Peace* (Washington, D.C., 1941), p. 66.

3. Notter, *The Origins of the Foreign Policy of Woodrow Wilson*, p. 342.

4. Dispatch from Robert Lansing to Walter Hines Page, Sept. 26, 1914; also Grey to Page, Feb. 10, 1915—Grey's summary of the British stand. Walter Hines Page Papers, Houghton Library, Harvard University.

5. Grey, *Twenty-Five Years*, II, pp. 102-103. Grey further elaborated: "We kept the rule against the use of poison gas till the Germans broke it, and when they did break it, we had neither gas nor protection against gas ready."

6. The lengthy dispatch from Lansing to Page dated September 26, 1914, a total of fourteen typewritten pages, which explained the background of the Declaration of London and the British modifications of it also asked Page to relay to the Foreign Secretary an American protest of British interpretation. Page kept it in his dispatch box until March 26, 1915, and then it was given to Page's secretary, Irwin Laughlin, to be filed. It never reached the Foreign Office. Walter Hines Page Papers, Houghton Library, Harvard University.

7. Page to House, Nov. 9, 1914, Walter Hines Page Papers, Houghton Library, Harvard University.

8. F. O. 800/84/1256, Grey to Spring Rice, Sept. 3, 1914; F. O. 800/84/1256, Spring Rice to Grey, Sept. 3, 1914. These documents were marked "Private and secret."

9.   Edward Buehrig, *Woodrow Wilson and the Balance of Power* (Bloomington, Indiana, 1955), pp. 102-104.

10.   Ibid.

11.   Robert E. Osgood, *Ideals and Self-Interest in American Foreign Relations: The Great Transformation of the Twentieth Century* (Chicago, 1953), pp. 179-181.

12.   Notter, *The Origins of the Foreign Policy of Woodrow Wilson*, p. 355; also Arthur S. Link, *Woodrow Wilson and the Progressive Era* (New York, 1954), p. 155.

13.   R. S. Baker, *Wilson*, V, pp. 276-277.

14.   Grey told Page that he was personally favorable to the idea of mediation, but the real question was: on what terms could the war be ended? And at this time there was no indication that Germany was prepared to make any reparation to Belgium—a necessity as far as the British were concerned. Grey to Spring Rice, Sept. 9, 1914, Walter Hines Page Papers, Houghton Library, Harvard University.

15.   Ernest R. May, *The World War and American Isolation, 1914-1917* (Cambridge, Massachussetts, 1959), pp. 72-75.

16.   House Diary, Sept. 20, 1914, Edward M. House Papers, Yale University Library.

17.   E. May, *The World War and American Isolation*, p. 23.

18.   House Diary, Sept. 5, 1914, Edward M. House Papers, Yale University Library.

19.   House to Page, Oct. 3, 1914, Walter Hines Page Papers, Houghton Library, Harvard University; also R. S. Baker, *Wilson*, V, p. 288.

20.   R. S. Baker, *Wilson*, V, p. 301. Baker wrote that of all the advisers around Wilson, Bryan's views at this time were the broadest and most constructive.

21.   E. May, *The World War and American Isolation*, p. 78.

22.   Ibid., pp. 78-79.

23.   Bakhmetieff to Sazonov, *Mezhdunarodnye Otnosheniya*, Series 3, VIII, No. 8, reprinted in E. May, *The World War and American Isolation*, pp. 79-80.

24.   House Diary, Dec. 20, 1914 and Jan. 13, 1915, Edward M. House Papers, Yale University Library.

25.   F. O. 800/84/1256, Spring Rice to Grey, Sept. 22, 1914. Spring Rice's pithy answer to House: "I said of course we were glad of American sympathy, but did not ask for it."

26.   F. O. 800/84/1256, Spring Rice to Grey, Sept. 28, 1914; Spring Rice to Grey, Oct. 17, 1914; Spring Rice to Grey, Dec. 24, 1914.

27.   House to Page, Dec. 4, 1914, and Jan. 4, 1914; also Page to House, indefinite date in January, 1914, Walter Hines Page Papers, Houghton Library, Harvard University.

28.   F. O. 800/84/1256, Grey to Spring Rice, Dec. 22, 1914; Spring Rice to Grey, Dec. 24, 1914.

29.   House Diary, Dec. 19, 1914, Edward M. House Papers, Yale University Library.

30.   Ibid.

31.   House Diary, Jan. 12, 1915, Edward M. House Papers, Yale University Library.

32.   R. S. Baker, *Wilson*, V, pp. 302-307.

33.   Ibid., p. 308.

34. Page to Wilson, Oct. 15, 1914, Walter Hines Page Papers, Houghton Library, Harvard University.

35. E. May, *The World War and American Isolation,* pp. 81-83.

36. Those in the British Foreign Office feared that a strong German influence in America was possible for this mission, and Bernstorff was called the "sinister element behind this . . . ." F. O. 800/84/1256, Notes on telegram from Spring Rice, Dec. 24, 1914, initialed E. G. and W. T. (Grey and Tyrrell).

37. George and George, *Woodrow Wilson and Colonel House,* p. 165.

38. Grey was often extraordinarily frank with Spring Rice, revealing perhaps more to him of his true feelings than to other British officials. F. O. 800/84/1263, Grey to Spring Rice, Jan. 2, 1915; F. O. 800/84/1263, Grey to Spring Rice, Jan. 18, 1915; also E. May, *The World War and American Isolation,* p. 84.

39. Spring Rice, to whom House referred by his code name, "Winkle," had arranged this meeting, and although House met with Page on February 6, he allowed him to think that he (Page) had arranged the first meeting which actually did not occur until several days later. House delighted in this kind of intrigue. House Diary, Feb. 6, 1915, Edward M. House Papers, Yale University Library; also F. O. 800/84/1263, Spring Rice to Grey, Jan. 26, 1915.

40. House Diary, Feb. 7, 1915, Edward M. House Papers, Yale University Library; also E. May, *The World War and American Isolation,* p. 87.

41. House Diary, Feb. 13, 1915, Edward M. House Papers, Yale University Library; also Grey, *Twenty-Five Years,* II, p. 124.

42. E. May, *The World War and American Isolation,* p. 87; also Charles C. Tansill, *America Goes to War,* (Boston, 1938), p. 446.

43. Buchanan to Sazonov, Feb. 14, 1915, *Mezhdunarodnye Otnosheniya,* series 3, VII, No. 190, quoted in E. May, *The World War and American Isolation,* p. 88. House told Grey on Feb. 11, 1915, that he had no intention of pushing the question of peace. House Diary, Edward M. House Papers, Yale University Library.

44. R. S. Baker, *Wilson,* V, p. 308.

45. *Papers Relating to the Foreign Relations of the United States, 1915, Supplement* (Washington, 1928), pp. 15-16.

46. House Diary, Feb. 12, 1915, Edward M. House Papers, Yale University Library.

47. House Diary, Feb. 13, 1915, Edward M. House Papers, Yale University Library.

48. R. S. Baker, *Wilson,* V, p. 311.

49. C. Seymour, *The Intimate Papers of Colonel House,* I, p. 378. This letter to Wilson, in the Yale Collection, was dated Feb. 18, 1915. In House's diary entry of the same day, he states that (after showing Gerard's letter to Grey) ". . . we concluded that Gerard was writing under the influence of some German . . ." which would indicate that House no longer believed in Gerard's avowals that Germany was ready for peace.

50. R. S. Baker, *Wilson,* V, 312-313. Wilson may have been moved by a message from Gerard to Bryan. Gerard no doubt felt panic at his inability to get House to Germany. He conveyed this to the Secretary of State: "Favorable moment is passing. Germans have gained great victory over Russians and are following it up and will soon turn and break through French lines. Germany will never make pro-

posal but if Colonel House can come here bringing secret reasonable proposal it will
be accepted in all probability but Germany will never pay an indemnity to Belgium
and on the contrary will probably expect all or part of Congo and perhaps indemnity from France for portion now occupied." Gerard to Bryan, Feb. 19, 1915, Page
Papers.

51.   R. S. Baker, *Wilson*, V, p. 314.

52.   Trevelyan, *Grey of Fallodon*, pp. 123-124; also C. Seymour, *The Intimate Papers
       of Colonel House*, I, p. 363.

53.   Notter, *The Origins of the Foreign Policy of Woodrow Wilson*, p. 392.

54.   C. Seymour, *The Intimate Papers of Colonel House*, I, p. 382.

55.   R. S. Baker, *Wilson*, V, p. 315.

56.   House Diary, Feb. 27, 1915, Edward M. House Papers, Yale University Library.
       House had other reasons (in addition to his friendship with Grey) for feeling
       satisfied about his mission. He had been sent about five hundred clippings from
       newspapers concerning his activities. He wrote in his diary on Feb. 22 that he
       found one particularly "amusing." The *Boston Transcript* had an editorial entitled
       "The House of Mystery" which read: "An assistant President of the United
       States, the itineraries of Colonel E. M. House arouse public interest unequalled
       by the comings and goings of mere officialdom."

57.   House Diary, March 7, 1915, Edward M. House Papers, Yale University Library.

58.   C. Seymour, *The Intimate Papers of Colonel House*, I, pp. 391-392.

59.   Ibid.

60.   F. O. 800/181/1800, Grey to Sir Francis Bertie, March 11, 1915. Bertie replied that
       Delcasse would see House because "I cannot well refuse but we do not want any
       intervention or mediation . . . ." F. O. 800/181/1800, Bertie to Grey, March
       12, 1915.

61.   R. S. Baker, *Wilson*, V, p. 318.

62.   Link, *The Struggle for Neutrality*, p. 223. Walter Hines Page, who may have felt
       some pique at the frequency of House's conferences with Grey, had a different
       comment on the shape of things in England. His diary reads: "E. M. House
       went to Paris this morning, having no message from this kingdom. This kind
       of talk (peace) here now was spoken of by the Prime Minister the other day as
       'the twittering of a sparrow in a tumult that shakes the world.'" Page Diary,
       March 11, 1915, Walter Hines Page Papers, Houghton Library, Harvard
       University.

63.   Link, *The Struggle for Neutrality*, p. 223.

64.   E. May, *The World War and American Isolation*, pp. 108-109; also Arthur D. H.
       Smith, *Mr. House of Texas* (New York, 1940), p. 132.

65.   C. Seymour, *The Intimate Papers of Colonel House*, I, pp. 405-411.

66.   C. Seymour, *The Intimate Papers of Colonel House*, I, pp. 405-411. See also Arthur
       Marsden, "The Blockade," pp. 503-504, in Hinsley, ed., *Sir Edward Grey*.
       Marsden writes that this was dangerous, speculative talk in view of the dissension
       among cabinet members. This excellent chapter by Marsden, University of
       Dundee, succinctly explains the dilemma of the English vis-a-vis the United States.

67. C. Seymour, *The Intimate Papers of Colonel House,* I, pp. 410-411; also A. D. H. Smith, *Mr. House of Texas,* p. 132; also House Diary, March 27, 1915, Edward M. House Papers, Yale University Library.

68. An example of House's naivete is his diary entry of March 28, 1915, Edward M. House Papers, Yale University Library: "The Foreign Office [in Germany] had done everything to make our journey comfortable and pleasant. Two entire compartments were reserved and the guard refused to allow any one else to enter them . . . . The conspicuous courtesy and generosity in which our trip was handled made me feel that my visit to Germany has been a success."

69. House Diary, April 16, 1915, Edward M. House Papers, Yale University Library. Lord Bertie wrote in his diary on April 14 about House's latest visit to Paris: "President Wilson's intimate friend who has been to London, Paris and Berlin on a fishing expedition to ascertain how American intervention would be appreciated, was at the Elysee yesterday . . . ." Bertie's comment may have been typical of most of those in France at that time: "Let the Americans mind their own business, and keep their own Germans in order." Lennox, ed., *The Diary of Lord Bertie,* I, pp. 144-145.

70. House to Grey, April 12, 1915, Edward M. House Papers, Yale University Library.

71. Link, *The Struggle for Neutrality,* p. 230.

72. The Conference between Grey and House at which this subject was discussed was held on February 10, 1915. House recorded that Grey agreed (with a slight amendment) to lanes of safety at sea. C. Seymour, *The Intimate Papers of Colonel House,* I, p. 369.

73. Grey to House, April 24, 1915, Edward M. House Papers, Yale University Library; see also Link, ed., *The Papers of Woodrow Wilson,* vol. 33, *April 17-July 21, 1915.* (Princeton, N. J., 1980), p. 124.

74. R. S. Baker, *Wilson,* V, pp. 318-319.

75. House Diary, April 30, 1915, Edward M. House Papers, Yale University Library.

76. House Diary, May 7, 1915, Edward M. House Papers, Yale University Library.

77. Hendrick, *Page,* II, pp. 1-2.

78. Ibid.

79. House Diary, May 14, 1915, Edward M. House Papers, Yale University Library; see also Link, ed., *The Papers of Woodrow Wilson,* vol. 33, *April 17-July 21, 1915,* p. 222.

80. C. Seymour, *The Intimate Papers of Colonel House,* I, pp. 446-451.

81. House Diary, May 14, May 19, May 26, 1915, Edward M. House Papers, Yale University Library. House and Grey were still interspersing their philosophic talks (which House found so appealing) among their political talks. On May 14, they discussed compatibility: "Grey said he saw very few people outside of his colleagues, and there were almost none with whom he talked as he did to me. He said it seemed that each individual was surrounded by some invisible substance that enveloped them—that when this substance was sympathetic to another it was easy to open up one's soul, but when it was not, and it was most of the time so— it was impossible for him at least, to give up that which was his inner most self . . . . I accepted this as a high expression of friendship and as an indication that he feels for me as I do for him."

82. House to Grey, June 1, 1915, Edward M. House Papers, Yale University Library.

83. R. S. Baker, *Wilson,* V, p. 320.

84. Page Diary, April 30, 1915, Walter Hines Page Papers, Houghton Library, Harvard University.

85. Page Diary, April 30, 1915, Walter Hines Page Papers, Houghton Library, Harvard University; House to Page, June 17, 1915, Walter Hines Page Papers, Houghton Library, Harvard University.

Chapter V

The Memorandum

The House-Grey Memorandum, a secret covenant, secretly arrived at, was an example of Wilson's and Colonel House's diplomatic work before the United States entered the World War. While in London House had reacted in a bellicose way to the dramatic sinking of the *Lusitania,* but underwent a marked change when he returned home.[1] His views on submarine warfare as a *casus belli* for the United States did not remain consistent; his new theory in the summer and autumn of 1915 was that any kind of American participation in the European conflict must turn on a larger issue than that of the German submarine—possibly on the more constructive purpose of shaping the peace.[2] The result of House's altered approach to American diplomatic problems, the Memorandum of February, 1916, sought an end to the hostilities with the United States assuming an active part in European politics. Such an approach was, however, far from a straightforward solution to wartime problems. Z. A. B. Zeman, in his *Diplomatic History of the First World War* (London, 1972), calls it one of the most unusual agreements in the annals of European diplomacy. Grey, House's co-author of the document, behaved like a character in a James novel in which the protagonist, seemingly straightforward, obscures all true meaning. And Wilson, for whom House acted as executive agent, appeared not to have understood what would have been his commitment to the Allies. The unspoken confusion between the President and his agent in the period preceding this agreement is reminiscent of Cordell Hull's later assumption that he knew the mind of President Franklin D. Roosevelt before he attended the London Economic Conference of 1933.

Misconceptions had begun in the autumn of 1915 when the tentacles of the European conflict began to touch the American shore. After the sinking of the *Lusitania* in May of that year the United States government had indulged in an exchange of notes with Imperial Germany protesting the loss of 128 American lives. The notes had proved unsatisfactory, and there seemed no doubt that German submarines would continue to sink ships on which there might be American passengers. The British press had expressed ridicule of the President's indecisiveness which the American Ambassador in London seemed to delight in repeating in letters to Wilson and House.[3] In the meantime, the blockade tightened and American commerce suffered. The American people, perhaps, had become unappeasable in their wants; they desired a firm policy toward Germany, without war; they wanted a cessation of the shipping problems with Britain.[4] Wilson felt himself to be in a labyrinth (he was also wholly absorbed in a love affair with Mrs. Edith Bolling Galt, and did not give these international problems his full attention) and he asked his political adviser, House, for a "way out."[5] House remembered a casual remark the President made in September, 1915 "that he had never been sure that we ought to take part in the conflict." This double-negative evidence of Wilson's desire for participation pleased House, for his British friend, Grey, had suggested intervention in a letter dated August 26: "if the end of this war is arrived at through mediation, I believe it must be that of the United States . . . Therefore I look forward to the help of your country under the guidance of the President."[6]

This letter, and Wilson's remark, had prompted House to present to Wilson—on October 8, 1915—a daring plan which had been taking shape in the Colonel's mind: either to compel a peace settlement or to bring the United States into the war on the Allied side. House's diary related that Wilson was startled, but seemed by silence to acquiesce—a habitual reaction of Wilson to House's suggestions (at least the reaction House was fond of drawing for his diary).[7]

The President made an address on October 11, 1915, which disclosed that if he had acquiesced he had done so with important reservations: "Neutrality is an obligation," he said, "to stand apart and maintain certain principles of action which are grounded in law and justice."[8] Although Wilson was convinced that the future of America was bound up in friendly relations with Great Britain and France, he felt that neutrality should be maintained because of the duty inherent in that concept. He did not accept House's plan of throwing the force of the United States on the Allied side behind a demand for peace; he did not wish to discard official neutrality for any reason.[9]

During this period—the autumn of 1915—House was in constant communication with Grey. The Colonel's *id'ee fixe* was American participation of some sort in the war ("I cannot keep my mind from the European stage which holds so much of fateful interest") and he kept the subject before Grey.[10] The latter replied to one of House's suggestions on September 22:

Dear Colonel House,

You ask me, in your letter of the 3rd, whether I think that the President could make peace proposals to the belligerents at this time, upon the broad basis of the elimination of militarism and navalism and a return, as nearly as possible to the "status quo," by which I understand is meant the "status quo" before the war.

That is a question I cannot answer without consulting the Cabinet here and the Governments of the Allies. It would not be easy to do that, unless I was in a position to say that the President really was prepared to make such a proposal . . . .

To me the great object of securing the elimination of militarism and navalism is to get security for the future against aggressive war. How much are the United States prepared to do in this direction? Would the President propose that there should be a League of Nations binding themselves to side against warfare on sea or land (such rules would of course have to be drawn up after this war); or which refused, in case of dispite to adopt some other method of settlement than that of war? . . .

I liked very much your saying that your people are awakening slowly but surely to the issues involved in this war and that you believe they will be found willing to go to limits heretofore unthinkable to bring about a just solution . . .[11]

Yours sincerely,

E. Grey

Whether Wilson saw this letter is debatable. He was certainly informed of Grey's delicate proposal for European and world security; this apparently impressed him, and he authorized House to prepare an encouraging reply. House's answer to Grey, dated October 17, outlined his own attitude. He considered it one of the most important letters he ever sent, and in keeping with his love of intrigue he sent it as a split message, that is, as two letters—with words alternately numbered "1" and "2"—not difficult for anyone (least of all a crytographer) to decipher. Put together it read:

. . . It has occurred to me that the time may soon come when this Government should intervene between the belligerents and demand that peace parleys begin upon the broad basis of the elminination of militarism and navalism. In my opinion it would be a world-wide calamity if the war should continue to a point where the Allies could not with the aid of the United States bring about a peace along the lines you and I have so often discussed . . . What I want you to know is that whenever you consider the time is propitious for this intervention I will propose it to the President. He may then desire me to go to Europe in order that a more intimate understanding as to procedure may be had.

It is in my mind that after conferring with your Government, I should proceed to Berlin and tell them that it was the President's purpose to intervene and stop this destructive war, provided the weight of the United States thrown on the side that accepted our proposal could do it.

I would not let Berlin know, of course, of any understanding with the Allies but would rather lead them to think our proposal would be rejected by them. This might induce Berlin to accept the proposal, but if they did not do so it would nevertheless be the purpose to intervene. If the Central Powers were still obdurate, it would [probably] be necessary for us to join the Allies and force the issue . . . .[12]

Here was a plan full of sophistry, to persuade the Germans into an acceptance of American mediation on Allied terms. It was not the unbiased approach toward peace a neutral country might be expected to make. Possibly House thought that the idealism of Sir Edward Grey could be counted on to assure a just peace.

The President's attitude toward this scheme was uncertain. He had read House's letter to Grey before it went off, and had returned it with an insertion—the word "probably" in the critical sentence above.[13] From this one might conclude that he preferred the aims of the Allies to those of Germany. It is possible that he meant by his limited approval of House's plan to go to the point of a threat of war to compel peace negotiations, a drastic action, but one founded on his own thinking that all the belligerents desired security rather than victory. With his insertion of the "probably" American intervention became questionable; the President had retained a free hand while making a move for peace. House held the view that the peace settlement should be favorable to the Allies, which meant, in fact, victory for them. Wilson's belief nonetheless was that peace did not mean victory to either side, and the President concentrated on his part as a peacemaker.[14] To underscore this part House sent Wilson a careful, indeed fulsome, message on November 10 containing these words: "This is the part I think you are destined to play in this world tragedy, and it is the noblest part that had ever come to a son of man."[15]

Grey seemed reluctant to accept his part in this new Anglo-American negotiation. He could not have failed to have been impressed with Wilson's qualification and was not sure he had made his point that an American guarantee against future aggression was necessary. With reference to this latter ambiguity on November 10 he cabled to ask if the proposal was to be taken in connection with his own suggestion of a league of nations.[16] Wilson and House answered quickly in the affirmative, House hinting that he might come to England to confirm the plan.[17]

In a somewhat tentative manner, American policy appeared to have moved toward participation in international affairs. Doubtless all these implications were not clear in the President's mind at this time, but he wrote House on November 12, 1915, that "I think the paragraph quoted from [Grey's] letter of Sept. 22 concerning a league contains the *necessary* programme."[18]

Grey's answer was full of caution; he informed Colonel House that "the Allies could not commit themselves in advance to any proposition without knowing exactly what it was and knowing that the United States of America were prepared to intervene and make it good if they accepted it . . . the situation at the moment and the feelings here and among the Allies, and in Germany so far as I know, do not justify me in urging you to come on the ground that your presence would have any practical result at the moment."[19] It seemed ironic that Grey was wavering over acceptance of American aid, and the Colonel was disappointed. Possibly he expected an immediate invitation to go to England. He complained to the President: [The offer] . . . "should have met a warmer reception . . . the British are in many ways dull."[20] But it appeared that Grey understood Wilson better than did House, for he realized the significance of Wilson's qualification which meant no commitment. Moreover, he wrote House that he felt the American protests against Allied shipping were unfriendly acts—that these protests might "strike the weapon of sea power out of our hands and thereby insure a German victory." He wanted more from House and Wilson than a half-hearted advocacy of disarmament and a league—he wanted a statement of unequivocal support.[21]

House refused to accept Grey's indecisive answer, and wrote again on December 7, 1915: "You are quite wrong in thinking that we have any desire to lessen the effectiveness of England's sea power at this time. It is the one reassuring potential element in the war . . . What is most needful at present is a better working understanding with you and how this is to be brought about is uppermost in our thoughts. The machinery we are using is not altogether satisfactory. Just why I cannot explain here, and perhaps it may be necessary for me to see you in person . . . ."[22] House had decided to make another trip to Europe; he explained in his diary that he and the President felt that their thoughts and intentions might be expressed more plainly by word of mouth than in writing.[23] It is difficult, however, to see how much more explicit one could get in expressing a preference for England's cause than in the Colonel's letter of December 7.

The machinery to which House referred in this letter—Ambassadors Page in London and Spring Rice in Washington—had kept the President in a state of agitation. Page's letters protested the blockade so vehemently ("In the meantime our prestige . . . in British judgment, is gone . . . . they will regard protests as really inspired by German influence . . . .") that Wilson was tempted to recall him.[24] Spring Rice, in late 1915, had become upset at what he considered pro-German coverage in American papers and "blew the lid off" against the State Department on November 17.[25] Wilson's respect for professional diplomats always had been limited; to explain that Americans were not unfriendly to the Allied cause, and to present the House plan of American intervention, he therefore concurred with the Colonel's wish to go to England "to save the British from their own obtuseness."[26]

There were, to be sure, other factors in American foreign policy at this time; one of them was Robert Lansing, who was just as pro-Allied as the President and House, despite his legal protests to London over shipping rights. Lansing became Secretary of State in early summer, 1915, and as Wilson had predicted to House, had proved himself capable of working in harmony with the President and the Colonel.[27] But even though House and Lansing and Wilson were pro-Ally they lacked understanding as to the direction of American policy. House, as conveyed by his plan, wanted a quick entente with Great Britain. Lansing's purpose was to avoid a breaking point over shipping rights with the Allies. His method for achieving this was to send verbose and legalistic complaints (short and emphatic notes were dangerous, he thought). Wilson believed "American object in the world . . . was to show men the paths of liberty and mutual serviceability to life the common man . . . and enable him to achieve the best development possible."[28] He felt a league of nations might achieve this. House had convinced him that Grey's hope for a peaceful, productive future matched his own. Neither the President nor House understood the forces that had molded European diplomacy; neither realized that Sir Edward would not have a free hand in the making of a European peace. Colonel House's mission was, they thought, to insure Grey's leadership. It was to provide for a triumph of ideals.

As for American public opinion, it was preoccupied with the general problems of war and peace and American relations thereto. Congress reflected the fact: during the week of December 6-12, 1915, representatives introduced ten bills to curtail munition sales from the United States. A resolution called for the appointment of a commission on universal peace to declare America's position on neutrality. Indignation over the British attitude toward neutral trade resulted in a recommendation for a congressional investigation. These were signs of popular discontent with the President's foreign policy. Something needed to be done; American neutrality did not appear positive and people wanted an active stand. Peace advocates sent a shower of telegrams to the White House in December, 1915, urging support for a neutral conference of nations. It was at this time that Henry Ford financed a Peace Ship (humorously known as the Peace Ark) to sail to Europe with a boatload of pacifists who believed they could stop the war by Christmas.[29]

The German ambassador in Washington, Bernstorff, felt the pressure of discontent, and urged Bethmann Hollweg to invite House to Berlin for an exploratory peace mission. After a talk with Bernstorff House thought "there seems to be some hope that Germany is coming to her senses."[30] He wrote the President that the Ambassador had heard from his government and "they would like me to come directly to Berlin to discuss peace upon the general terms of military and naval disarmament . . . . I said . . . that we were not concerned regarding territorial questions . . . which involved not only the belligerents but the neutrals also . . . . I said I believed if they would consent to a plan which embraced general disarmament you would be willing to throw the weight of the Government and demand that war cease."[31]

Wilson may have felt the time had come to take a step toward peace. He had no better alternative than House's device: Germany had manifested interest in ending the war by inviting the Colonel to Berlin, while Grey's suggestions relative to a league also seemed a hopeful method. He agreed therefore that House should undertake a mission.[32] In a letter of approval the President added these affectionate words: "You need no instructions. You know what is in my mind and how to interpret it, and will, I am sure, be able to make it plain to those with whom you may have the privilege of conferring."[33] House's diary entry on Christmas day, 1915, makes evident that he was not displeased with this state of affairs. "The President clearly places the whole responsibility back on my shoulders where I would gladly have it, for if I am to act, I wish to act with a free hand."

House did receive more definite instructions before he left, which indicates that the President had given the mission some thought. A letter, written on December 24 and mailed from Virginia where he and the former Mrs. Galt—now Mrs. Woodrow Wilson—were spending their honeymoon, revealed the President's attitude toward a peace settlement: "We are concerned only in the future peace of the world and the guarantees to be given for that. The only possible guarantees . . . are (a) military and naval disarmament and (b) a league of nations to secure each nation against aggression and maintain the absolute freedom of the seas. If either party to the present war will let us say to the other that they are willing to discuss peace on such terms, it will clearly be our duty to use our utmost moral force to oblige the other to parley, and I do not see how they could stand in the opinion of the world if they refused."[35]

Despite such efforts at clarity, it is important to point out there were several misconceptions between House and Wilson at this time. House in December, 1915, believed that Wilson meant to back Great Britain, that the President believed that the British cause was also the American cause; in truth, these instructions of December 24 displayed no partiality, and did have a sentence which suggested that House press England about American neutral rights.[36] There was nothing stating that Wilson intended the United States to enforce mediation—only moral pressure was indicated. There was not the slightest reference to that aspect of House's plan which contemplated entering the war against Germany as a possible contingency. These unresolved divergences of view were serious. But House replied to Wilson's letter from Virginia, "I think we agree entirely," and prepared to sail for Europe on December 28.[37]

Once more there was to be the aura of mystery. Why was the Colonel making this trip (it was his third) to Europe? David Lawrence in the New York *Evening Post* suggested that the Colonel's visit to Europe was to "canvass the prospects for peace." Other headlines began to refer to House and the trip: "Commonsense Diplomacy," "An Interesting Mission," and "Discreet Envoy."[38] Reporters besieged the envoy as he boarded the *Rotterdam*. "I was perfectly pleasant acceding to their demands and posing for photographs for something like five minutes." At the same time he denied that his trip had any diplomatic significance.[39]

After a terrific storm at sea (House's journeys were always full of drama) the President's friend received a royal welcome on his arrival in London on January 6, 1916. House had written Ambassador Page that he expected to be in London in January for a few days—then to

Paris and Rome, returning to England. House told Page that "this is absolutely between us and the angels and to be mentioned to no one." He denied that his trip had anything to do with plans for peace, and asked the Ambassador to release an explanation to the press so stating.[40] Page's initial rapport with House had begun to disappear, because he felt the Colonel was behaving as if he were the Ambassador to Britain.[41] Nevertheless, he entertained House at lunch and dinner within a week of the Colonel's arrival. Others, including Grey and Balfour, lunched with House. On these occasions House initiated discussions of his specific plan for peace. Since the plan seemed to guarantee American support to the Allies, House was surprised to be confronted with arguments. Balfour wanted to know, almost sharply, if the President would be able to carry out such an agreement. With all the confidence in the world House spoke then of the manipulative process he used with the President: "I told them it would be easier for me to persuade the President to accede to what I would be willing to agree to, than it would be for them to succeed with their colleagues. I had only one man to convince and I knew him sufficiently well to know what he would accept and what he would refuse."[42]

British statesmen had their reasons for not accepting House's word as Wilson's word. The President had cabled House on January 12, 1916, that it looked as if the German submarine controversy was going to be settled. He indicated that the Senate would demand pressure on England "to make at least equal concessions to our unanswerable claims of right."[43] Wilson appeared to have no thought of coming to the aid of the Allies at the expense of American neutral rights. In House's absence the President and Secretary thus had embarked on an independent diplomacy which could have impinged on House's mission. And in addition to the strain the blockade placed on Anglo-American relations there was a new dispute over armed merchantmen. Moved by what Wilson termed "an impartial attitude," the President and Lansing, on January 18, 1916 sent a circular to the Allies threatening to exclude such merchantmen from American ports.[44] Lansing then offered a new plan for regulating wartime commerce. For some time the Secretary of State had seen logic in Germany's contention that a submarine could not come to the surface and stop an enemy vessel if there was a danger of the vessel firing on the submarine. In a proposed *modus vivendi* he suggested disarming all merchantmen as consistent with the regulations of visit and search imposed on the Germans. This perhaps was like trying to impose restraining orders during a riot.[45] The British felt that it was not impartial—indeed, that it favored the submarine. Impartial or not, it seemed to be an ill-timed proposition, coming at a moment when Wilson's emissary was advocating peace via Anglo-American cooperation. Lansing's demarche also, of course, revealed the confusion of the President's policies.[46]

Lansing's proposal may have had a far-reaching effect on the British Foreign Secretary's reaction to House's plan. The Secretary of State's suggestion had increased Sir Edward's natural gloom. Two documents attest to this. Grey's immediate reaction appeared in a telegram to Spring Rice who had sent a message attempting to clarify the position of the United States. The normally reticent Grey told the Ambassador that the American attitude afforded him a "most painful surprise." He elaborated: "It had seemed incredible that the upshot of controversy about German submarine warfare would be that the United States Government would propose to justify and legalize wholesale sinking of merchant vessels by German submarines and to deprive British vessels of a chance of defense which United States have hitherto recognized as legitimate . . . . I cannot adequately express the disappointment and dismay with which such an attitude on the part of the United States will be viewed here . . . It confronts us with a most serious situation . . ."[47] Ambassador Page wrote the President that Grey regarded Lansing's proposal as "a great calamity." Grey seemed to equate the seriousness of the situation with that in August, 1914, just prior to the beginning of the war.[48]

The British Government, of course, needed the cooperation of the United States in any blockade of Germany. Yet at the beginning of the year 1916, Lansing and the President appeared to be proposing to withdraw their previously cooperative attitude and behave in a more neutral fashion. Grey may have thought he saw a way to keep the support and friendship of America through Colonel House, who was in London attending luncheons and talking about ending the war through mediation. House had discussed what he considered a basis for a fair peace: retrocession of Alsace-Lorraine to France, restoration of Belgium and Serbia, Constantinople for Russia, and a league of nations to prevent aggressive war. If he promised American military intervention on the side of the Allies, there was no mention of such an eventuality. Nevertheless, House's general attitude was pro-Ally. Grey continued to encourage House, the President's friend. House had intended to go to Germany.[49] Page did not approve,[50] but Grey may have been playing a more devious game than was the more direct Ambassador. The Germans, Grey knew, were sensing victory in the beginning months of 1916 and would be in no mood to accept an unfavorable peace offer presented by a visitor from the United States with no official standing. Grey perhaps counted on this far-from-peaceful atmosphere in Germany to consolidate House's British sympathies.

With Grey's blessing, therefore, House left for the Continent on January 20, 1916. During his stay in Germany the Colonel remained close to Ambassador Gerard at the Embassy, to avoid Admiral von Tirpitz, whom he considered the cause of "frightfulness on the high seas."[51] The civil leaders of the Imperial Government, from Bethmann Hollweg down, were impeccably polite. European leaders naturally would want to make a good impression on President Wilson's friend. But after four days the Colonel left Berlin hurriedly—even though he recorded that the Chancellor wanted him to stay to see the Kaiser ("I have little more desire to meet the Kaiser than von Tirpitz")[52] Perhaps it was Bethmann's copious beer drinking, but he had become convinced that the Germans would not agree to any moderate peace terms.[53] House's diary does not reveal that he suggested to the Germans a conference of neutrals; nor did he mention in his reports to the President that he talked about the two general peace terms (military and naval disarmament and the formation of a league of nations) Wilson had instructed him to emphasize. He simply stated that he thought further talks futile, and left, apparently with relief, for Paris.[54]

Aristide Briand and Jules Cambon—the former was premier, the latter foreign minister—received House cautiously. Cambon sent several secret messages to the British Foreign Office reporting the meetings with House; he said that while the Colonel had showed two letters from the President, neither appeared to contain instructions.[55] This was true, but House proceeded as if he had instructions. His remarks to French officials were definite and daring. He said there was a sentimental American attachment to the Allies, particularly France. America wished to help their cause. He then made his commitment: "If the Allies obtain a small scale success this spring or summer, the U.S. will intervene to promote peaceful settlement, but if the Allies have a setback, the United States will intervene militarily and will take part in the war against Germany."[56] House's diary added the following to Cambon's report: "They [Cambon and Briand] agreed not to let the fortunes of the Allies recede beyond a point where our intervention could save them."[57]

House did inform Wilson of this conversation, and explained his diplomacy apologetically in a letter on Febraury 9: "The way out seems clear to me and when I can lay the facts before you, I believe it will be clear to you also."[58]

What was the French reaction to this tremendous commitment?

It was unbelieving. "They would keep in touch with House by letters and messages."[59] The Colonel, however, felt that his visit with the French was "surprisingly satisfactory." He hastened back to England to impress upon Grey the need for an immediate decision.[60]

On the morning of February 10, 1916, House held a long discussion with Grey, upon whom he now placed reliance for cooperative action. he wrote the President afterward that "Grey was interested in what I told him of my interview with Briand and Cambon, and felt that my interview with them would relieve his Government of the suspicion of being the one desiring peace."[61] There was a temporary dissension, for Grey urged a more positive and immediate American action toward Germany as a result of the *Lusitania* incident (the problem was still smoldering, months after the great liner had gone down in May, 1915). But as House explained later—modestly—to the President, "in ten minutes I had brought him around." With the Colonel's persuasion, Grey agreed that "it would be best for you to demand that the belligerents permit you to call a conference for the discussion of peace terms."[62]

How effective had House been? It seems unlikely that House convinced Grey to drop the *Lusitania* issue after ten minutes of gentle persuasion. It was one of the Colonel's defects that he believed that he could change other peoples' beliefs with a few minutes of conversation. He felt that he had such rapport with Grey that he may have thought they agreed. Grey, for his part, once had said that [House] "had a way of saying "I know it," in a tone and manner that carried conviction of both his sympathy with and understanding of what was said to him."[63] In this conversation early in 1916, each man might have thought he had convinced the other; manipulation and counter-manipulation were never more evident between the two negotiators, House and Grey, than in these conversations concerning the proposed American intervention.

House was the sole executive agent of the American President, but Grey had to consult members of the Cabinet. Accordingly, on February 14, the Colonel lunched with the Foreign Secretary, with Balfour, and with Prime Minister Asquith. That evening he dined with David Lloyd George, at this time Chancellor of the Exchequer, and with the Lord Chief Justice, Lord Reading. On both occasions House found his hosts cordial, if cautious. Those Cabinet members convinced of ultimate victory were unwilling to accept a compromise peace until the hope of success had disappeared. They doubted the willingness of their French Allies to cooperate in House's plan of mediation or intervention.[64] There was a distrust of President Wilson which had been encouraged by Ambassador Page. Page disapproved of the plan; he felt it a scheme in which America would enter the war, not on the merits of the cause, in which he believed, but by a trick. "No member of the Government," Page wrote in his diary, "can afford to discuss such a subject, not one of them had any confidence in the strength of the President for action . . . The vanity of House for the President sticks out and is offensive."[65] The Colonel, aware of Page's disapproval, wrote in his diary," [The Ambassador] hinders me in my work because he tries to discourage me, and would totally do so if I were of a different temperament."[66]

Page was right about the attitude of the British popular mind toward peace. For Cabinet Members it was necessary to conduct meetings with House in secrecy. Persons attending always left the meetings separately. Page was wrong, however, about the Cabinet's refusal to discuss House's plan. On Febraury 14, Lord Reading gave a dinner for House with Asquith, Grey, Balfour, and Lloyd George present. Page did not attend the meeting.[67] House described the occasion in his diary: "The conversation was general while dinner was being served . . . When the butler withdrew there was a discussion of the war, the mistakes that had been made, and possible remedies . . . . It was 10:30 before we got down to the real purpose of the meeting."[68] House presented his ideas regarding the summoning by President Wilson of all the belligerents to discuss peace terms. He then invited free discussion. The result would have intrigued a student of the psychology of personality.

House's dinner party produced a remarkable colloquium. Grey, melancholy, appeared earnestly in sympathy with House's plan; Asquith was pompous and authoritative. Reading, the perfect Lord Chief Justice, tolerant and impartial, drew out one individual after another. Balfour, floridly benign, used his rich oracular voice to steady the conversation.[69] According to House's account of the meeting, Lloyd George was willing to agree to the intervention of the President immediately. In his *War Memoirs,* however, Lloyd George states that he wanted some preliminary understanding with the President as to the minimum terms the Allies were to insist upon. "A conference without such an agreement would have been productive of the most serious consequences to the morale of the Allied countries in the event of its failure."[70] As stated in Lloyd George's memiors, the terms included restoration and independence of Belgium and Serbia, and surrender of Alsace-Lorraine to France, provided that loss of territory thus incurred by Germany would be compensated outside Europe. There were to be adjustments of frontiers between Italy and Austria to liberate Italian communities under Austrian rule. Russia was to have an outlet to the sea. There were to be guarantees against the recurrence of such a catastrophe as the World War.[71]

These terms, recalled by Lloyd George, tallied closely with those indicated to Grey earlier by House as being his and Wilson's tentative terms. [72] The question of timing, brought up by Asquith, could not be so easily settled. Finally, as the hour approached midnight, it was understood that the American offer would not be made until an "opportune moment," and that was left to the Allies to decide.[73] With this latter point settled (or unsettled), the meeting adjourned.

House felt the dinner party had been a success, that the major point—the President calling a halt to the war and demanding a conference—had been agreed upon. He was content. In retrospect one can see there were important areas left untouched. House did not know about the Allied secret treaties which had allocated many of the war's spoils;[74] this omission alone made the terms so deftly enumerated by Lloyd George a high-water mark in hypocrisy. Lloyd George apparently had paid no attention to the prospective league of nations, as an essential basis for peace and Wilson's "necessary programme." The timing, left to the Allies, robbed the President of an important decision, and did in fact leave the future of the whole proposal to the British. And there was almost a conspiracy of silence on the most important item of all. The sweeping promise of American support to the Allies in case Germany refused to sanction a conference, made to Cambon by House on February 7, and to Grey on February 10, was not mentioned in accounts of the meeting given in the memoirs published after the war by House, Grey, and Lloyd George.

Three days after this epochal meeting, namely, on February 17, 1916, House and Grey drafted their later well-known memorandum embodying the general and tentative agreement of the Cabinet leaders. In this memorandum they incorporated the promise that the United States, under stated conditions, would enter the war on the side of the Allies. They showed the document to the French Ambassador who questioned whether House was serious (House recorded this fact in his diary, apparently seeing nothing sarcastic about the question).[75] A copy dated February 22 received the approval of Asquith, Balfour, and Lloyd George; Grey alone initialled it, and gave it to House to convey to the President.

> Confidential:
>
> Colonel House told me that President Wilson was ready on hearing from France and England that the moment was

opportune, to propose that a conference should be summoned to put an end to the war. Should the Allies accept this proposal, and should Germany refuse it, the United States would probably [sic] enter the war against Germany.

Colonel House expressed the opinion, that, if such a conference met, it would secure peace on terms not unfavorable to the Allies; and if it failed to secure peace, the United States would leave the Conference as a belligerent on the side of the Allies, if Germany was unreasonable. Colonel House expressed an opinion decidedly favorable to the restoration of Belgium, the transfer of Alsace and Lorraine to France, and the acquisition of Russia of an outlet to the sea, though he thought that the loss of territory incurred by Germany in one place would have to be compensated to her by concessions to her in other places outside Europe. If the Allies delayed accepting the offer of President Wilson, and if, later on, the course of the war was so unfavorable to them that the intervention of the United States would not be effective, the United States would probably [sic] disinterest themselves in Europe and look to their own protection in their own way.

I said that I felt the statement, coming from the President of the United States to be a matter of such importance that I must inform the Prime Minister and my colleagues; but that I could say nothing until it had received their consideration. The British government could under no circumstances, accept or make any proposal except in consultation and agreement with the Allies. I thought that the Cabinet would probably feel that the present situation would not justify them in approaching their Allies on this subject at the present moment; but as Colonel House had had an intimate conversation with M. Briand and M. Jules Cambon in Paris, I should think it right to tell M. Briand privately through the French Ambassador in London, what Colonel House had said to us; and I should, of course, whenever there was an opportunity be ready to talk the matter over with Briand if he desired it.[76]

Itd. E. G.

House was victorious. The Memorandum existed. The question afterward would arise, however, of why British officials sanctioned such a document at this time, when mediation with the Germans seemed impractical to the British and impossible to the French.[77] Page expressed the British point of view when he wrote the President three weeks later that, after a year's discussion about the *Lusitania,* the consensus in England was that, short of an invasion of American territory, the Wilson Administration would not go to war for any cause whatsoever.[78]

Lord Bertie, the Ambassador in Paris, wrote Grey expressing another opinion about House's purpose: "I think that that sheep-faced but fox-minded gentleman was out on an electioneering mission and that President Wilson wishes for his Presidential candidature while preserving peace for the United States to pose as the arbiter of the destinies of Europe and at the same time to obtain great advantages for America."[79]

Grey was aware of these points of view, yet he continued to give House all signs of esteem and affection. House wrote a diary entry for February 23 that the Foreign Secretary "was affectionate in his expressions of friendship saying I could never know how much my coming into his life has meant."[80] One conclusion could be that Lansing's proposed *modus vivendi* of early 1916—the removal of armament from British merchantmen—had given Grey a fright, and that he felt he must make an effort to maintain American support. This theory would seem to be borne out by a letter he sent to Bertie on March 5 in which he spoke in an unusually plain manner about his purposes as far as concerned the House mission: "As long as the Military and Naval authorities of the Allies say they can beat the Germans there need be no talk of mediation but if the war gets to a stalemate, the question to be asked will be, not whether the mediation is good electioneering for President Wilson, but whether it will secure better terms for the Allies than can be secured without it. It is therefore in my opinion a great mistake not to treat Colonel House seriously; though if the Allies can dictate terms of peace in Berlin without the help of the United States, nothing will come of Colonel House's proposals. These . . . do not seem to me to be times in which to neglect any profitable friend."[81]

Unaware that he was regarded as both "sheep-faced" and a "profitable friend," the Colonel, meanwhile, had left happily for home.[82] Each day, en route to New York, House received wireless messages from Wilson to keep him abreast of the news. On March 4, House recorded in his diary: "I find that the President and Lansing have gotten themselves into deep waters brought about by their ill-timed proposal as to the disarming of the merchantmen."[83] It was true that Wilson's and Lansing's independent diplomacy had caused consternation among the Allies and revitalized the German's submarine campaign. Using Lansing's suggestion as a pretext, the Germans had announced on February 10, 1916 that submarines would attack all enemy merchantmen without warning after February 29. Lansing had thought he was close to agreement with the Central Powers over the legality of the *Lusitania* affair, but this new statement made the situation acute again and caused the Secretary of State to revert to the orthodox American position which sanctioned the arming of merchantmen for protection.

Wilson had to ride out a storm in Congress over the right of Americans to travel on armed belligerent ships—Senator Gore and Representative McLemore both introduced resolutions forbidding Americans to travel aboard belligerent vessels—and the President had to exert himself to defeat these proposals.[84] His concern is obvious in the Marconi messages sent to House on shipboard. He also asked House to come at once to Washington.

Upon arrival in New York, House was glad to comply with Wilson's summons. After handling reporters with his usual aplomb (an article in the *Tribune* said he was both elusive and significant), he went straight to Washington.[85] Wilson had sent a White House automobile to meet his friend at the station, and the Colonel breakfasted with the President and Mrs. Wilson. Afterward, the three went for an automobile ride and discussed every detail of the House mission.[86] That evening, at the White House, the President saw the Memorandum for the first time.[87]

It would be interesting to know what the President thought when he read this fascinating document. It may be that Wilson saw only what he wanted to see (throughout his tempestuous academic career he had been known to do this)—an opening toward peace negotiations, with which he could start a reasonable discussion with the belligerents. He may have seen how tentative the proposal was with two safeguarding "probablys." The President then added the now-famous third "probably." The phrase, "the United States would leave the Conference as a belligerent" with Wilson's new insertion read: "the United States would [probably] leave the Conference as a belligerent . . ."

Wilson then authorized House to reply to Grey in the following manner typing out the words on his typewriter for House to sign:

> I reported to the President the general conclusions of our conference of the 14th of February, and in light of those conclusions he authorizes me to say that so far as he can speak for the future action of the United States he agrees to the memorandum with which you furnished me with only this correction—that the word "probably" be added after the word "would" and before the word "leave" in line number nine."[88]

This presidential change created a tenuous and highly conditional document, and perpetuated the misconception between House and Wilson. The Colonel could not be sure what the President meant by his new qualification: Evidently there was no discussion between House and Wilson concerning the third "probably;" Wilson was following the pattern of his personality which allowed little explanation. He avoided subjects which could result in controversy with friends, and his affection for

House was such that he would not have entered into an argumentative debate because of fear that it might cause a change in the friendship.[89] The link between the two friends remained strong; the Memorandum's strength was considerably weakened.

For the Colonel's purposes, however, the President's reply to the British Foreign Secretary seemed satisfactory. His next move was to make sure that Grey believed it to be so. He knew that Grey had appeared to doubt an American commitment to the Allies in correspondence with him during October and November, 1915. But he believed that his personal diplomacy while in England had persuaded Grey that Wilson meant to be unequivocal in his commitment (after all, Grey had initialled the Memorandum containing two "probablys"). Now his problem was to explain the third qualification. He did this quite deftly: he followed the cable sent to Grey by Wilson and himself with a personal letter to Grey assuring him that the President had completly approved of everything which had been done "at our conferences," and he explained "He [Wilson] inserted the word "probably" which was merely overlooked in our original draft as it occurs in the sentence above and with the same meaning."[90] Would this trick of rhetoric, this careful blending of two "probablys," succeed in assuaging any doubts Grey might have?

Apparently, House's ploy was successful. Grey seemed unconcerned over the American qualifications. A private note to the British War Cabinet some months later, in November, 1916, shows him remarking flatly that the proposal by Colonel House was confirmed by President Wilson. His other correspondence in 1916 displayed no special concern over Wilson's third "probably," or indeed over "probably" number one and "probably" number two. In his *Twenty-Five Years,* Grey treated the offer of February 1916 as unequivocal.[91] For him Wilson's third "probably" in the final draft was no warning sign, and perhaps had no significance whatever beyond the implication that the President shared control of foreign policy with Congress and could not make an absolute guarantee.[92]

The true meaning of the Memorandum may have been more subtle than a few words, even qualifying words. Whether Grey was seeking intervention by the United States in the war in the early months of 1916 is questionable, but one might assume that he was seeking proof of an American bias for the Allied cause—which would allow the British navy to continue its pressure against Germany without interference. Colonel House's Memorandum, for all its cautious phrasing, did provide Grey with a document to that effect. Grey must have felt he had done the best he could do for his country at this stage of the war.

On the American side there seemed to be a feeling of satisfaction.

House was satisfied, for the Memorandum was the culmination of his wishes and desires at the beginning of his 1916 mission. And the enigmatic Wilson may have felt that the Colonel had made a move for peace which the American public had wanted.[93] Walter Lippmann, in an article in *Foreign Affairs* for April, 1926, gave an interpretation of Wilson's actions: that the President, through the Memorandum, committed himself to a conference to end the war, with certain benevolent sympathies for the Allies acknowledged. According to Lippmann, Wilson could have said: "I will recommend to Congress that the United States enter the war on the side of the Allies." He did not say that. It is possible to conclude, however, that Wilson in early 1916 had high hope that if the Allies invoked the Memorandum and a Conference were to assemble, the warring nations might find it difficult to resume hostilities.[94]

In France at this time a battle had begun to rage around the fortress of Verdun, one which would last through most of the year and bring an enormous toll of soldiers killed and maimed. The high significance of this battle was anticipated from the beginning. Lord Bertie put the British apprehension succinctly: "I do not like the look of Verdun. It may not be taken by the Germans, but their big guns will destroy it, which will have a bad moral effect in neutral countries and a good one in Germany and other enemy countries."[95]

This was the condition of Europe, then, when on March 10, 1916, Colonel House wrote Sir Edward Grey from America: "Be assured my dear friend, that I am thinking of you always, and I wish I could in some way lighten the load which bears so heavily upon you."[96] House's way of lightening the load lay through the Memorandum, and he had no doubt that Grey would, in the near future, utilize their joint diplomatic effort.

Notes

1. Proximity to the scene may have caused House's reaction. Page, stationed in London, consistently agitated for war on the basis of German violation of neutral rights via the submarine. Ross Gregory, *Walter Hines Page: Ambassador to the Court of St. James* (Lexington, Kentucky, 1970), pp. 95-100.

2. Buehrig, *Balance of Power*, pp. 200-202.

3. Gregory, *Walter Hines Page*, pp. 109-110; also Page to House, Aug. 4, 1915, Walter Hines Page Papers, Houghton Library, Harvard University.

4. Wilson's personal sympathy continued to be with the Allies. In a letter to Bryan on June 2, 1915, the President wrote: "It is interesting and significant how often the German Foreign Office goes over the same ground in different words and always missing the essential point involved that Englan's violation of neutral rights is different from Germany's violation of the rights of humanity." He did, however, understand the dilemma of American shippers. William Jennings Bryan's Letter Books, Bryan Papers; also R. S. Baker, *Wilson*, V, pp. 386-372.

5.   Link, ed., *The Papers of Woodrow Wilson*, vol. 33, *April 17-July 21, 1915.*
      Beginning on page 87 and continuing throughout this volume, the copies of the
      letters from the President to Mrs. Galt reveal his growing love for her, and Wilson
      writes that this love had complete possession of him to the exclusion of other
      thoughts. (See, for example, the letter dated June 4, 1914, p. 339.)

6.   House Diary, July 31, 1915 and Sept. 22, 1915, Edward M. House Papers, Yale
      University Library; also C. Seymour, *The Intimate Papers of Colonel House*, II,
      p. 84; also Grey to House, Aug. 26, 1915, Edward M. House Papers, Yale Univer-
      sity Library. Grey had sent an earlier letter to House on August 10 which mention-
      ed peace and said that sources from Germany indicated there might have been
      a peace last February "if we had made proposals then"—this is interesting in view
      of the fact that Grey kept House in England so these proposals would not be made.
      Grey to House, Aug. 10, 1915, Edward M. House Papers, Yale University Library.

7.   House Diary, Oct. 8, 1915, Edward M. House Papers, Yale University Library.

8.   Ray Stannard Baker and Willaim E. Dodds, eds., *The Public Papers of Woodrow
      Wilson* (6 vols., New York, 1925-1927), III, p. 375.

9.   Notter, *The Origins of the Foreign Policy of Woodrow Wilson*, p. 445; also Charles
      Seymour, *American Diplomacy During the World War* (Baltimore, 1934), p. 140.

10.   House to Page, July 15, 1915, Walter Hines Page Papers, Houghton Library,
      Harvard University.

11.   Grey to House, Sept. 22, 1915, Edward M. House Papers, Yale University
      Library. This letter was handed to House personally by Spring Rice on October
      13, 1915. See also C. M. Mason, "Anglo-American Relations: Mediation and
      Permanent Peace," in Hinsley, ed., *Sir Edward Grey*, p. 474.

12.   The Edward M. House Papers, Yale University Library contains both the split
      letters and the integrated copy.

13.   House Diary, Oct. 18, 1915, Edward M. House Papers, Yale University Library;
      also R. S. Baker, *Wilson*, VI, 127-128; also Link, ed., *The Papers of Woodrow
      Wilson*, vol. 35, *October 1, 1915-January 27, 1916*, pp. 81-82.

14.   Notter, *The Origins of the Foreign Policy of Woodrow Wilson*, pp. 447-448.

15.   R. S. Baker, *Wilson*, VI, p. 131.

16.   Grey to House, Nov. 10, 1915, Edward M. House Papers, Yale University
      Library; also Buehrig, *Balance of Power*, p. 209.

17.   House to Grey, Nov. 11, 1915, Edward M. House Papers, Yale University Library;
      also Link, ed., *The Papers of Woodrow Wilson*, vol. 35, *October 1, 1915-January 27,
      1916*, pp. 186-187.

18.   The underlining is Wilson's. This letter can be seen in the Ray Stannard Baker
      collection, Series I, Library of Congress.

19.   Grey to House Nov. 11, 1915, Edward M. House Papers, Yale University Library.

20.   C. Seymour, *The Intimate Papers of Colonel House*, II, p. 98.

21.   Grey to House, Nov. 11, 1915, Edward M. House Papers, Yale University Library.
      Grey, of course, was not being "dull" as House suggested, or even reluctant
      because of the Anglo-American problems concerning the blockade, as he intimated
      in his letter; he was being intensely practical. He wished to find out if this proposal
      from the United States was a blanket approval which might accept the secret
      treaties made by the Allies—about which U. S. officials knew little—and might

reject on a moralistic basis. Two important treaties had already been signed by Great Britain: in March, 1915, the treaty with France and Russia in regard to the annexations of the Straits and Constaninople by Russia; in April, 1915 the Treaty of London promising Italy Trentino, Trieste, and other territory if she entered the war on the Allied side. R. S. Baker, *Wilson*, VI, pp. 132-133. See also C. M. Mason, "Anglo-American Relations: Mediation and Permanent Peace," Hinsley, ed., *Sir Edward Grey*, pp. 475-476.

22.   House to Grey, Dec. 7, 1915, Edward M. House Papers, Yale University Library.

23.   House Diary, Nov. 28, 1915, Edward M. House Papers, Yale University Library.

24.   Hendrick, *Page*, III, pp. 96-97.

25.   Stephen Gwynn, ed., *The Letters and Friendships of Sir Cecil Spring Rice* (2 vols., Boston, 1927), II, p. 300, note 1; C. Seymour, *The Intimate Papers of Colonel House*, II, pp. 100-101.

26.   Tansill, *America Goes to War*, p. 454.

27.   William Jennings Bryan had resigned in June, 1915, ostensibly because of Wilson's bellicose notes to Germany following the sinking of the Lusitania. It is true that he felt the British were as much at fault as the Germans (as early as February 15, 1915, he wrote Wilson "that the British position is without justification") but he also resented House's position with Wilson. When he resigned, he told Wilson "with a quiver in his voice . . . Colonel House has been your Secretary of State, not I . . . . Bryan Papers, General Correspondence, Library of Congress; also House Diary, June 24, 1915, Edward M. House Papers, Yale University Library. According to this diary entry, Wilson told House that he "had explained to Lansing our relations, and he did not believe we would have any trouble with him."

28.   Tansill, *America Goes to War*, p. 452; Robert Lansing, *War Memoirs of Robert Lansing* (Indianapolis, 1935), p. 128; Notter, *The Origins of the Foreign Policy of Woodrow Wilson*, p. 464.

29.   Notter, *The Origins of the Foreign Policy of Woodrow Wilson*, pp. 464-466. Page in London, who wanted America in the war on the Allied side, had a caustic remark to make about the Peace Ship: "The Ford crank ship is at Christiania, and Ford is— sick! They've had some sort of mutiny among the crazy folk aboard." Page Diary, Dec. 14, 1915, Walter Hines Page Papers, Houghton Library, Harvard University.

30.   Notter, *The Origins of the Foreign Policy of Woodrow Wilson*, pp. 464-466; also House Diary, Dec. 21, 1915, Edward M. House Papers, Yale University Library.

31.   C. Seymour, *The Intimate Papers of Colonel House*, II, p. 107. The last two sentences are transposed.

32.   One can assume that House had been exerting steady pressure on the President to get him to agree to the trip. On December 15, House recorded: "I cannot quite get him up to the point where he is willing to take action." It may have been difficult for House to get Wilson's attention since he was preoccupied with plans for his wedding to Mrs. Galt to take place on December 18, 1915. House Diary, Dec. 15, 1915, Edward M. House Papers, Yale University Library.

33.   R. S. Baker, *Wilson*, VI, p. 138.

34.   House Diary, Dec. 25, 1915, Edward M. House Papers, Yale University Library.

35.   A. S. Link, *Confusion and Crises*, pp. 112-113; R. S. Baker, *Wilson* VI, p. 138.

36.   R. S. Baker, *Wilson*, VI, p. 139. Wilson told House to put "further, immediate, and imperative pressure" upon the British.

37.   Buehrig, *Balance of Power*, p. 213; also R. S. Baker, *Wilson*, VI, p. 139.

38.   C. Seymour, *The Intimate Papers of Colonel House*, II, p. 112.

39.   House Diary, Dec. 28, 1915, Edward M. House Papers, Yale University Library. The reporters were not the only ones from whom House kept his purpose secret. Spring Rice was told unequivocally that House "had no special mission of any description, would convey no proposals, would not even make a suggestion of a political character." F. O. 800/85/1263, Spring Rice to Grey, Dec. 23, 1915.

40.   House to Page, Dec. 1, 1915 and House to Page, Dec. 17, 1915, Walter Hines Page Papers, Houghton Library, Harvard University. On the statement which House asked Page to release to the press denying peace parlays, Page has written: "Why lie to me about it?"

41.   Page complained bitterly about House and his mission in a letter to the President written sometime in December, 1915, but never sent. Walter Hines Page Papers, Houghton Library, Harvard University.

42.   House Diary, Jan. 10, 1916, Edward M. House Papers, Yale University Library.

43.   Page Diary, Jan. 12, 1916, Walter Hines Page Papers, Houghton Library, Harvard University.

44.   A. S. Link, *Woodrow Wilson and the Progressive Era*, pp. 205-208.

45.   R. S. Baker, *Wilson*, VI, pp. 159-160.

46.   Henry Cabot Lodge at this early date was writing to his friends in England that "the Administration was vacillating and shifty in its dealings with foreign relations." Lodge to Colonel Arthur Lee, Feb. 14, 1916, F. O. 800/108/1771.

47.   Grey to Spring Rice, Jan. 25, 1916. The telegram is labelled: "This Document is the Property of His Majesty's Government . . . ." Nevertheless, it is in a folder among the Walter Hines Page Papers, Houghton Library, Harvard University.

48.   Page to the President and Secretary of State, Jan. 25, 1916, Walter Hines Page Papers, Houghton Library, Harvard University.

49.   C. Seymour, *The Intimate Papers of Colonel House*, II, pp. 135-136; also House Diary, Jan. 19, 1916, Edward M. House Papers, Yale University Library.

50.   Page's disapproval was directed toward House, but some British officials were also criticizing Grey, albeit quietly. Captain W. R. Hall, Director of Intelligence at the Admiralty had succeeded in breaking House's private cypher to Wilson and had decyphered his telegrams. Hall relayed these to Maurice Hankey, Secretary of the War Committee who confided to his diary on January 27, 1916 his feelings about the talks between House and Grey: "What really horrified me was that Grey seems to have given House the impression that he would bargain the 'Freedom of the Seas' against German Militarism—a most ridiculous idea when one remembers that we keep our treaties and the Hun don't." Stephen Roskill, *Hankey, Man of Secrets* (London, 1970), vol. I, p. 247.

51.   House Diary, Jan. 27, 1916, Edward M. House Papers, Yale University Library.

52.   Ibid.

53.   "The Chancellor drank copiously of beer which was served to us from time to time. I contented myself with mineral water, matching him glass for glass. The beer did

not apparently affect him for his brain was befuddled at the beginning as at the end. Into such hands are the destinies of the people placed." House Diary, Jan. 28, 1916, Edward M. House Papers, Yale University Library.

54. On January 29, House recorded in his diary that he and German officials had discussed better treatment for German prisoners in Russia, a worthwhile subject no doubt, but hardly the reason for House's mission. House Diary, Jan. 29, 1916, Edward M. House Papers, Yale University Library. Also R. S. Baker, *Wilson,* VI, pp. 147-148.

House told the editor of the *Spectator,* John St. Loe Strachey, at lunch on February 15, 1916, that he loathed going to Germany—that while there he scarcely moved out of the American Embassy. Strachey felt he was "an absolutely sincere man and would not lend himself to any intrigue [detrimental to England] even if he were pro-German which he certainly is not." Lewis L. Gould, ed., "A Texan in London: A British Editor Lunches with Colonel Edward M. House, February 15, 1916," *The Southwest Historical Quarterly,* 1980-1981, 84 (4), p. 433.

55. F. O. 800/381/1814, Conversation avec M. House 2 Fevrier, 1916. This document from the French is in the Arthur Nicolson file, misc. corres., 1916. According to Cambon, the letters stated only that House was Wilson's dearest friend and adviser.

56. F. O. 800/181/1800, Deuxieme Entrevue Du Colonel House, 7 Fevrier, 1916.

57. House Diary, Feb. 7, 1916, Edward M. House Papers, Yale University Library. House's underlining.

58. C. Seymour, *The Intimate Papers of Colonel House,* II, p. 165.

59. C. Seymour, *The Intimate Papers of Colonel House,* II, p. 165; also F. O. 800/181/1800. House ended one interview with Cambon by complementing him on the excellent work Jusserand had done in Washington. Cambon replied laconically that he was happy to hear this. This was typical of these conversations with the French—House attempting to flatter them, the French remaining aloof. F. O. 800/381/1814, Cambon conversation with House.

60. C. Seymour, *The Intimate Papers of Colonel House,* II, pp. 164-165.

61. C. Seymour, *The Intimate Papers of Colonel House,* II, pp. 171-173; also House Diary, Feb. 10, 1916, Edward M. House Papers, Yale University Library. House apparently thought that his was the only report of his conversations with the French (Grey encouraged this by professing ignorance of the French attitude toward House's proposal), but a steady exchange of letters between French officials and the British Foreign Office concerning House continued all during February.

62. C. Seymour, *The Intimate Papers of Colonel House,* II, pp. 171-172.

63. Grey, *Twenty-Five Years,* II, p. 125.

64. Lloyd George, *War Memoirs,* I, p. 408.

65. Page Diary, Feb. 9, 1916, Walter Hines Page Papers, Houghton Library, Harvard University.

66. Hendrick, *Page,* III, pp. 284-285; House Diary, Feb. 9, 1916, Edward M. House Papers, Yale University Library.

67. Hendrick, *Page,* III, p. 282. House wrote in his diary that it suited his purpose to leave Page out of the Conference. House Diary, Feb. 11, 1916, Edward M. House Papers, Yale University Library.

68. House Diary, Feb. 14, 1916, Edward M. House Papers, Yale University Library; also C. Seymour, _The Intimate Papers of Colonel House,_ II, pp. 179-180.

69. A. D. H. Smith, _Mr. House of Texas,_ p. 168; also H. Sidebotham, _Pillars of the State,_ pp. 45-49. Concerning the Prime Minister's air of authority, his eccentric wife, Margot Asquith, once told Page that "nobody but God could put Herbert out of office."

70. Lloyd George, _War Memoirs,_ I, p. 411-412.

71. Ibid.

72. C. Seymour, _The Intimate Papers of Colonel House,_ II, p. 135.

73. C. Seymour, _American Diplomacy During the World War,_ p. 151.

74. R. S. Baker, _Wilson,_ VI, p. 152.

75. House Diary, Feb. 21, 1916, Edward M. House Papers, Yale University Library.

76. F. O. 800/181/1800, Titled "Memorandum," Feb. 28, 1916, initialled by Grey. In Seymour's _Intimate Papers of Colonel House,_ this memorandum is dated Feb. 22, 1916; however, in the Foreign Office Papers in London, the date is Feb. 28, 1916.

77. Lennox, ed., The Diary of Lord Bertie, I, p. 312.

78. Page to Wilson, March 20, 1916, Walter Hines Page Papers, Houghton Library, Harvard University.

79. F. O. 800/181/1800, March 2, 1916. Cambon told Nicolson that he thought "Colonel House wished to create a good opinion in European capitals of President Wilson in view of the approaching electoral campaign and he was not inclined to attach much importance to the suggestions of Colonel House." F. O. 800/381/1814, Feb. 15, 1916.

   Another point of view was expressed to Prime Minister Asquith in a lengthy letter written by E. S. Montagu, Minister of Munitions to Prime Minister Asquith dated March 18, 1916, and entitled "Mission of Colonel House" (Asquith Papers, Bodleian Library, Oxford). Montagu wrote that he felt the memorandum might be diplomacy but that it was not essentially honest. Furthermore, Montagu added, even if House could insure American intervention for peace on the side of the Allies by hoodwinking the Germans "the goods are not good enough." The Munitions Minister cautioned his friend Asquith that political victory would not be satisfactory—only a complete moral victory over Germany would suffice—"and that I think House cannot secure us."

80. House Diary, Feb. 23, 1916, Edward M. House Papers, Yale University Library.

81. F. O. 800/181/1800, Grey to Bertie, Mar. 5, 1916. These words written by Grey to Bertie and found by this author in the Bertie file at the Foreign Office could be interpreted as damaging to Grey's integrity showing his deliberate manipulation of the "profitable" friend, House. The letter is handled in an interesting fashion by two British sources: V. H. Rothwell in his _British War Aims and Peace Diplomacy_ (Oxford, 1971), p. 36, cites the letter as being in the Hardinge MSS (Hardinge was permanent Undersecretary from 1905-1910 and was replaced by Arthur Nicolson, Bart., in 1910). This citation reads "copy of letter from Grey to Bertie" and the words are the same with one exception: the last line including the words "profitable friend" is deleted. Rothwell, however, in the text of his book following this letter writes that House was treated with dishonesty.

C. M. Mason, "Anglo-American Relations: Mediation and Permanent Peace," in Hinsley, ed., *Sir Edward Grey*, p. 477, also uses this letter to Bertie, again citing the Hardinge Papers as the source. Mason explains that the Hardinge Papers contain copies of letters between Grey and Bertie. In the text, however, Mason says that Grey sharply rebuked Bertie telling him that he regarded the Colonel as a "trusted friend." The term "trusted friend" is not a direct quote but one gets an entirely different picture of Grey's attitude toward House by the use of different adjectives. Apparently Mason chose to use the term "trusted friend" instead of "profitable friend" which is the precise wording in the Bertie letter.

82. He left behind a disgruntled Ambassador, Walter Hines Page, who wrote in his diary: "Last night, House left London for Falmouth to sail for New York on Friday. He cannot come again or—I go!" Page Diary, Feb. 24, 1916, Walter Hines Page Papers, Houghton Library, Harvard University.

83. C. Seymour, *The Intimate Papers of Colonel House*, II, p. 218.

84. Buehrig, *Balance of Power*, p. 217.

85. *Tribune* quoted in John Dos Passos, *Mr. Wilson's War* (Garden City, New York, 1962), p. 159.

86. House Diary, March 6, 1916, Edward M. House Papers, Yale University Library. Mrs. Wilson accompanied her husband everywhere—to golf courses and conferences alike.

87. C. Seymour, *The Intimate Papers of Colonel House*, II, p. 199.

88. C. Seymour, *The Intimate Papers of Colonel House* II, p. 202; also R. S. Baker, *Wilson*, VI, pp. 152-153.

89. R. S. Baker, *Wilson*, VI, p. 322.

90. House to Grey, March 10, 1916, Edward M. House Papers, Yale University Library.

91. Grey, *Twenty-Five Years*, II, pp. 124-132.

92. C. Seymour, *American Diplomacy During the World War*, p. 155.

93. Wilson's notes to House during this period indicate his appreciation for House's diplomatic accomplishments which implied approval of the House-Grey Memorandum. See, for example, Wilson to House, March 9, 1916, in Link, ed., *The Papers of Woodrow Wilson*, vol. 36, *January 27-May 9, 1916* (Princeton, N. J., 1980), p. 276.

94. Walter Lippmann, "The Intimate Papers of Colonel House," *Foreign Affairs*, IV (April 1926), pp. 383-393.

95. Lennox, ed., *The Diary of Lord Bertie*, I. p. 312.

96. House to Grey, March 10, 1916, Edward M. House Papers, Yale University Library.

Chapter VI

Failure and Success

Walter Hines Page, the forgotten man as far as House and Wilson were concerned, did not see the Memorandum before the Colonel left for America. He knew about its contents, and he strongly disapproved. Part of his disapproval stemmed from the fact that House had held secret meetings with Allied leaders which Page did not attend. The Ambassador commented caustically about the conversation at these seminars between House and the Allied leaders: "I wonder if they understood what *he* said, or if he understood what *they* said."[1] This may have been a discerning remark. And even if understanding did exist between House and his Allied friends it did not survive time and distance. House believed, as he sailed for America, that Grey had given him assurances that Wilson's mediation would be welcome by summer. Throughout the spring and summer the Colonel and the President waited in Washington for Grey to go ahead with the Memorandum.

Wilson, whose single-word revision of the Memorandum had greatly modified it, nevertheless came to regard it as a device for mediation which might end the war and extricate the United States from an almost insoluble difficulty.[2] He was far from accepting House's interpretation of mediation as an adjunct of an Allied victory. He did not even regard victory as an ultimate goal, but wanted the war to end. He was influenced by domestic political considerations; a successful peace move would make him irresistible to the Democratic party in June and to the American electorate in November. He wished also to commit his party to a league of nations, and to use this as a leading issue in the campaign.[3] Ambassador Spring Rice described the President's mood in a letter to Grey in the spring of 1916: "If the President can appear before the country as the great pacificator before the end of October, his re-election is almost certain. Consequently it is not surprising to see that his mind is turning that way. His standpoint seems to be that the world is mad and can only be saved by a few sane men who are left in it. As one of the madmen, you will form your own opinion, presumably a mad one, as to the claims of our sane Savior . . . ."[4]

Spring Rice, in his own way, was being as caustic as Page, for he, too, had felt that in his position as Ambassador in Washington he had been circumvented by the diplomacy between House and Grey. He had complained bitterly in April, 1916 to Theodore Russell in the Foreign Office that the letters he was asked to transmit to House from Grey had instructions on them "to be unopened." This he regarded as a "serious imputation" and was hardly appeased by Russell's reply that Grey was trying to comply with the Colonel's wish that their correspondence "should be seen by only four eyes."[5]

House may have been aware of the dissatisfaction among the ranks in the Anglo-American diplomatic structure; this had never bothered him before, and did not do so now. He had only one purpose— to carry out the Memorandum. He thereby would accomplish what he had tried to do since he became Wilson's adviser: make Wilson's influence felt in Europe.[6] In 1914 he had attempted to establish the President as the pacifist who prevented the war; in 1915 his mission had been to see if Wilson could become the mediator who could stop it. Now, in 1916, he wished for the President the role of the belligerent who could go in and win it, through a working agreement between Great Britain and the United States.[7] His motives no doubt were the highest, for he, like Page, had faith in the advantages and virtues of a Pax Anglo-Americana. He had revealed this faith as early as 1912, in his fanciful romance, *Philip Dru, Administrator*. A super-reformer, Dru was able to accomplish great things by an international league of peace based on cooperation between the two great English-speaking peoples.[8] In the spring of 1916 House was not tormented by suspicion of Allied war aims or distrust of European power politics. He waited with Wilson for his English friend Grey to give the word which would put the Anglo-American scheme into operation.[9]

At this point he encountered the somewhat different viewpoint of Grey, whose philosophy of the war remained constant from August, 1914, until his resignation in December, 1916. Grey believed that victory over Germany was by far the best solution, provided it was followed by a reasonable peace, negotiated with a beaten enemy. He was never certain that victory was possible; he had moments when he felt defeat conceivable. Only an American alliance would make victory swift and sure.[10] Therefore America must not be alienated, the idea of negotiating must not be vetoed. To give America, or its President, or its President's friend, the idea that England stood in the way of a negotiated peace would be to play the game of German propaganda.[11] Grey's object in connection with the House-Grey Memorandum was to seem to acquiesce in a cooperative move with America while giving reasons why England could not cooperate. Barbara Tuchman in *The Proud Tower* has described British Liberals during this era as statesmen for whom it was necessary to find a moral reason to fortify a natural policy of self-interest, "a practice no one carried to higher perfection or more obscure expression than Sir Edward Grey." This technique was perfectly illustrated by the obscurity of Grey's replies to House in 1916 after the Colonel had gone back to America.

The cross-purposes of the co-authors of the Memorandum, House and Grey, and of the silent, sometime reluctant partner, Wilson, made it improbable that the plan of mediation and intervention could be made operable. Other factors entered. During the four months after the drafting of the plan, diplomacy was dominated not by statesmanship but by military events.[12] On the Continent, the fighting around Verdun stiffened the French and British resolve to "see the war through." The Allies became convinced that they must make a great new attack along the Somme. On the seas, the Germans revived the submarine campaign. In opposition to high political authority, German naval commanders were taking matters into their own hands and torpedoing ships without warning. Such was the fate of the unarmed French channel steamer *Sussex* on March 24, 1916. The killing of eighty persons, mostly passengers, again brought to a focus the submarine issue, to where it had been following the sinking of the *Lusitania,* and House reacted in the same bellicose manner, wanting immediate action against Germany. This time he had an instrument he believed he could use—the House-Grey Memorandum—which stipulated intervention with a demand for peace negotiations backed up by assurance that the United States otherwise would (probably) go to war against Germany.[13]

During the two weeks following the sinking of the *Sussex,* House bombarded the President with advice, all of which seemed to point to a break with Germany. On April 3 he made his suggestion as to the Memorandum: "Before it [the break] comes do you not think it would be well to cable Grey telling him the status of affairs and asking him whether or not it would not be wise to intervene now rather than to permit the break to come?"[14] Wilson did not want to make an issue of the *Sussex;* but with pressure from House (and Lansing, too)

he looked for a loophole for peace negotiations. Because he had nothing
better in mind he agreed to House's suggestion to explore the possibilities of the House-Grey Memorandum.[15] The result was this message,
typed by Wilson and sent to Grey over House's signature on April
6, 1916:

> Since it now seems probably that this country must break
> with Germany on the submarine question unless the unexpected
> happens and since if this country should get its teeth in the war
> would undoubtedly be prolonged I beg to suggest that if you
> had any thought of acting at an early date on the plan we agreed
> upon you might wish now to consult with your allies with a view
> to acting immediately.

> (Endorsement by House:
> This is a joint composition of
> the President's and my own. I
> suggested elimination "get its
> teeth in" and substituting
> "become a belligerent.")[16]

The above cablegram must stand as the strangest of all the diplomatic products of House and Wilson. In effect it said to the Allies
that if the submarine situation continued America would have to go
to war against Germany, and the Allies should take the step that
would keep the United States from doing so. Here was what the
British were hoping for—that the submarine would drive the United
States into the war.[17]

Grey's reply, written on April 7, appeared a masterpiece of
restraint. He said that he did not feel that the time had come for a
conference—nor did the French since the German attack at Verdun.
He understood the dilemma about the *Sussex* and "ruthless torpedoing
of neutral ships"—that is, if the United States Government took a
strong line about these acts it would become difficult to propose a
conference to Germany; if these acts were ignored by the American
Government, the Allies would lose faith in the United States government. He added that he did not think the entry of the United States
into the war would prolong it, and closed by saying that "My personal
touch with you and through you with the President makes me more
hopeful, but amid such tremendous forces an individual opinion
formed in private knowledge can count for little."[18]

While reaffirming his friendship with House, Grey said politely
that he intended to do nothing at this point, and indeed it is hard to
see what House expected him to do. The torpedoing of the *Sussex*
had been a German action. The sensible American reaction appeared

to be an appeal to the Germans. Wilson—with Lansing's help—composed and sent a virtual ultimatum to Germany on April 18 on the *Sussex* affair. The President attempted to base his demand on a broader issue than American rights alone.[19] "Unless the Imperial Government should now immediately declare and effect an abandonment of its present methods of submarine warfare against passenger and freight-carrying vessels, the Government of the United States can have no choice but to sever diplomatic relations with the German Empire altogether. This action the Government of the United States contemplates with the greatest reluctance, but feels constrained to take in behalf of humanity and the rights of neutral nations."[20]

The German reply on May 4 ended the crisis temporarily, for the Kaiser had decided to accede to American demands even though this meant that submarine warfare in the war zone would cease. The note expressed hope that the United States would proceed to restore "the freedom of the seas" and insist that Britain observe international law regarding the blockade.[21]

The situation remained fundamentallly precarious. American neutrality was at the mercy of the struggle to control the seas. Nothing had been settled, and when House proposed writing Grey again, Wilson agreed. He suggested that House protest the blockade and indicate a desire for a peace conference. On May 10 Colonel House dispatched a long cable:

> There is an increasing insistent demand here that the President take some action toward bringing the war to a close. The impression grows that the Allies are more determined upon the punishment of Germany than exacting terms that neutral opinion would consider just. This feeling will increase if Germany discontinues her illegal submarine activities . . . . If the President is to serve humanity in a large way, steps should be taken now rather than wait until the opportunity becomes less fortunate. His statement would be along the lines you and I have so often discussed and which you express in your letter to me of September 22, 1915 . . . . I am sure this is the psychological moment for this statement to be made . . . If it is not done now the opportunity may be forever lost.[22]

House followed with a curious letter to Grey the next day, May 11:

> We have been on the eve of a break with Germany so long that I have not written as it seemed it would come each day. For the moment matters are quiet, and, unless Germany transgressed further, there will probably be no break . . . . If we get into the war, I feel sure it would not be a good thing for England . . . .

It would probably lead to the complete crushing of Germany . . .
The wearing down process, as far as Germany is concerned, has
gone far enough to make her sensible of the power we can wield . . . .
this is the psychological moment to strike for those things which
the President and you have so near at heart. Delay is dangerous
and may defeat our ends . . . . Therefore England should be
immediately responsive to our call. Her statesmen will take a
great responsibility if they hesitate or delay, and in the event of
failure because thay refuse to act quickly, history will bring a
grave indictment against them.[23]

Once more the British government took refuge in delay. Sir
Edward—who could follow the submarine controversy as well as
House—apparently did not feel that delay was dangerous for England;
nor did he appear worried that history would bring a grave indictment
against him. To act now under the House-Grey Memorandum, Grey
implied in his answering cable, would be premature, and if the President
should summon a peace conference without indication of a basis for
peace, it would be construed as German in origin. Grey carefully
forgot that the President, through House, had suggested terms by
no means unfavorable to the Allies, and that he, Grey, had agreed
to such terms on February 22 when he initialed the Memorandum.
He sympathized with the President's aspirations regarding a league
of nations, but conveyed the impression that he was removed from
that idea, and that his letter of September 22, 1915, referred to by
House, contemplated the diminution of arms. To remove himself
further from a joint responsibility with House he closed with these
impersonal words: "I hope you will realize this telegram is a purely
personal opinion sent in reply to your request without consulting
my colleagues, not even the Prime Minister, who is now in Ireland,
but if you desire it I will consult him upon his return."[24]

Consulting had not been the course in his diplomacy with House
throughout the preceding years. To House this commentary appeared
as a personal as well as official rebuff. On May 13 he noted bitterly
in his diary: "For two years Grey has been telling me that the solution
of international well-being depended upon the United States being
willing to take her part in world affairs. Now that we indicate a willingness to do so, he halts, stammers, and questions. . . ."[25]

While House was confiding his frustration to his diary in his
apartment on East Fifty-Third Street in New York, over 125,000
citizens of that city were marching in a demonstration of dissatisfaction
with the progress of the war. The group—the largest parade since
the Grand Review at the close of the Civil War—seemed to have
"Preparedness" as its slogan. Actually, patriotism may have been its

theme. The largest American flag ever made hung between the St. Regis and Gotham hotels, and in hundreds of towns throughout the country there was a similar sort of flag-waving.[26] The American public affirmed its identity, and wanted in, or out, or something. From the Verdun front the news was that French losses had been 120,000; British about 90,000, and German losses (according to Marshal Pétain) over 450,000.[27] These casualities stirred world leaders into talk of peace. The King of Spain and the Pope declared their willingness to cooperate with such a movement. Gerard reported from Germany that he feared an official renewal of unrestricted submarine warfare; he advised the President to demand peace.[28]

Moved by both the unrest in the United States and by the frightfulness of the war itself Wilson wrote to House on May 16, 1916, stating his views, one of the most vigorous letters of his career, a letter he considered a turning point in his approach to problems of the war. It contained all the things he was to say in speech after speech from that time on:

> Washington
> 16 May, 1916
>
> My dearest friend,
>
> I have been giving some very careful thought to your question how we should deal with Sir Edward and his Government at this turning point,—for it really is that.
>
> It seems to me that we should really get down to hard pan.
>
> The situation has altered altogether since you had your conference in London and Paris. The at least temporary removal of the acute German question has concentrated attention here on the altogether indefensible course Great Britain is pursuing with regard to trade to and from neutral ports and her quite intolerable interception of mails on the high seas carried by neutral ships. Recently there has been added the great shock opinion in this country has received from the course of the Britain Government towards some of the Irish rebels.
>
> We are plainly face to face with this alternative, therefore. The United States must either make a decided move for peace (upon some basis that promises to be permanent) or, if she postpones that, must insist to the limit upon her rights of trade and upon such freedom of the seas as international law already justifies her in insisting on as against Great Britain, with the same plain speaking and firmness that she has used against Germany. And the choice must be made immediately. Which does Great Britain prefer? She cannot escape both. To do nothing is now, for us, impossible.
>
> If we move for peace, it will be along these lines 1) Such a settlement with regard to their own immediate interests as the

belligerents may be able to agree upon. We have nothing material of any kind to ask for ourselves and are quite aware that we are in no sense parties to the quarrel. Our interest is only in peace and its guarantees; 2) a universal alliance to maintain freedom of the seas and to prevent any war begun either a) contrary to treaty covenants or b) without warning and full inquiry,—a virtual guarantee of territorial integrity and political independence.

It seems to me to be of imperative and pressing importance that Sir Edward should understand all this and that the crisis can not be postponed; and it can be done with the most evident spirit of friendliness through you. Will you not prepare a full cable putting the whole thing plainly to him? We must act, and act at once in the one direction or the other.

With affectionate messages from us all.

Faithfully yours,
Woodrow Wilson[29]

House at once used the letter as a basis for new messages to Grey, sent on May 19 and May 23, warning that if England refused to support a peace move there would be trouble with the United States. "Your seeming lack of desire to cooperate with us will chill enthusiasm here." He said there was no intention of calling a conference immediately; the Allies would have "ample" time to test the endurance of the Germans; and then in a sprightly paragraph House said that "if England is indeed fighting for the emancipation of Europe, we are ready to join her." Ray Stannard Baker has suggested that House diluted the President's sternness, but when Wilson's letter to House is compared with House's cable to Grey, it appears that House was doing more; he was reassuring Grey of American partiality to the Allied cause.[30]

Houses's cable gave Grey little cause for alarm, and the Foreign Secretary continued his campaign of polite evasion. With somewhat peculiar logic, but impeccable rhetoric, he answered that "a premature announcement of intervention by the President might be dangerous to the cause he and we have at heart because it would be interpreted as meaning that he desired peace on a basis favorable to Germany . . . No such peace could secure a reliable and enduring organization of the kind he contemplates."[31] That same week Grey on May 24 had made an impromptu speech in Commons proclaiming—to the accompaniment of "Hear! Hear!"—a fight to the finish: "The prowess of the French Army during the long battle of Verdun is saving France and her allies, too . . . . deeply as we desire to see the fruits of peace established . . . I believe the duty of diplomacy at the present moment is to maintain, as it has completely maintained, the solidarity of the

Allies and to give the utmost support it can to the military and naval measures which are necessary . . . ."[32]

Page wrote House enthusiastically about this speech: "No utterance by anyone has stirred this kingdom for many months as Sir Edward's impromptu speech last night in the House of Commons when he called the German Chancellor a first-class liar . . . . As you know, he is the most gentle of all the Cabinet, yet he felt moved to say that there can be no peace until the German despotism is broken."[33] The Colonel may have thought Grey unsure of Wilson's commitment to the Allies.

This speech in Commons raised questions. House thought he knew how gentle and peace-loving Grey was—at least, such was the impression from their many talks before the fireplace in Grey's study. For one so devoted to peace the Foreign Secretary's behavior toward Houses's communications suggesting use of the Memorandum seemed inconsistent. A public speech by the President stating his attitude toward mediation might provide the stimulus to move the British.

There followed a move from the American side. An occasion for a speech presented itself when Ex-President Taft, head of the League to Enforce Peace, invited Wilson to address a League meeting on May 27.[34] House wanted Wilson to use the occasion to demand a conference, indicating at the same time a willingness of the United States to share responsibilities for maintaining peace. On the eve of delivery of the speech House and Wilson decided it would be better to leave out the appeal for an immediate conference (the Allies might denounce such a move as a German trick—Spring Rice constantly intimated this possibility to House and others), and make the address a general exposition of American foreign policy with all of Wilson's idealistic hopes for the future.[35]

Wilson's speeches were often masterpieces (House once said that Wilson was the greatest orator the world had ever known). On May 27, 1916, in the new Willard Hotel, the President had something to say and said it extremely well. He threw away the traditional isolationist policy of the United States, and outlined three points of a plan for world peace: (1) the right of self-determination for important national groups; (2) the right of small nations to enjoy international respect for their sovereignty; (3) the right of the whole world to be free from disturbance of its peace, and to enforce this right there should be an association of nations which would make war impossible. Of the war he said (and it might be a fair supposition that this was the result of his oratorical technique and not necessarily a planned phrase), "The obscure fountains from which its stupendous flood has burst forth we are not interested to search for or explore."[36]

The British ignored Wilson's masterful statements and seized on the latter sentence—that the United States was not concerned with the war's causes. Their press reacted violently.[37] *Punch* wondered how anyone who had maintained even a casual contact with the course of history since July, 1914, could discuss the situation with such "Olympian detachment and conspicuous moderation." *The Saturday Review* once more declared Britain's determination to vindicate her sacrifices by destruction of German militarism.[38] Ambassador Page said the President was speaking to the gallery filled with peace cranks— Bryans, Fords, Jane Addamses.[39] Grey wrote House that he read the speech "in the light of my talks with you and welcomed it. But the phrase about not being concerned with the objects and causes of the war was sure to chill the Allies."[40]

The attitude of the British chilled, and since this was the determinative factor in realizing the House-Grey plan, progress seemed impossible. The speech of May 27 had an adverse effect on Anglo-American diplomacy. But late in May, House still was dreaming of intervention on the British side. He had written a private letter to Grey on the day of Wilson's address: "There is one thing to which I wish to call your attention and that is the German Chancellor's statement that Germany would make peace on the basis of the map as it stands today. This cannot mean anything except a victorious peace for Germany. If England and France, under our invitation, should go to a peace conference, now, it would probably lead either to German's abandonment of this position or war with us. I thought I would call your attention to this, although I take it you have considered it."[41]

Sir Edward Grey had considered all angles, and was looking at the moment at the French angle. His standard reply to House and Wilson was that he could do nothing without the French, and that they should be approached directly rather than through British auspices. He had stated this again in his message to House on May 29, pointing out that separate negotiations were impossible, and that "even separate interchange of ideas with a friendly neutral is not easy."[42] House had not found it easy, and although he approached the French Ambassador— as Grey obliquely had suggested—on the possibility of an American peace proposal, he found that the French were not interested in peace until the Germans were defeated. House reported this to Grey, commenting that he wondered if the Allies knew that their position in the United States might materially change after November.[43] Grey (back to the French again) replied on June 28 that no Englishman could urge the French to make peace after their own effort on the western front.[44] House wrote Grey on July 15 that there was nothing

further the President could do "for he gets but little support or encouragement outside of America."[45] Grey ended this useless exchange
on August 28 stating that England would not contemplate peace until
all the Allies agreed—that Germany might be able to speak for her
allies "because she was absolutely predominant," but that England's
allies were equal and independent. As for his own part, Grey explained
that he shared responsibility for daily conduct of the war, and since
the very existence of his country was at stake, "I cannot force the pace
any more."[46]

It was not easy for Wilson to give up the role of peacemaker at
this time. When a friend displeased him he ceased to like that person.
So it was with the Allies. He became angry. There had been many
causes of irritation. For two years the British had discouraged his
attempts at mediation. At the same time they sought every financial
and commercial advantage. They had interfered with American
shipping, to the point of regulating trade with the neutral nations
of Europe. On July 19, 1916, the British Government had published
a black list of more than eighty American firms with whom Britishers
were forbidden to trade, this in retaliation for trade by those firms
with the Central Powers. To Wilson such tactics appeared an invasion
of American rights.[47]

The result was a summer of tension in Anglo-American relations.[48]
The President manifested his anger at the British rejection of his peace
offers and the pressure against shipping by a change of policy. He
brought Ambassador Page home "to get some American atmosphere
into him"[49] The State Department's protests were no longer friendly.
A harsh note on July 26 charged that Great Britain had disregarded
well-defined international practices and called attention to serious
consequences of the black list. Wilson warned American bankers
through the Federal Reserve Board to use caution in financing Allied
trade.

Colonel House had taken to the woods, literally and figuratively,
after the Allied refusal of the offer of mediation. He spent the summer
in an isolated spot in New Hampshire, nine miles from a railroad,
four miles from a post office. The mail did go through, and in addition
to his unsatisfactory correspondence with Grey he kept up a flow of
advice that Wilson "keep balance in regards relations with England."[50]
He resented British behavior, and recorded a conversation in which he
let Page know upon the ambassador's return, that he felt the British,
as well as the Germans, dealt in hypocrisy.[51]

House's friend Grey, who had just been raised to the peerage
as Viscount Grey of Fallodon, was disturbed at the worsening of

Anglo-American relations, but unconciliatory about the black list. Grey pointed out to Wilson that "it was an exercise of the sovereign right of an independent state over its own citizens."[52] His letters to House during July and August, refusing mediation, had not been his usual graceful efforts. His health had given away—he was living on spoonfuls of bread and milk in July—and his eyesight was failing rapidly.[53] It was becoming more difficult to maintain friendship with America, and appease public opinion in Britain. It was abundantly clear that mediation talk was not popular. The battle on the Somme which had begun in June seemed to be going well in late summer; there were signs of some deterioration of the German army. The *Spectator* on September 16, 1916 indicated the British attitude: "We will tolerate no pliable, good-natured congress where all belligerents could kiss and be friends; there must be no great, flat, flabby over-grown international Pow-wow, with intrigue of every form where a bribing, wheedling, threatening Germany might gain advantages." It was plain that the Allies wanted to impose the conditions of peace upon a Germany bereft of the power to bargain.[54]

Grey still believed in placating America, unlike many British statesmen who felt Wilson should be presented with the iron logic of facts. Lloyd George illustrated this latter approach in an interview to an American reporter on September 28, in which he said that any peace move by a neutral such as the Vatican or the United States would be regarded as pro-German: "President Wilson . . . must understand that there can be no outside interference at this time . . . The fight must be to the finish—to a knockout!"[55] Grey thereupon wrote Lloyd George one of the sharpest letters he ever penned, that he felt a public warning to the President of the United States had been unnecessary and could close the door on Wilson's mediation which the Allies might desperately need.[56] Grey, of course, had never spoken so plainly against any proposals by the United States (this was not his sort of diplomacy) and feared that Lloyd George's remarks might have undone months of subtle machinations with the Colonel and the President.

The presidential election in November slowed Wilson's diplomatic efforts, for during the weeks leading to the election the President had advised Lansing that only routine matters should be taken up at that time—"because all foreign statesmen are waiting to see which way the election goes, and in the meantime they know that settlements will be inconclusive."[57] At the convention in June, Wilson had been pictured as a bulwark against the tides of war. The slogan "He kept us out of war," first used by Governor Glynn of New York, later by the Democratic party, was a legitimate claim, but interpreted as a promise to "keep us out of war in the future." Wilson interpreted it that way, and considered his re-election a mandate from the people to make a peace move. He had other reasons for wanting peace in addition to campaign promises and humanitarian purposes. He had become aware of a controversy in Germany between the military staff and the civil government over resumption of unrestricted submarine warfare. If U-boat war were resumed he would find a break with Germany inevitable as a result of his *Sussex* note.[58] At last the election occurred, a close affair, turning on the vote in California which for one reason or another went to Wilson. The President found the way open for mediation.

In late November and early December, 1916, Wilson, House, and Lansing held discussions on the best way to approach the mediation. If Wilson had no confidence in Lansing's advice, his dependence on House was still great. Aside from Mrs. Wilson and Dr. Grayson, the White House physician, House was the only person the President trusted. But he had begun expressing beliefs even when they conflicted with those of House. It had been a year of revelation for Wilson—the year of 1916—and the motives of the Allies seemed as selfish as Germany's motives, the new "War Cabinet" in Britain as militant as the German Government. House's friend, Sir Edward Grey, was replaced by Balfour on December 5, and Lloyd George, proponent of the "knock-out blow," became Prime Minister.[59] House remembered that Lloyd George, in February, 1916, had seemed eager for Wilson's mediation. He suggested to Wilson on December 7 that it might be a good time to revive the House-Grey Memorandum. Wilson then revealed his intermost thoughts for the first time since discussions of the Memorandum had begun. The Memorandum had been based on the assumption of Anglo-American cooperation, and this now was out of date, he told House emphatically. He planned to stand for peace alone, independent of others. If the Germans responded favorably he would work with them, and if the Allies resisted he would attempt to force them. "We cannot go back to those plans, we must shape new ones!"[60]

This was the final word on the House-Grey Memorandum, spoken as perhaps it should have been by the President of the United States. The President at last had made up his mind about the ambiguous proposal which with the addition of his "probably" had become triply ambiguous, and which the British obviously had no intention of using. With the President's words the Memorandum was gone forever.

Wilson attempted an independent peace move on December 18, 1916, when he sent a message to the belligerent capitals calling on both sides for a statement of terms on which they would conclude the war. Wilson had risen above personal feeling.[61] It was an effort of statesmanship.

It was also an effort on which Colonel House had not been consulted. After the mediation proposal had been sent, Wilson informed House, who was in New York, saying that the time had been too short to summon him.[62] House's diary reveals the Colonel's resentment. House recorded on December 20 that Wilson did not seem to understand why the Allies were fighting. "I find with this note the President has nearly destroyed all the work I have done in Europe."[63] The note certainly made it appear that the President no longer required the Colonel's political guidance, and its tone was so neutral that the special position heretofore held by the British vanished. This did not prove fatal to British interests, for the timespan between Wilson's peace appeal and German announcement of unrestricted submarine warfare on January 31, 1917 was so short that relations never reached the breaking point. Wilson thus severed relations with Germany. As a matter of chance rather than policy, Lloyd George and Balfour evaded the dangers of an unfriendly America which, throughout 1916, had plagued Asquith and Grey.

That imbroglio of misunderstanding, the House-Grey Memorandum, so one must conclude, had been at the center of Anglo-American relations in 1916. It has generally been accepted that the Memorandum was a saddening failure, and many historians have lamented that if it had been carried out thousands of lives and billions of dollars could have been saved by virtue of a shorter war. The theory is that the British were presented with a great opportunity, and muffed it. But a hard look at the Memorandum and its creators reveals its improbability, from beginning to end.

First there had been a wide gap between Allied war objectives and the kind of peace the government of the United States intended to support. No one knew this better than Grey, but House and Wilson seemed incredibly unaware of that fact in the first half of 1916. Allied war objectives were such that they had to be imposed on a beaten foe rather than having the victor and vanquished reason together.[64] The tentative terms of the Memorandum set forth by House as acceptable to Wilson contained no indemnities or reparations, no German colonies for the victors, no destruction of the German navy. House's terms were all right as far as they went—no one could argue about the restoration of Belgium—but they stopped short of what British officials felt was necessary. The moderate terms suggested by the Colonel would only have been acceptable to the Allies if their coalition were in danger of military defeat; in that case something would be better than nothing.[65]

Second, Grey had told House and Wilson many times that Britain could do nothing toward carrying out the Memorandum without approval of the Allies. It is true that Britain's Allies did not push for action on mediation. Russia was not fully informed, so there was no encouragement from that quarter. The British Ambassador to France, Bertie, reported that Cambon had "laughed it to scorn."[66] With French territory at stake, France would scarcely have been interested in a moderate peace. It did appear that Grey had almost a monomania about keeping the French Government satisfied within the Entente. After conclusion of the Entente of 1904, when Edward VII and British statesmen had visited Germany, Grey always had assured the French that such visits had no "new political significance." He informed Cambon of Haldane's visit to Germany in 1912, telling him, according to Cambon, that there was no intention of negotiating a naval program with Germany.[67] In the current situation Grey felt that the brunt of the fighting had fallen upon the French—that the British had been accused of husbanding their own army—and to prove this was not so Britain would be obligated to fight when the French desired it. During the spring and summer of 1916, when French troops were fighting desperately, peace without French acquiescence would not only have been premature but impossible.[68]

What was Grey's purpose in initialing the Memorandum, if he knew it was unworkable? Grey revealed this purpose in a letter to Bertie in which he called House "a profitable friend." He needed the cooperation of America, and House, because of association with the American President, was the closest representative of American cooperation with whom Grey had contact. He liked House. He needed him as a channel to America. He needed to know how far Britain could go in interfering with American shipping. The Memorandum did not guarantee a supine United States government, as far as concerned maritime rights, but it did indicate toleration. The Memorandum showed whose side America was on.

There was a time in the summer and autumn of 1916 when Grey faced the possibility that the Memorandum did not indicate what he thought it did—support by the United States. His rejections had been cautious and careful, but danger lay in the thoughts of the unaccountable, inscrutable, or, at least, unpredictable President. Wilson's reactions were certainly not as predictable as those of House. Grey thought House could be stalled and would manitain loyalty to the Allies. Rejection or stalling often caused Wilson to become angry, and now he began to push the very real complaints of the United States against England. No wonder Grey was living on bread and milk in the summer of 1916. Had he, for all his careful diplomacy, alienated the President?

House's actions concerning the document are perhaps the most easily understood. He was so intrigued with the part he played in creating the Memorandum that he did not see the futility of it. He had written in his diary on March 10, 1916 immediately after his return from England: "The life I am leading transcends in interest and excitement any romance. I cannot begin to outline here what happens from day to day, how information from every quarter pours into this little unobtrusive study."[69] House's philosophy was that the good of mankind could best be served by Anglo-American co-operation, and he believed Wilson should head this powerful influence for good. He persuaded Wilson into partial agreement. Wilson did not commit himself altogether—a fact House did not understand until December, 1916 when he heard the President say that the Memorandum could not be used.

Should the Memorandum be labelled a failure? Since it was never carried out, since the United States did not enter the war through this instrument, House's diplomacy failed. But Grey, in creation of the document, and by judicious stalling, was able to prevent a breakdown between the two countries. Shortly after the end of the crucial year 1916 (in fact, in the first weeks of 1917), as he had hoped, Germany broke the *Sussex* pledge and the United States entered the war against the Central Powers because of the submarine issue. This result fulfilled the fondest wish of the British. House's diplomacy had failed but, paradoxically, the other creator of the Memorandum, Grey, and his diplomacy, proved successful.

Notes

1. Page Diary, Feb. 9, 1916, Walter Hines Page Papers, Houghton Library, Harvard University.

2. W. Lippmann, "The Intimate Papers of Colonel House," p. 392.

3. Osgood, *Ideals and Self-Interest in American Foreign Relations,* p. 188; also A. S. Link, *Woodrow Wilson and the Progressive Era,* p. 233.

4. Gwynn, ed., *Letters of Spring Rice,* II, pp. 331-332.

5. F. O. 800/242/1776, Spring Rice to Russell, April 7, 1916, and Russell to Spring Rice, April 19, 1916.

6.   During this period House had no interest in what he termed "local situations" which the President wanted to discuss: "I myself am so little interested in them that I talk of them with reluctance." House Diary, March 29, 1916, Edward M. House Papers, Yale University Library.

7.   L. J. Maxse, "Colonel House as Potential President of the U. S. A." *National Review,* 87 (May, 1926), pp. 377-378.

8.   In 1911-1912, House wrote the novel *Phillip Dru, Administrator,* which was published anonymously. The hero, Dru, barred by ill-health from a military career became dictator of the United States. The Georges conclude that the handsome, dashing Dru was everything House wished to be and that Dru's political philosophies were precisely those of House. George and George, *Woodrow Wilson and Colonel House,* p. 131.

9.   Osgood, *Ideals and Self-Interest in American Foreign Relations,* p. 162.

10. Grey once told Winston Churchill that "the United States is like a gigantic boiler. Once the fire is lighted under it there is no limit to the power it can generate." Winston Churchill, *The Grand Alliance* (Boston, 1950), p. 608.

11. Trevelyan, *Grey of Fallodon,* pp. 353-354.

12. R. S. Baker, *Wilson,* VI, p. 154.

13. Ibid., pp. 178-181.

14. C. Seymour, *The Intimate Papers of Colonel House,* II, pp. 229-230.

15. A. S. Link, *Confusion and Crisis,* pp. 236, 237; also R. S. Baker, *Wilson,* VI, p. 182.

16. Cable from House to Wilson and Grey, with addition by House, April 6, 1916, Edward M. House Papers, Yale University Library.

17. A. S. Link, *Confusion and Crises,* pp. 237-238; also R. S. Baker, *Wilson,* VI, p. 182.

18. Grey to House, April 6, 1916, Edward M. House Papers, Yale University Library.

19. Notter, *The Origins of the Foreign Policy of Woodrow Wilson,* pp. 501-502.

20. Secretary of State to Ambassador Gerard, April 18, 1916, *Papers Relating to the Foreign Relations of the United States, 1916, Supplement* (Washington, D. C., 1929), pp. 232-237.

21. The decision made by the Kaiser was, in the final analysis, a political one, in which the Chancellor was able to influence him to the chagrin of the militant Falkenhayn. A. S. Link, *Confusion and Crises* pp. 269-271.

22. House to Grey, May 10, 1916, Edward M. House Papers, Yale University Library.

23. House to Grey, May 11, 1916, Edward M. House Papers, Yale University Library.

24. Grey to House, May 12, 1916, Edward M. House Papers, Yale University Library.

25. House Diary, May 13, 1916, Edward M. House Papers, Yale University Library. C. M. Mason, "Anglo-American Relations: Mediation and Permanent Peace," in Hinsley, ed., *Sir Edward Grey,* p. 480, adds to this that House was too much under Grey's spell to accuse him of deception, but he was bitter toward the lack of cohesiveness in British government.

26. *New York Times,* May 14, 1916.

27. Lennox, ed., *The Diary of Lord Bertie,* I, p. 350.

28. R. S. Baker, *Wilson,* VI, p. 210.

29. Link, ed., *The Papers of Woodrow Wilson*, vol. 37, *May 9–August 7, 1916*, pp. 57-58. Also R. S. Baker, *Wilson*, VI, pp. 221-213.

30. House to Grey, May 19, 1916, May 23, 1916, Edward M. House Papers, Yale University Library; also R. S. Baker, *Wilson*, VI, pp. 213-214.

31. Grey to House, May 29, 1916, Edward M. House Papers, Yale University Library.

32. Extracts from Grey's speech reprinted in *Current History*, IV (July 1916), pp. 730-731.

33. Page to House, May 25, 1916, Walter Hines Page Papers, Houghton Library, Harvard University.

34. The League to Enforce Peace, a non-partisan group organized in June, 1915, attempted to influence the American public to orient their thinking toward a constructive and active participation for peace throughout the world. R. S. Baker, *Wilson*, VI, p. 119. See also Ruhl J. Bartlett, *The League to Enforce Peace* (Chapel Hill, North Carolina, 1944).

35. C. Seymour, *The Intimate Papers of Colonel House*, II, pp. 293-298.

36. Link, ed., *The Papers of Woodrow Wilson*, vol. 37, *May 9–August 7, 1916*, pp. 113-116; R. S. Baker, *Wilson*, VI, pp. 220-224.

37. In an American Press Resume prepared periodically for use by the British Cabinet, the New York *Herald* is quoted as saying that the attitude of British newspapers toward the President's speech was "as cold and academic as Mr. Wilson himself." F. O. 899/16/1813, June 21, 1916. This comment, of course, revealed the *Herald's* attitude toward Wilson as well as that of the British press.

38. Rappaport, *The British Press and Wilsonian Neutrality*, p. 112.

39. Page to House, May 30, 1916, Walter Hines Page Papers, Houghton Library, Harvard University.

40. Grey to House, June 28, 1916, Edward M. House Papers, Yale University Library. Before this letter arrived, House commented in his diary that Grey had sent an earlier cable saying that House's letter of June 1 had just arrived, and that he was preparing an answer. House then wrote one of his few criticisms of the British: "I hope to get it between now and autumn, so slowly do the English move . . . ." House Diary, June 29, 1916, Edward M. House Papers, Yale University Library.

41. House to Grey, May 27, 1916, Edward M. House Papers, Yale University Library.

42. Grey to House, May 29, 1916, Edward M. House Papers, Yale University Library.

43. House to Grey, June 8, 1916, Edward M. House Papers, Yale University Library. House referred to Wilson's possible defeat in the November elections.

44. Grey to House, June 28, 1916, Edward M. House Papers, Yale University Library.

45. House to Grey, July 15, 1916, Edward M. House Papers, Yale University Library.

46. Grey to House, Aug. 28, 1916, Edward M. House Papers, Yale University Library. In this letter, which must have been eminently unsatisfactory to House, Grey also mentioned again that the President's statement of indifference as to the causes of the war (in Wilson's speech of May 27) was responsible for part of the lack of enthusiasm the British displayed toward America.

47. Wilson wrote on July 23, 1916 "I am, I must admit, about at the end of my patience with Great Britain and the Allies . . . ." Baker Papers, Series I, Letters of Wilson to House, Library of Congress; also R. S. Baker, *Wilson*, VI, pp. 312-316.

48.   A. S. Link, *Woodrow Wilson and the Progressive Era*, pp. 220-221; also Notter, *The Origins of the Foreign Policy of Woodrow Wilson*, pp. 543-545.

49.   One of the contributing factors to Page's recall might have been a letter Page wrote House on July 21, 1916, expressing the British attitude toward mediation, and indirectly, of course, his approval of this attitude: "[The English] remind me that there has not been any mediation in any modern war. T. R. beat his drum and kept up a howling dance while the Japs and Russians were arranging their peace-terms; but that was not mediation; it was merely giving them both the hospitality of the United States to make their own terms. The belligerents in this war, the Allies think, are going to get together and make their own peace-terms, as belligerents always do . . . ." Page to House, July 21, 1916, Walter Hines Page Papers, Houghton Library, Harvard University.

50.   House to Wilson, Oct. 9, 1916, R. S. Baker Papers, Chronological Notes, Series II, Box 152, Library of Congress.

51.   House Diary, Sept. 25, 1916, Edward M. House Papers, Yale University Library. Page referred continually to the "high purposes" of the British. Also C. Seymour, *The Intimate Papers of Colonel House,* II, pp. 313-320.

52.   Tansill, *America Goes to War*, p. 544.

53.   Grey's eyesight had been impaired since 1914. He suffered from degeneration of the retina which gradually grew worse with use. He had been advised by oculists to give up work involving reading, but this he refused to do, although periodically he would take a few weeks off to rest his eyes. Trevelyan, *Grey of Fallodon*, pp. 309-310, 373.

54.   Rappaport, *The British Press and Wilsonian Neutrality*, p. 115.

55.   *New York Times*, Sept. 29, 1916.

56.   Lloyd George, *War Memoirs*, I, p. 511.

57.   Notter, *The Origins of the Foreign Policy of Woodrow Wilson*, p. 556.

58.   Forster, *The Failures of Peace*, p. 72. House wrote Grey "in confidence" on October 24, 1916 that he had received unofficial notification that the U-boat warfare might soon be resumed. House to Grey, Oct. 24, 1916, Edward M. House Papers, Yale University Library.

59.   Notter, *The Origins of the Foreign Policy of Woodrow Wilson*, pp. 582-585; also Rappaport, *The British Press and Wilsonian Neutrality*, p. 117.

60.   House to Wilson, Dec. 6 and Dec. 7, 1916; Wilson to House, Dec. 8, 1916, Edward M. House Papers, Yale University Library; also Notter, *The Origins of the Foreign Policy of Woodrow Wilson*, pp. 586-587. Spring Rice had written Grey that he saw the election as a desire on the part of the people to keep out of the war. At this time, so Spring Rice wrote, "public opinion demands strong words but shrinks from deeds." The British Ambassador then accurately described Wilson's attitude toward the war: "Whatever happens the decision lies with the President who seeks inspiration from popular opinion as expressed in the mass but takes no individual into his counsel." F. O. 800/86/1281, Spring Rice to Grey, Nov. 24, 1916.

61.   Notter, *The Origins of the Foreign Policy of Woodrow Wilson*, pp. 590-591.

62.   Wilson wrote House: "I sent yesterday to *all* the belligerent governments the message of which I enclose a copy. Things have moved so fast I did not have time to

go over it with you . . . ." (Underlining Wilson's.) Baker Papers, Series I, Letters of Wilson to House, Dec. 19, 1916, Library of Congress.

63. House Diary, Dec. 20, 1916, Edward M. House Papers, Yale University Library.

64. A. S. Link, *Wilson the Diplomatist,* p. 64.

65. Ibid., p.65.

66. Lennox, ed., *The Diary of Lord Bertie,* I, p. 311.

67. Herman Lutz, *Lord Grey and the World War,* translated by E. W. Dickes (London, 1928), p. 163.

68. F. O. 800/86/1281, Grey to Spring Rice, July 29, 1916.

69. C. Seymour, *The Intimate Papers of Colonel House,* II, p. 339.

Chapter VII

The Colonel and the Ambassador

Many eventful months were to pass between December, 1916, and the next diplomatic encounters between Colonel House and his friend Grey, and it is impossible to detail them in the present pages. Suffice it to say that American intervention in the war brought a new activity for House—dealing with the nations which Wilson carefully denominated the Associates (not the Allies; the United States Government refused to subscribe formally to the Treaty of London of 1914 which bound the Allies). The Colonel happily set off on this new diplomacy, and his influence with the President was never higher, or seemed never to have been so high. Whenever two or three Allied diplomats gathered together they spoke of the activities not merely of the American President but of the American Colonel, and the singularity of this official-unofficial diplomacy did not subtract from its importance. At last the war was over, and the making of the peace began at Paris, and in the summer of 1919 the treaties were signed, one after the other, with the German treaty signed first in a great cermony at Versailles on June 28. It was only some months thereafter, and under circumstances far different from those encountered by House and Grey in the months of neutrality, that the interesting Anglo-American friendship between the Colonel and the Britisher again entered the realms of diplomacy.

Lord Grey, described by Lloyd George as the most insular of British statesmen, overcame his reluctance to cross the seas in 1919; he accepted the ambassadorship to America in August of that year.[1] He did not go gladly into this assignment for his eyesight had failed to the point that he could see objects only indistinctly, and travel to new places was very awkward. He felt out of touch with the ebullient Prime Minister and the Coalition Government.[2] After leaving the Foreign Office in December, 1916, Grey had written House that he would not accept a public position again until he thought there was confidence and sympathy between the Government and himself so as "to give me weight and importance."[3] In August, 1919, he was not sure such a bond existed ("I am not sanguine about the mission"). But the sense of duty which had prevailed throughout his life took him again into public service.[4]

Grey had spent the months between December, 1916, and the summer of 1919 in semi-seclusion at Fallodon. American's entrance into war on the side of the Allies and the subsequent Allied victory over the Central Powers had been for him the complete justification of his policies while Foreign Minister.[5] In the months of hiatus, his only participation in public life had been to espouse the cause of a league of nations, which he considered a translation into practical form of the old Concert of Europe. He published a booklet in May, 1918, pointing out the virtues of a league, and made many effective speeches in the House of Lords for this cause.[6] It was, in fact, his deep concern for such a league which brought him out of retirement.

Colonel House, definitely not retired, had actively participated in Anglo-American wartime and postwar diplomacy.[7] He had gone to England following the signing of the Versailles Treaty and with his usual propensity for seeing problems on both sides of the ocean thought he saw trouble for the League of Nations in America. Visiting with his old friend Grey, House found they shared this same anxiety. And while it is true that the British Government had been urging Grey to accept the ambassadorship to America, it was probably the Colonel's insistence that Grey alone could ease the tense situation between President and Senate on Treaty ratification—threatening America's entrance into the League—which persuaded Grey to accept.[8]

House had stayed in Europe in the summer of 1919 at the request of the President, who had asked him to meet with the commission appointed by the Peace Conference to work on technical details for equitable distribution of colonial mandates.[9] House did what he was asked to do, and perhaps a little more, for his interest lay not with the mandate system, but with establishment of the League of Nations as an operating organization. During his visit to London he talked with British officials about arrangements for the first meeting of the League Assembly. Robert Cecil and Eric Drummond of the Foreign Office suggested holding the meeting that autumn in Washington.[10] It was universally accepted that the Peace Treaty, which included the Covenant of the League of Nations, would receive the consent—perhaps with some advice, but not too much—of the United States Senate. By August, however, it became apparent to House and British officials that the Senate had no intention of rubber-stamping the Treaty as presented to them on July 10.[11]

This realization came slowly and reluctantly to the President. He had traveled to Europe to participate in the Peace Conference. His triumphal tour preceding the Conference, when he was accompanied by the purple-gowned and purple-plumed Mrs. Wilson, had indicated that the people of Europe regarded him as their savior. Another spectacular Wilson triumph had occurred when members of the Peace Conference voted to incorporate the League of Nations into the Peace Treaty.[12] The League, though not original with Wilson, had become the mystic embodiment of all his ambitions and dreams.[13] His religious background persuaded him that a pact among nations to insure worldwide tranquility was just and right. His desire for world acclaim, which House had encouraged and capitalized on to promote earlier peace missions, would be satisfied when as leader of the League's most powerful nation he could publicly guide the world's destiny in a legitimate way. Assured as to the rightness of his position, and of acceptance of his position by the people and statesmen of Europe, he surely could gain the approval of the Senate of his own nation. He had reason to think so. In March, 1919, thirty-four of the thirty-six state legislatures, and thirty-three governors, had endorsed the League. These endorsements did not guarantee the two-thirds majority vote necessary in the Senate, but Wilson was sanguine. When Clemenceau questioned him about the possibility of a change in attitude of American opinion, Wilson confided imperturbably, "America has taken much from me. She will take this also."[14]

In the hot summer of 1919 it gradually became apparent to the President that America might not take the League of Nations. The Senate, focal point of the controversy, was composed of men who also needed to satisfy their ambitions, who would go to considerable lengths to preserve their self-esteem. Wilson's relation with the Senators or, for that matter, with other government officials had never been cordial; little communication of ideas existed between them. Wilson had become more aloof after his second marriage. Walter Hines Page, home on leave in August and September, of 1916, wrote in his diary that after five weeks he was finally invited for lunch at the White House, but that he couldn't talk to the President because he and Mrs. Wilson sat side by side in two high-backed chairs while guests (in low-backed chairs) sat opposite them. He complained: "The President is entirely surrounded by women . . . there is no social life at the White House . . . Houston told me that he had never given the slightest token in a social way that he knew of [any government officials'] existence . . . . Wilson does his own thinking, untouched by other men's ideas. He receives nothing from the outside . . . . His . . . life is spent with his own—nobody else, except House occasionally . . . ."[15] In a conversation with Charles Seymour, Colonel House later verified the fact that Wilson would not see Congressmen. House said that although the press had accused him, the Colonel, of keeping visitors away, the contrary was true. He had urged Wilson to talk with the Senators when controversial questions arose. Wilson always refused. The President felt that if a measure was right, a Senator ought to vote for it without an interview.[16]

An example of Wilson's insensitivity toward Republican points of view was his appeal to the nation to return a Democratic majority to the Senate and House of Representatives in order to give him the solid support he needed with Allied leaders abroad.[17] Theodore Roosevelt may have revealed the anger of many Republicans when he wrote: "The President's statement is an announcement that he is a partisan leader first and President of all the people second."[18] Disastrous results for Democratic candidates followed. The President became defiant toward those persons who spoke criticism of him and his policies, and would not choose a Republican for the Peace Commission who was hostile to him personally. No leading Republican met his qualifications. Wilson named himself as head of the Commission, and chose three Democrats—Lansing, House, and General Tasker H. Bliss; there was one pale Republican, the retired diplomat Henry White. The Commission was referred to as four Wilsons and one White.

Certainly the Treaty was looked upon as the President's Treaty, and hostile Senators reacted with vindictiveness, guided by Wilson's foe, the Senator from Massachusetts. It is a well-known story that a feud had arisen between Wilson and Henry Cabot Lodge; each regarded himself as a scholar and the other as a charlatan. In his role as head of the Foreign Relations Committee, Lodge insinuated that the Treaty, with the Covenant, violated American rights. Ultimately, the Committee tacked on fourteen reservations which, they said, would preserve American prerogative. It was one way of making the Treaty no longer Wilson's, of sharing the glory and frustrating the President.

In England, the President's friend House had felt for some time that Wilson needed some kind of support on the League issue. House wanted to go home to testify in behalf of the League before the Foreign Relations Committee. He thought his testimony "would do a great deal of good." Wilson, whose own experience with that Committee had been demoralizing, asked him to stay away.[20] With an ocean between them House searched for a way to help the President. It seemed that Grey, deeply admired by Wilson and by the American public, could, as British Ambassador, invoke a calm atmosphere which would provide a background for compromise. This was, in fact, the type of delicate assignment at which Grey had so long excelled.

British officials, sensing the reluctance of the United States regarding the League of Nations, seemed to concur. Lloyd George later wrote that "We pressed Lord Grey to seek a personal interview with the President."[21] Lord Curzon, who had assumed control of the Foreign Office, urged Grey to go. In addition to the questions of the League there was the matter of Anglo-American naval competition, and the ever-present Irish issue. After several conferences with House, Grey apparently decided there was a need for his kind of diplomacy in the United States.[22]

On other occasions Grey had turned down such a request. Lloyd George had written an ingratiating letter in 1917 asking him to accept appointment to America. The Prime Minister had said that no one could better promote a friendly understanding between the two countries; since Grey's house had just burned, Lloyd George added a note of his calculated personal charm: "I was so sorry to hear of Fallodon. I do hope the squirrels are alright [sic]."[23] The reference to Grey's beloved wildlife on his estate, however, did not persuade him to accept the position in 1917. Grey wrote his successor at the Foreign Office, Balfour, that what Lloyd George "really wanted was someone to speed up war services." Grey implied that this was not his proper task and that what he could do best when necessary was "to discuss ideals with Wilson."[24] One might surmise that in August, 1919, House may have pointed out that someone had better talk to Wilson about ideals or else those ideals would never materialize.

Grey asked that the appointment as Ambassador to the United States be regarded as temporary. It was thus announced, causing a question in Parliament as to "why this distinguished statesman cannot be permanently appointed?" Bonar Law answered in a manner which revealed the esteem in which Grey was held: "I do not think an answer is necessary to that. I need only say that the Government would have been only too glad if he could have accepted a permanent post, but everyone who knows what the disabilities of Lord Grey are, will share in the gratitude that the Government feel toward him.[25] The press had warm praise for the selection. According to the London *Times,* "Lord Grey's acceptance of the position even if only for a time, commands universal approval . . . . The Government is fortunate in his acceptance."[26] *The Observer* commented: "The Prime Minister's offer of the Washington Embassy is on a level with his proposal of Marshal Foch as Generalissimo. Now, as then, there is a campaign to be fought. The League of Nations has been shaped, but has yet to be quickened into life."[27] And on the other side of the Atlantic the President expressed delight. Wilson wrote House: "We have been very much interested to learn within the last two or three days through the newspapers, that we are likely to have Viscount Grey as the Ambassador of Great Britain. I am delighted to believe that his health permits him to accept this appointment and shall look forward with great pleasure to being associated with him."[28]

In spite of these glowing and hopeful remarks the Grey mission added another puzzling dimension to the arabesque of relations between Grey and House—including the President of the United States.

Lord Curzon had recognized areas of discord between the United States and England, including the increasing naval strength of America. Should the two countries establish a limit to their navies? Another area, as mentioned, centered around Ireland. Only the outbreak of hostilities in 1914 had prevented a revolt in Ulster against Liberal Home Rule Bill; but in 1916 and 1918 revolts and terrorism in Ireland convinced England and the world that Ireland wanted independence. The United States was in a unique position because the many Irish-Americans retained loyalty and emotional commitment to the homeland. These citizens pressed Wilson to obtain self-determination for Ireland at the Peace Conference.[29] England stalled, and this problem, among other difficulties, was left unsettled. The "Irish question" hung uneasily over Anglo-American relations in the last half of 1919.

Josephus Daniels, Secretary of the Navy in Wilson's cabinet, later criticized the Lord Grey mission severely as interference rather than diplomacy, because, he implied, Grey did not come to discuss real issues between the two countries. "There is no evidence that Viscount Grey sought to discuss 'the Naval building program' or the 'Irish question.'"[30] He was wrong, because Grey had a long letter of instruction from Lord Curzon dealing with these subjects. Written on September 9, 1919, the letter dealt in a conciliatory manner with the threat of a naval race between the two countries: "The unanimous opinion of the British Government is that in framing their own naval estimates they would take no account of the United States naval programme and would not build against the United States Navy as against that of a possible rival or enemy." On granting independence to Ireland, Curzon made a commitment "to give to Ireland the most complete control—legislative and administrative of its own affairs" with the stipulation that army and navy and foreign policy would remain in British hands. Recognizing the delicate situation in the United States in September, 1919 concerning the League, Curzon advised Grey to assure Americans that the British Government would not use the League to further national interests, "that His Majesty's Government believes that the League of Nations can be made the means of achieving great good . . . . But to secure this it must be made a reality . . . ."[31]

Curzon's statements on the League coincided with Grey's beliefs. Throughout correspondence with House there ran the theme of the necessity of a postwar league. He believed it necessary for the United States to belong to such a league. In early 1917 Grey had written Balfour: "Without the United States a league would be at best but a revived Concert of Europe liable at any time to split into rival groups."[32] He believed that he was performing a service for his country by going to America. This belief was evidenced by one of his letters to the Foreign Office concerning remuneration. The British Treasury had set up a £2,000 outfit allowance for him. When informed, Grey answered that £50 would cover his personal outfit, that he wanted no salary, and that he had so stipulated to the Prime Minister when he accepted the mission.[33] No doubt believing he was doing one last work for his country the Ambassador sailed on the *Mauretania* in mid-September, accompanied by Sir William Tyrrell who had served for eight years as his secretary when Grey was in the Foreign Office. Tyrrell had made the trip to America in November, 1913, to talk over the Mexican situation with the President whom he then had found friendly. Another official in the party, Major Charles Kennedy Crauford-Stuart, had been attached to Lord Reading, the previous ambassador. Grey was told that he ought to bring Crauford-Stuart along because of the major's special knowledge of America.[34] On board were three cases of a blend of tea which Grey had been informed he would be unable to get in the United States.[35] One might assume the Ambassador thought his stay would be longer than a few weeks.

Wearing dark glasses to protect his eyes, Grey disembarked in New York on September 26, 1919; he proceeded to the British Embassy in Washington. Another man who looked upon the world darkly also arrived in Washington at this time, after a long trip: the President of the United States, who had suffered a collapse in Pueblo while on a speaking tour in behalf of the League.[36]

In August the President had been in such a highly nervous state that the head of the British secret service in the United States, Sir William Wiseman, with whom both House and Wilson had a com-

fortable familarity, had been warned by Mrs. Wilson "to keep off
serious questions" while at the White House.[37] If by "serious questions"
she meant talk of the League, it was foolhardy for the President to
attempt the tour during which the topic would be the League. The
obstinate Wilson may have decided to become a martyr (he told H. H.
Kohlsaat that he did not care if the trip killed him, so long as he could
get the Treaty ratified).[38] Having returned in a state close to physical
collapse, Wilson on October 2, 1919 suffered a thrombosis which
paralyzed his entire left side.[39]

While the President lay near death in the White House, his friend
House in Europe made the decision to return home. The Colonel
had gone from London to Paris in September and, according to a
letter to the President on September 20 had discussed the readjusting
of finances of the Allies with Clemenceau and Tardieu. Warned by
cable of Wilson's breakdown he felt the situation demanded his
presence; the forces battling for the Covenant had lost their leader, but
House was ready to step in.[40] The Colonel himself then fell ill with
an attack of gallstones. The New York *Times*, sensing a human interest
story, kept readers advised of House's progress from Paris to Brest
to New York. On October 6 it was reported: "Colonel E. M. House
"left Paris" and will sail from Brest tomorrow morning for New York.
Much of the mystery about what Colonel House has been doing . . . has
been cleared up by his own statement that he has been keeping the
League plans from going ahead too fast, until the United States can
sit in."[41] The *Times* reported his illness on October 13 with another
quotation from the Colonel: "I was attacked in Paris with a recurrence
of the gravel for which I suffered a year ago." When the transport
Northern Pacific, docked in New York, readers heard of his slow
descent down the gangplant aided by "Dr. Albert Lamb, the Colonel's
physician, and an army officer." The Colonel told reporters optimistically: "I want to get home and in bed where I can rest comfortably
until I have recovered my health . . . [and I] expect to go to Washington
next week."[42]

The Colonel's optimism proved unfounded. He wrote Mrs. Wilson
asking to see the President. She replied to Mrs. House that she had
not informed the President of House's arrival since her husband
had wanted him to remain in Europe.[43] House, acting independently,
as he had for six years during the Wilson-House relationship, took
the initiative in an attempt to resolve the differences between Senator
Lodge and Wilson. He sent Colonel Stephen Bonsal, who had acted
as an interpreter for Wilson and House at the Peace Conference, to
Washington to confer with Lodge about the Senator's minimum

demands for changes in the Covenant. According to Bonsal's account of a quarter-century later, Lodge took a printed copy of the Covenant and made the changes and additions he considered necessary (in Bonsal's opinion they were far less severe than those he was publicly backing). Bonsal mailed the document to House who sent it to the White House.[44] The Colonel, as in the past, then waited for a summons from Wilson. From the White House, which had been turned into a hospital, all that came was silence.

The weeks passed. To close observers it seemed unusual that the Colonel was remaining in New York while his friend was seriously ill in Washington. Rumors circulated. In early December an article by Louis Siebold in the New York *World* declared that House had been shorn of the diplomatic powers he once enjoyed. The Colonel remained quiet "in deference to propriety" but friends were busy denying the story, pointing out a rumor to this effect each year, and that is usually appeared earlier, "about August."[45] In truth there had been a rumor in August, 1919. At that time House was in England, and wrote the President that the Foreign Office had informed him they had received from their sources in the United States a cable pertaining to ". . . our annual falling out." This Foreign Office cable, sent August 14, said the Colonel no longer represented the President's views because Wilson felt House's British sympathies "were responsible for three months delay of [the] Peace Conference."[46]

Wilson had cabled House to treat this "malicious story" with "silent contempt."[47] From the continuation and friendliness of the correspondence between the two men in August it seems probable that a break did not occur. On August 15, Wilson had written House a warm letter on the work regarding the mandates and signed it "Affectionately Yours."[48] But there had been a change in the friendship at the Paris Conference in the spring of 1919 due in part to the presence of Mrs. Wilson, who, as H. G. Wells once said, brought a "tourist quality" to the peace talks.[49]

The second Mrs. Wilson, unlike the first, did not approve of the friendship between House and her husband. A willful woman, she insisted on attending the discussions House had with the President on matters of policy. With the advent of a third party the intimacy between House and Wilson disappeared. House found himself unable to direct and guide the President as in the past.[50] Outwardly, Mrs. Wilson and House were friends, but it was a silent truce. In her memoirs Mrs. Wilson made disparaging references to House's "Yes, yes" characteristic. She described the Colonel as insignificant looking, with intelligent eyes. She imbued House with a sinister quality. She raised doubts in her husband's mind about House's effectiveness and loyalty.[51]

There was a period in February and March of 1919 when the President left the Peace Conference to return home, and House remained in charge, and the President's absence had led to trouble. During the absence, House, empowered by Wilson to continue drafting the treaty with Germany, pushed for a quick conclusion. He considered that each day of delay brought problems, and consistent with his personality compromised with the Allies. Ray Stannard Baker, Wilson's biographer, charged later that House betrayed the President's trust.[52] Such may well not have been Wilson's view at the time. The deeply prejudiced Mrs. Wilson years later would give the only extant report of the President's immediate reaction to House's summary of the business conducted in his absence. According to her story the President had "aged ten years" and told her bitterly that House had given away everything he had won before he left Paris. In her memoirs Mrs. Wilson told another tale about House's infidelity, in the course of which Wilson defended House—which may show that he sometimes disagreed with his wife's opinions. As Mrs. Wilson related the story, she had reproached House about an article in a newspaper which said that the only constructive work of the American delegation had been done while President Wilson was away and House in charge. Apparently expecting House to react violently in defense of Wilson, she was shocked when he simply "turned crimson" and "fled as though pursued." She told her husband of the incident, and he exclaimed, "Oh, I am sorry you hurt House, I would as soon doubt your loyalty as his."[53]

Despite Wilson's avowed faith in House there undoubtedly was a lack of congeniality between the men during the rest of the Conference. The Colonel found reasons. He believed it part of the general perturbation Wilson felt toward the negotiations, for the President was forced to compromise and it was much against his nature to do so.[54] The conference ended with the signing of the treaty, and Wilson left for America. House went to the station to see him off. Many historians have since noted House's recollection: "My last conversation with the President yesterday was not reassuring. I urged him to meet the Senate in a conciliatory spirit. In reply he said, 'House, I have found one can never get anything in this life that is worthwhile without fighting for it.' I combated this, and reminded him that Anglo-Saxon civilization was built up on compromise."[55]

Whatever the confusions of the Peace Conference, after Wilson returned to America, made his tour of the West, and was struck down, the situation became more confusing. After the President's illness Mrs. Wilson, in her attempts to prolong her husband's life, assumed control of his activities. Grayson had told her that Wilson should not confront problems which required "constructive thought;" accordingly, she censored messages and people alike.[56] In November, 1919, although the President's condition was much improved, his knowledge of the controversy raging over the reservations to the Treaty was limited. Due to Lodge's maneuvering, fourteen reservations were adopted by the Senate, and the question became: Would Wilson and his followers accept the Treaty with the Lodge reservations? Because of lack of information about the desires of the Senate and the people, and also because of stubborness, fortified by illness, the President's position remained the same as in September. He instructed the Democratic leader, Senator Hitchcock, to have followers vote against the Treaty with the reservations. On November 19, Lodge and his coterie voted down unconditional ratification; then those senators loyal to the President voted against the Treaty with the reservations. The Sixty-sixth Congress adjourned *sine die,* the Treaty neither ratified with or without reservations.[57]

Colonel House had been one of those persons censored by Mrs. Wilson, for what she considered disloyal behavior at the Peace Conference. The Colonel had written several letters to the President during November urging him to reach some compromise with Lodge. There is no evidence that Wilson saw these letters, but Mrs. Wilson's reaction to one of them which House had sent by Attorney General Thomas W. Gregory was that House was urging the President to surrender his principles.[58] From this time on, House probably had as much chance to see the President as did Henry Cabot Lodge.

In early December, 1919, when the story of an alleged break appeared in the New York *Times,* the Colonel had not given up hope of seeing the President. But another report in the *Times,* appearing that same week, gave every indication that House's influence with Wilson had ceased. According to the *Times,* Lord Grey, House's special friend, having been greatly embarrassed by his inability to see the President, was returning to England. "This," the *Times* reported ominously, "is the first instance in the history of the United States when an Ambassador or Minister from Great Britain has not been formally received by the President."[59]

Grey's arrival had coincided with the President's illness. The Ambassador had sent the Secretary of State an announcement of arrival, but wrote three days later that he did not expect to see the President right away "in view of reports of his health." Lansing as well as Grey expected this situation to be temporary, and his answer to Grey's announcement was that "I will be glad to accord you provisional recognition as Ambassador . . . formal recognition to be granted when the President receives you in audience."[60]

The President did improve, and in the last days of October, Mrs. Wilson allowed a select few to see him. Among the first were (a curious choice) the King and Queen of the Belgians.[61] The distinguished British Ambassador received no invitation, and must have wondered. He soon became enlightened, for it seemed that a member of his entourage, Crauford-Stuart, had slandered the First Lady.

It was an unusual situation indeed. Grey was notified by the State Department that the President wanted Crauford-Stuart sent home. The message had been passed along by Lansing to Sir William Tyrrell and apparently had originated with Dr. Grayson.[62]

The Crauford-Stuart story is an intriguing one and, although Colonel House deplored the whole situation as "trivial and unworthy of the grave situation facing us at this time," its political implications were not trivial.[63] As mentioned, Major Charles Crauford-Stuart had been attached to the Embassy headed by Lord Reading during the war. A versatile man, his accomplishments included photography and polo. He was a talented musician, and in addition to playing the piano he composed songs of some note ("At Gloaming Tide" and "Make-Believe Land"). The Musical Major played his compositions at Washington parties in late 1918, and allegedly spoke indiscreetly about Mrs. Wilson. Ambassador Reading and all the attaches returned soon afterward to England, and the episode was considered closed.[64]

The Major's reappearance on the American scene with Lord Grey caused consternation to Mrs. Wilson. Moreover, a new indiscretion was now attributed to him. it seemed that the Major told a few friends that the reason Mrs. Wilson wanted to go to the Peace Conference was to acquire social prestige which she had lacked in the United States.[65] Grey's first knowledge of the whole situation came when he confronted the demand, ostensibly from the President, that he must send his attache back to England. Crauford-Stuart denied the allegation in a formal statement which is now in the National Archives, although curiously it does not mention Mrs. Wilson. In the statement the Major named the people present at a dinner party given by Mrs. James B. MacDonald, and said that at the party there had been some comparison of the President's powers and ability with those of Balfour, Asquith, and Lloyd George. Crauford-Stuart said he gave no opinion, and concluded his statement somewhat passionately, also somewhat ambiguously: "I would like to point out that I have all along denied having discussed the President not only at Mrs. MacDonald's but at any time, nor have I discussed any member of the Administration. If I am sent back to England, I am simply being punished for an offense I have never been guilty of."[66]

Grey refused to send the Major home, but changed his status from that of attache to a member of the Ambassador's household, hoping to appease those persons who objected to him; at the same time, however, he was indignant about the whole matter, and told Curzon he would resign if compelled to part with Crauford-Stuart.[67]

Lord Grey probably needed his specially blended tea to bring him comfort. The Crauford-Stuart problem was just one of many he encountered in America during his mission. Surely, in the annals of diplomacy, no British Ambassador ever faced such an unduly delicate situation. Colonel House, who had persuaded him to assume this responsibility and who had predicted that he and Grey working together with Wilson could have Anglo-American relations "upon an absolutely firm basis" within three months, did not arrive in America until mid-October.[68] During that time Wilson's illness placed moratorium on the work of ambassadors. And then the Crauford-Stuart silliness occurred. Grey did not know what provision would be made if Wilson proved incapacitated.[69] He could not have anticipated that Mrs. Wilson would have reacted to her husband's illness by erecting a Chinese Wall around him, making decisions about who could reach him, and that in her capacity as sole judge of the selected few she eliminated Colonel House, whom Grey had counted upon for his entrée to the President.

Nor could Grey have anticipated that the fight for the League, with or without reservations, would have engendered so much emotionalism, which extended far beyond party loyalty and manifested itself in admiration of or hatred for the stricken President. Almost all individuals in Washington during this complicated period, even those persons who moved as cautiously as Grey (he wrote Curzon that until the debate was over he did not dare to mention the League of Nations in public) found themselves labelled as for or against Wilson. In late November, 1919, Grey found himself not only in the midst of a kind of domestic imbroglio over Crauford-Stuart but accused by Wilson's loyal cabinet members as having come on a special mission to "take sides against the President."[70]

The man who had served as Foreign Secretary for Great Britain from 1905 to 1916, handling the complicated European diplomacy of that period, found his position in America almost beyond belief.[71]

Notes

1. Lloyd George, *War Memoirs*, I, p. 60.

2. House Diary, Aug. 12, 1919, Edward M. House Papers, Yale University Library; also Trevelyan, *Grey of Fallodon*, pp. 397-399. This did not include Balfour for whom Grey had much respect. He wrote the new Foreign Secretary on Dec. 8, 1916; "From a letter of Robert Cecil, I gather that the Foreign Office is to be in your hands . . . ." Balfour Papers, British Museum.

3. Grey to House, Feb. 15, 1917, Edward M. House Papers, Yale University Library.

4. Grey to House, Aug 12, 1919, Edward M. House Papers, Yale University Library.

5. Hendrick, *Page*, II, p. 233.

6. Trevelyan, *Grey of Fallodon*, pp. 394-396. An excerpt from this booklet reads: "The establishment and maintenance of a League of Nations such as President Wilson has advocated, is more important and essential to a secure peace than any of the actual terms of peace that may conclude the war: it will transcend them all." Viscount Grey of Fallodon, *The League of Nations* (London, 1918), available in Walter Hines Page Papers, Houghton Library, Harvard University; also H. Sidebotham, *Pillars of the State*, p.41.

7. After Grey left office, House maintained a close association with British officials through the auspices of William Wiseman who became head of British intelligence operations in the United States in 1917. Wiseman, only thirty-three years old and less than five feet in height, displayed (according to House) "extraordinary discretion, perfect loyalty and an extraordinary degree of impartiality" which enabled House to keep in touch with all details of British policy. Conversations. Charles Seymour and Edward M. House. May 26, 1922, Charles Seymour Papers, Yale University Library. See also W. B. Fowler, *British-American Relations, 1917-1918: The Role of Sir William Wiseman* (Princeton, New Jersey, 1969.)

8. House to Wilson, Aug. 8, 1919, 701.4111/282 1/2 National Archives, Washington D. C.

9. C. Seymour, *The Intimate Papers of Colonel House*, IV, p. 490.

10. Conversations. Charles Seymour and Edward M. House. May 14, 1922, Charles Seymour Papers, Yale University Library.

11. Trevelyan, *Grey of Fallodon*, p. 399; also Thomas A. Bailey, *Woodrow Wilson and the Great Betrayal* (rpt., Chicago, 1963), p. 233.

12. Robert Lansing wrote in his Confidential Memorandum on November 22, 1919, that he thought Colonel House hatched this idea—a shrewd scheme to make the treaty unworkable without the League. Robert Lansing Papers, Library of Congress.

13. George and George, *Woodrow Wilson and Colonel House*, p. 228.

14. Harold Nicolson, *Peacemaking 1919* (Boston, 1933), p. 206. Wilson was also aware that a Senate had never before rejected a peace treaty.

15. From a section entitled "On Leave," Aug. and Sept., 1916, Walter Hines Page Papers, Houghton Library, Harvard University.

16. Conversations. Charles Seymour and Edward M. House. March 17, 1920, Charles Seymour Papers, Yale University Library.

17.   *New York Times*, Oct. 26, 1918.

18.   Ibid.

19.   Robert Lansing, Confidential Memorandum, Nov. 22, 1919, "An Intimate and Frank Consideration of the Causes of Non-Ratification of the Treaty of Peace," Lansing Papers, Library of Congress. Lansing, however, in retrospect, wrote that he did not consider the fact that Wilson did not choose a Republican Senator "a menace," only an "embarrassment."

20.   Conversations. Charles Seymour and Edward M. House. May 12, 1922, Charles Seymour Papers, Yale University Library. The Foreign Relations Committee questioned about sixty witnesses (among them the President of the United States— he voluntarialy chose to appear) presumably for the edification of the Senators on the League. Lodge was so adroit that most of the testimony proved embarrassing to League partisans. Bailey, *Woodrow Wilson and the Great Betrayal*, pp. 79-85.

21.   David Lloyd George, *Memoirs of the Peace Conference* (2 vols., New Haven, Conn., 1939), II, p. 818.

22.   C. Seymour, *The Intimate Papers of Colonel House*, IV, pp. 494-498.

23.   F. O. 800/383/1865, Prime Minister to Lord Grey of Fallodon, May 11, 1917. Grey further elaborated: "I got on well with Page and House who are Wilson's friends and should very likely get on well with Wilson."

24.   F. O. 800/380/180, Lord Grey to Balfour, Oct. 17, 1917.

25.   F. O. 371/4251/1777, Extract from Parlimentary Debates, Aug. 13, 1919. Bonar Law was referring to Grey's diminishing sight. Grey described his affliction in connection with his capability as a fisherman: "By 1918 I had ceased to be able to see a small fly floating in the water . . . . When the season of 1919 came I could no longer see rises." Viscount Grey of Fallodon, *Fly Fishing* (London, 1930), p. 228.

26.   London *Times* quoted in *New York Times*, Aug. 15, 1919.

27.   *The Observer*, Aug. 17, 1919, 701.4111/288, National Archives, Washington D. C.

28.   Wilson to House, Aug. 15, 1919, Woodrow Wilson Papers, Letterbook 57, Series III, Library of Congress.

29.   Daniel M. Smith, *The Great Departure: The United States and World War I, 1914-1920* (New York, 1965), p. 180.

30.   Josephus Daniels, *The Wilson Era: Years of War and After, 1917-1923* (Chapel Hill, North Carolina, 1946), p. 455.

31.   F. O. 800/4251/1777, Curzon to Grey, Sept. 9, 1919.

32.   F. O. 800/211/1868, Grey to Balfour, Feb. 19, 1917.

33.   F. O. 371/4251/1777, C. H. Montgomery to Tyrrell, Oct. 2, 1919; Grey to Montgomery, Oct. 3, 1919.

34.   Conversations. Charles Seymour and Edward M. House. May 12, 1922, Charles Seymour Papers, Yale University Library.

35.   *New York Times*, Sept. 19, 1919.

36.   Benjamin Abeshouse, M. D., *A Medical History of Woodrow Wilson;* this original manuscript written by Dr. Abeshouse, whose lifetime avocation was the collection of medical data of famous men and women, is now in the Smithsonian Institute in Washington D. C. In 1969 Eaton Laboratories published this manuscript on Wilson in the form of a booklet. Dr. Abeshouse wrote that in Seattle, President

Wilson suffered from severe frontal headaches which impaired his vision. These headaches increased in intensity, and on September 25, in Pueblo while addressing an audience, he could scarcely see. Dr. Grayson, the President's physician, warned him that further speechmaking would be fatal. Thus the return to Washington.

37.   Sir Arthur Willert, *The Road to Saftey: A Study in Anglo-American Relations* (London, 1952), pp. 63, 181.

38.   H. G. Kohlsaat, *From McKinley to Harding* (New York, 1923), pp. 218-219.

39.   Dr. Abeshouse, *A Medical History of Woodrow Wilson.* See also Edward Weinstein, *Woodrow Wilson: A Medical and Psychological Biography*, pp. 355-357.

40.   C. Seymour, *The Intimate Papers of Colonel House*, IV, pp. 501-503.

41.   *New York Times*, Oct. 6, 1919.

42.   *New York Times*, Oct. 13, 1919.

43.   Conversations. Charles Seymour and Edward M. House. May 11, 1922, Charles Seymour Papers, Yale University Library. This letter, which Mrs. Wilson wrote to Mrs. House, was dated Oct. 17, 1919.

44.   Stephen Bonsal, *Unfinished Business* (Garsden City, N. Y., 1944), pp. 270-276; also Bailey, *Woodrow Wilson and the Great Betrayal*, pp. 175-176. Colonel House thought highly of Bonsal, and of his ability to suborinate himself to the situation. House, as a master of what appeared to be self-effacement, recognized this quality in Bonsal, calling it his "low visibility."

45.   Robert Lansing, Confidential Memorandum, Dec. 9, 1919, Lansing Papers, Library of Congress. Lansing's assessment: Someone was throwing javelins at House as they had at David three thousand years ago, and since the President was too sick, it might have been Mrs. Wilson; also the *New York Times*, Dec. 9, 1919.

46.   E. L. Woodward and Rohan Butler, eds., *Documents on British Foreign Policy, 1919-1939* (17 vols., First Series, London, 1954), V, p. 1022. Hereafter cited as Woodward and Butler, ed., *British Documents.* See also C. Seymour, *The Intimate Papers of Colonel House*, IV, p. 515.

47.   C. Seymour, *The Intimate Papers of Colonel House*, IV, p. 515.

48.   Wilson to House, Aug. 15, 1919, Letterbook 57, Series III, Wilson Papers, Library of Congress.

49.   H. G. Wells, quoted in Jonathan Daniels *The End of Innocence* (Philadelphia, 1954), p. 284. In one sense, Mrs. Wilson must have given the impression that she was a tourist—she spent a lot of time acquiring a Paris wardrobe. One woman reporter described the First Lady as "all smiles and new clothes," and advised her feminine readers: "If you are very, very smart and League of Nationy you wear a big blowsy all-tulle hat with an all-tulle scarf attached that winds around your throat coquet-tishly." From a clipping in Scrapbook of Edith Bolling Wilson, listed in Woodrow Wilson Papers, Series 9, vol. 4, Library of Congress.

50.   George and George, *Woodrow Wilson and Colonel House*, pp. 185-187. The Georges say that the friendship may have revealed a weakness in her husband which was distasteful to Mrs. Wilson, and that she sought to make Wilson inde-pendent of House in order to make reality conform with her idealized image of her husband.

51.   Edith Bolling Wilson, *My Memoir* (Indianapolis, 1938), pp. 155, 245-246. According to Tom Shecktman, author of *Edith and Woodrow* (New York, 1981), Mrs. Wilson was actually motivated to write her memoir because she was angered at Colonel House's *Intimate Papers*, published in the late 1920s, which she felt glorified House.

52.   C. Seymour, *The Intimate Papers of Colonel House*, IV, p. 330; also A. D. H. Smith, *Mr. House of Texas*, pp. 304-313.

53.   E. B. Wilson, *My Memoir*, pp. 245-246, 250-252.

54.   A. D. H. Smith, *Mr. House of Texas*, p. 382. This seems to be substantiated by Mrs. Edith Benham Helm's diary for the months of March and April, 1919. She often described Wilson as being irritated and irritable with everyone and she felt that the obstructiveness of Clemenceau and other Allied leaders was the cause. Edith Benham Helms Papers, Paris Peace Conference Notes, Library Congress.

55.   C. Seymour, *The Intimate Papers of Colonel House*, IV, p. 487.

56.   Lansing to Frank Polk, Nov. 14, 1919, vol. 49, Lansing Papers, Library of Congress. According to White House usher "Ike" Hoover, even Dr. Grayson had no influence in getting people in to see the President. Hoover states that the President's secretary, Joe Tumulty, made repeated efforts to see Wilson, that Grayson like Tumulty and apparently tried to intervene on his behalf, but Mrs. Wilson was adamant about Tumulty and "Grayson could not insist." "Notes on the President's Illness," The Papers of Irwin H. Hoover, Boxes I and II, Library of Congress.

57.   Gene Smith, *When the Cheering Stopped: The Last Years of Woodrow Wilson* (New York, 1964), pp. 118-120; also John M. Blum, *Joe Tumulty and the Wilson Era* (Boston, 1951), p. 228.

58.   Conversations. Charles Seymour and Edward M. House. May 12, 1922, Charles Seymour Papers, Yale University Library; also House conversation with George S. Viereck, Oct. 13, 1930, George S. Viereck Papers, Yale University Library. In the R. S. Baker Papers, Container 7, Series I, Library of Congress, there is a note from Mrs. Wilson to House dated Nov. 18, 1919 in which she mentions that the President had heard that House had been ill and was sorry. She added: " . . . I fancy he still thinks you are in Paris."

59.   *New York Times*, Dec. 12, 1919.

60.   Grey to Lansing, Sept. 30, 1919, and Lansing to Grey, Oct. 3, 1919, 701.4111/289, National Archives, Washington D. C.

61.   Gene Smith, *When the Cheering Stopped*, pp. 113-115.

62.   Robert Lansing Desk Diary, Oct. 30, 1919, Lansing Papers, Library of Congress.

63.   House Diary, Nov. 20, 1919, Edward M. House Papers, Yale University Library.

64.   Jonathan Daniels, *The End of Innocence*, pp. 294-298; also Gene Smith, *When the Cheering Stopped*, p. 116; also recorded House conversation with Seymour, May 12, 1922, Charles Seymour Papers, Yale University Library.

65.   Conversations. Charles Seymour and Edward M. House. May 12, 1922, Charles Seymour Papers, Yale University Library. Mrs. Wilson's first husband owned a jewelry store in Washington.

66.   Statement by Major Charles Crauford-Stuart, Nov. 4, 1919, 701.411/314 1/2, National Archives, Washington, D.C. Under the same number in the Archives,

there is also a statement by Mrs. Isabelle MacDonald, the hostess at the dinner party, stating that the Major gave no opinion about the President.

67.   John Davis to Lansing, Nov. 24, 1919, 701.4111/303, National Archives, Washington, D.C. Curzon told American Ambassador Davis about Grey's threat to resign. Davis relayed this to Lansing.

68.   Conversations. Charles Seymour and Edward M. House. May 12, 1922, Charles Seymour Papers, Yale University Library.

69.   Grey to Curzon, Oct. 4, 1919, Woodward and Butler, eds., *British Documents*, V, p. 1003.

70.   Ibid. p. 1004.

71.   Grey, in reporting his frustration of his American experience to Lloyd George, said that his situation "was more intolerable to me than any position I have ever been in." George W. Egerton, "Britain and the Great Betrayal: Anglo-American Relations and the Struggle for United States Ratification of the Treaty of Versailles, 1919-1920," *The Historical Journal*, vol. 29, 4 (1978), p. 899.

Chapter VIII

La Danse est Terminée

"It is inconceivable how many blunders E. Grey always commits . . ."[1] So spoke Alexandra, widow of Edward VII, in 1912. The Dowager Queen did not care for the Foreign Secretary and thought he had mishandled the tense situation in the Balkins. In America, seven years later, many persons would have agreed with Alexandra—that Grey made blunders; his short stay was troubled indeed (on at least two occasions he threatened to resign); Anglo-American relations had not been improved by his presence. But it is hard to see how any British Ambassador could have behaved much differently, given the situation in Washington at that time.

The question which Grey had to face daily was, "Who is running the Government?" The President was an invalid in October-November 1919, incapable of running the country, but Vice President Marshall did not take over. The Constitution does not provide for automatic transfer of authority, and no one wished to take responsibility for declaring the President incompetent. The question before the country concerning the League of Nations colored the thinking of individuals who otherwise might have taken the initiative to replace Wilson: the Democrats would not discredit their leader, which would have produced certain defeat on the League question, and the Republicans found they could strengthen their own position at expense of the President's obvious incapacity.[2] A workable alternative existed, for Wilson could have resigned, but his wife and his doctor vetoed this course, the latter feeling it "would have a bad effect on the country, and a serious effect on our patient."[3]

Mrs. Wilson tried to transact some of the business of government, asking her husband for instruction if, in her judgement, the subject would not upset him, but Cabinet members had been intimidated by the threat that undue strain would cost the President his life; they stayed away and solved their problems as best they could. Ironically, it may have been the combined efforts of Mrs. Wilson and Secretary of State Lansing that kept the President in office. The two did not like each other, but Lansing, in attempt to maintain a facade of government, possibly prevented a congressional investigation of Wilson's ability to perform his duties.[4] The Secretary of State called the Cabinet together in October, and thereafter met with them twice a week. His Confidential Memoranda now in the Library of Congress record his schedule during the President's illness: "On Tuesday and Friday the Cabinet meets at eleven a.m. at which meeting I preside. We generally sit between two and two and a half hours." This use of the Cabinet as an executive device reassured the public and made the President's illness more acceptable. Another part of Lansing's schedule included Diplomatic Day, as he labelled each Thursday. "From eleven to twelve-thirty or later I receive diplomats who come."[5]

Lansing received Grey more frequently than the schedule would indicate. His desk diary for the month of October, 1919, is full of reference to sessions with the Ambassador. Much of the conversation centered on reservations to the Treaty. Although the Secretary had worked in behalf of the League he had become convinced that the Treaty would never secure Senate approval without concessions to the Lodge reservationists. From Grey he attempted to determine the position of the British Government toward a League bound by American qualifications.[6]

There were two problems concerning the Covenant which would affect the British—the Johnson Amendment, later called the Lenroot Reservation, and the preamble to the Lodge reservations. The preamble stated that the Treaty would not go into effect, even if ratified by the United States, until at least three of the four principal Allies, Great Britain, France, Italy, or Japan, agreed to the reservations.[7] Britain's acceptance seemed chancy since one of the reservations appeared a slap at England and the colonies. According to the arrangement at the Paris Peace Conference by Wilson, Lloyd George, and Clemenceau, the Empire would have a total of six votes in the proposed Council of the League of Nations—one for England, and one for each of the Dominions. This "unequal voting" was emphasized by the wily Lodge and other opponents of the League as one way of denouncing Wilson, Versailles, and internationalism. Their calculated assault was successful and the American people rebounded from the internationalism apparent in 1918 into a great surge of isolationism.[8] The Lenroot Reservation which declared that the United States would assume no obligation in any finding of the League Council in which "any member of the League and its self-governing dominions, colonies, or parts of empire have more than one vote"—in other words, the aggregate votes of the British Empire—was a sample of the isolationism and Anglophobia in the United States at that time.[9]

Lansing wanted to assure passage of the Treaty by the Senate, and at the same time secure acceptance of the reservations by the major powers as stipulated in the preamble. He asked Grey, with whom he dined occasionally during October, to contact his Government and suggest a public statement in which the British Government would say that Empire votes would not be used in a dispute in which any part of the Empire was involved.[10] Lansing perhaps naively assumed that such a disclaimer would appease both those Senators who wanted reservations, and those who felt any reservations would be intolerable, and thus make possible some sort of a compromise. His explanation to Grey was that he felt such a statement "would ease the situation." It did not ease the situation, and Grey's letter to Curzon indicated that he found the request awkward.[11] Was Lansing speaking for the President when he asked for cooperation on the six votes? It was common knowledge that Mrs. Wilson and Lansing did not get along. Grey must have concluded that it would be better if no one knew of his discussions with Lansing concerning the reservations. His communication to Curzon on November 7, 1919, ended: "Fact that Secretary of State consulted me must on no account leak out."[12]

Grey's feelings toward the League had changed like those of Lansing. One of his detractors, David Houston, reported that Grey had been seen talking to Lodge at a dinner party. Houston, as did Daniels, interpreted this talking as meaning that Grey sympathized with Lodge and the Reservations, and was therefore against Wilson.[13] It should be remembered that Grey had come to America to support the League. While Colonel House may have urged Grey to make the journey in order to use a moderating influence on the President, hoping to speed acceptance of the League, Grey's primary purpose was the same as Wilson's—to make the League a reality. His early stand on reservations paralleled views held by the President. As he wrote Curzon on October 26, "My general line is that all reservations are to be deprecated . . ."[14] Unlike Wilson, Grey became exposed to forces wishing to make changes in the Covenant, and came to know their strength. The only other source of leadership working for the League, in addition to partisans of the President, was the League to Enforce Peace headed by such moderates as William Howard Taft and Lawrence Lowell of Harvard.[15] After several soul-searching meetings, those individuals who wanted the Treaty passed at any cost persuaded the others to accept reservations. On November 13 the executive committee of this group, which had always worked staunchly for the League, voted to support the Treaty with the Lodge Reservations.[16] This action most certainly influenced Grey. And so did his talks with Lodge. How much he saw of Lodge is uncertain, and what his opinion of him was is uncertain, but there can be no doubt that he was convinced by Lodge that reservations were necessary to get the Treaty passed. In a letter to House many years later Grey unveiled what he had discovered in conversation with Lodge: "When I was in Washington in the Autumn of 1919, Senator Lodge talked to me very freely about the situation in the Senate in regard to the League of Nations . . . The situation was then very critical . . . [the Senator] said to me that it was a mistake to talk as if the reservations could be made the starting point for a compromise. He said the reservations themselves were a compromise between those who held extreme views for or against the Covenant. They were a compromise which would secure the passage of the Covenant . . ." Grey related that Lodge had told him that any attempt to modify the reservations would upset this compromise, and would be tantamount to giving up on the Treaty.[17]

Grey had encountered Lodge and his obsession and the Senator's intensity must have convinced him that the only profitable action he could take (in view of his inability to see the President) was to follow Lansing's request and persuade his country to take a lenient attitude toward the reservations.[18] And this could be best expressed by the public statement he suggested Curzon should make.

Curzon, in the meantime, had been sounding out the Dominions to determine their position on ratification of the treaty with reservations and had received divergent replies, causing him to delay sending an answer.[19] Grey felt that Curzon did not understand that the future of the League was in danger—perhaps the totality of Anglo-American relations. He sent the Foreign Secretary a long telegram attempting to explain:

> Reasons which still make an announcement desirable are that, though such an announcement would not apparently have any effect at this juncture upon fortunes of treaty and League in Senate, it is possible that after present stiff reservations are passed a deadlock may arise on point of ratification which may lead to a compromise on enforcement of milder resolutions as an alternative to complete failure of treaty in Senate. In such a contingency, if announcement now suggested had been made by His Majesty's Government, it might then help to ease situation . . . Supporters of League in America have to defend British six votes

in Assembly, and considerable odium is being however unfairly, fastened on them by their political opponents on this ground both in Senate and their constituencies. Whether they succeed or fail in their fight for League they will feel, if we withhold this announcement, that we have not played up to help them, and their soreness will probably be even more in the event of failure than if they had won in Senate.[20]

It was at this point—beset by doubt about the League as expressed by Taft and Lowell and Lodge, concerned about misunderstanding with Curzon—that Grey turned to his old friend House, who was recovering from illness in New York. The Ambassador had met the Colonel in October, but House had been ill and out of contact with the President.[21] In November, Grey sensed that House was not going to be the entrée to Wilson that both men had counted on. Grey put his opinion of House's position in a delicate way to Curzon: "President being still too ill to see Colonel House[—]latter has not been to Washington and is I fear entirely without political influence at present. I . . . will discuss situation fully with him and telegraph to Your Lordship again as his opinion will be valuable though his influence is suspended."[22]

Although House may have suspected that his influence with the President had waned, he had not lost hope that he could again become a go-between, acting with the same attractive individual with whom he had dealt in the past. Encouraged by the deadlock over the Treaty (the Senate had refused the Treaty in two votes on November 19), he had sent the two letters of advice to the President through Mrs. Wilson. He intended to follow up by proposing changes in the reservations which would be acceptable both to Lodge and Wilson. Grey was to be included in House's scheme. The Colonel planned in his diary, with assistance from the arts of psychology, that "if Lodge is properly approached in this matter, I feel confident his vanity will lead him to acquiesce. The next move would be to get the President to acquiesce, so the Democratic vote in the Senate might be thrown in behalf of the reservations as amended by Grey and myself."[23]

It was a noble psychological plan, and Grey was willing to work with House, but he needed the approval of his Foreign Office. He reported his meetings with House to Curzon, and asked for instruction concerning a compromise on reservations. The Ambassador felt he needed support. One of his communiques had a defiant ring: "I am absolutely committed in private here on 2 points (1) that any reservation inconsistent with triple letter to R. Borden must be repudiated by H. M. G. (2) that no British votes in League of Nations assembly can be used in a dispute to which any part of Empire is a party . . . . if H. M. G. feel they cannot support his view they ought of course to accept my resignation to avoid future misunderstandings. . ."[24]

Curzon's reply was of doubtful help. It ignored the deadlock in the Senate and ignored Grey's plea for support. It took a pious view of the problems in America. It compared the United States desire to be accepted in the League on a "different footing from the other Powers" to the dangerous desires of the countries in prewar Europe. It told Grey that "what we hope for is acceptance by the United States of the Treaty as it stands."[25]

This may have been the crowning frustration in a series which Grey encountered in what proved to be a two-month ambassadorial stay. He told House on December 5, prior to a luncheon the Colonel was giving in his honor, that he planned to return to Britain on January 2, 1920; the Ambassador and his secretary, Tyrrell, enumerated the problems facing them. Grey said the British Government did not understand the situation on ratification and he hoped to "persuade them to accept the Treaty with such reservations as were almost certain to be appended." It was impossible to see the President, and work through Lansing had been useless because "Lansing himself had not seen Wilson for three months." The trouble over Crauford-Stuart remained, with Grey being pressed by Bernard Baruch and by Dr. Grayson (both acting for the President, they said) to send the Major home. Grey probably related these troubles to House in his usual low-keyed way, but Tyrrell had a sharp remark about the President's treatment of Grey: he called Wison's action on the Crauford-Stuart affair "a high-handed procedure" and told House that "even the Kaiser, at the height of his arrogance and power would not have acted so."[26]

This conference so discouraged the Colonel that he made no other attempts to reach the President on political matters. He faced the fact that the Grey mission was a failure, and felt responsibility because "Lord Grey came to the United States largely . . . upon my advice."[27] He then placed most of the responsibility on the shoulders of Mrs. Wilson who had become angry over Grey's refusal to send Crauford-Stuart home and, in retaliation, so House's diary hinted, refused to allow the Ambassador to see the President.[28]

It appears that the Colonel had assessed this situation correctly. He knew (surely no one knew better) that Mrs. Wilson made the decisions about whom the President would see in the months of October, November, and December, 1919. While her selections of suitable visitors were supposed to be based on concern for the President's health, her prejudices and biases complicated her decisions. She disliked House and kept him away. She believed Lansing had been disloyal to the President when he had called Cabinet meetings; although she continued to see the Secretary of State, and remained outwardly pleasant ("she is always charming"), she did not allow him to see her husband. In like manner, Lord Grey was denied an audience with the President. The Secretary of State, disturbed over Wilson's failure to receive the Ambassador, made a special plea that the President see Grey. Mrs. Wilson reacted by inquiring if Grey had sent Crauford-Stuart home. Lansing informed her that the guests at the dinner party at which the Major made his supposedly slanderous remarks about Mrs. Wilson had refused to sign affidavits incriminating himself, and that because of this evidence of his innocence or lack of evidence of his guilt, Grey had refused to send him back to Great Britain. Mrs. Wilson then simply said that the President would not see Grey if Crauford-Stuart remained in America.[29]

On such a note—one might say, a woman's pique—the Grey mission ended. Grey wrote the Foreign Office on Christmas Day, 1919, shortly before he left for home, giving his final assessment of the political situation in the United States. He again expressed belief that the six British votes was the most popular argument used by opponents of the Treaty, and he was afraid this opposition would assume an increasingly anti-British character. He wrote that "there are other aspects of general situation . . . which cannot be adequately explained by telegram or letter."[30] Presumably he meant the hostility of Mrs. Wilson, and that this, indeed, had proved the most impenetrable barrier to Anglo-American cooperation.

After Grey's return to England he chose to make public his thoughts on the impasse in the United States concerning the Treaty in a long letter published in *The Times* on January 31, 1920. Reprinted in the New York *Times* on February 1, it stated that the observations were entirely Grey's; it indicated, however, that he felt that the United States should enter the League on whatever terms were necessary.[31] On February 3 *The Times* commented that "publications of Grey's letter . . . has given rise to the opinion that had the opportunity been given he would have indicated to the President that Great Britain would accept the Treaty with material reservations."[32] Since one of the strongest Wilsonian arguments had been that other powers would reject the Lodge reservations, the letter caused a furor among those individuals still engaged in argument over the Treaty. It appeared to knock the props out from under the Democrats, but it also confused those who wanted the reservations as a safeguard against foreign influence.[33] Lloyd George, moving with his customary expediency, hastened to disassociate himself and the British Government from the sentiments expressed in the Grey letter, informing the Secretary of State that he had not been consulted.[34]

The President and Mrs. Wilson reacted snappishly to what they concluded was interference in United States affairs. Apparently they regarded the letter as an attempt to influence the Senate and American public into passage of the Treaty with reservations.[35] Grey's purpose could have been different. He may have been using the London *Times* as an instrument to reach the President when all the ordinary channels which he had tried during his stay in America had failed. The President, whose illness had magnified his worst qualities (partisanship and ego), and encouraged by the solicitousness of Mrs. Wilson, could not be reached by anyone no matter by what means.[36] The Treaty again failed to pass the Senate on March 19, 1920, and Wilson did not resubmit it, hoping for a "great and solemn referendum" on the Treaty and the League in the presidential election in November. The presidency of Warren G. Harding, who had made a recording simultaneously deploring the League and extolling "Beautiful Ohio," was the answer to Wilson's last plea.[37]

When Grey left for England in early January, 1920, House departed for Texas. The New York *Times* quoted the Colonel's reasons: "I am going to Texas to see my friends and to attend to some personal matters that long have been neglected. What I want more than anything else is a period of quiet, and I'm going home to seek it."[38] Texas seemed about the only place suitable for the Colonel. Lansing has visited him in New York shortly before and wrote in his Confidential Memoranda (not without some complacency) that the Colonel knew he had lost influence with the President although House blamed Mrs. Wilson. "The Colonel was in better physical condition than I have ever seen him, but he did not seem so sure of his opinions as of old .... He seemed to me rather chastened in spirit and to seek sympathy for having advised the President wrongly as to certain matters ...."[39]

The rupture of the friendship had caused members of the Cabinet and other officials, who had perhaps resented House's unofficial position of authority, to point out publicly his mistakes and minimize his service to the President.[40] House's first reaction to this sort of criticism had been the one Lansing had observed—a feeling of humiliation, and a reassessment of his actions during the years with Wilson. He was probably more introspective and self-critical during this period than in any other time in his life. It would have been interesting to have known in what manner he thought he had advised the President incorrectly, but Lansing, to whom apparently he had confessed some bad advice, did not elaborate. House felt hurt for many years, perhaps the rest of his life, because he never saw the President again. However, in retrospect, he chose not to enumerate mistakes of advice, but to stress what he considered to be politically malefic influences surrounding the President after September, 1919—such individuals as Grayson, Baruch, and (notably) Mrs. Wilson.

In this manner, he regained his aplomb, and his recorded conversations in the early 1920s with Charles Seymour who edited his papers, and with George S. Viereck who wrote a book about the House-Wilson relationship, *The Strangest Friendship in History*, are full of confidence. *The Intimate Papers of Colonel House*, edited by Seymour, containing extensive passages from House's diary, letters to Wilson, and other correspondence dealing with matters of state, did not begin to appear until two years after Wilson's death in 1924. In these volumes, four in number, published between 1926 and 1928, House accepted substantial responsibility for whatever glory there was to be had in the Wilsonian Administration, by hinting that most of Wilson's domestic and foreign policies originated with him. At the same time he covered his tracks by removing himself from the national scene whenever things went wrong. One reviewer wrote in the New York *Tribune* on March 7, 1926, that the impression he received from *The Intimate Papers* was that Woodrow Wilson sat by the domestic hearth reading aloud the poems of Wordsworth while the private citizen, Colonel House, ran the government—except, of course, when mistakes were made, and at those times the Colonel could be found on the high seas.[41] Modesty, a trait which President Wilson thought he saw in House, and which many other individuals referred to when they called House self-effacing, was hard to find in the memoirs. The Colonel maintained the pose in a letter to Lord Grey soon after his first two volumes reached the public in 1926. "You can never know," he wrote Grey, "how much I have disliked the publicity which has come to me through the publication of these two volumes."[42]

The two men, House and Grey, had continued to correspond after they had gone into retirement. House made it a point to see Grey whenever he visited England. Both men were writing their memoirs in the early '20s and sometimes sent each other excerpts from their manuscripts before publication. In the *Intimate Papers* no one was referred to with more deference and admiration than Grey. Indeed, the series began with a quotation from Grey at the top of page one of Volume I. Recording their first meeting House called Grey "supremely distinguished" and remarked that it was due to "his sincerity of purpose and honesty of method."[43] In the descriptions of each mission to England, House presented Grey as possessing both wisdom and charm.

Despite these accolades Grey, when asked by House to comment after publication of the first two volumes, had a few bones to pick. He wrote that the two main criticisms in England were that House's view of the British attitude "is harsh and that some sentences about Spring Rice are unkind." He hinted that some persons had mentioned the exaltation of House at the expense of Wilson (he did not present it as his view), adding that "this is quite contrary to the impression you gave me at that period."[44]

Grey's two-volume memoir of his public life, *Twenty-Five Years,* published in 1925, contained a section on British relations with America, and he gave the manuscript of this section to House to read in late summer of 1924 when House was in Europe. In a supplement to his diary House recorded his reaction:

> Grey mentions in the chapter Whitelaw Reid, Theodore Roosevelt, Page and myself, speaking pleasantly of all of us. What he said of me was very cordial but he apologized when he saw me by saying that he did not write of me half as strongly as he felt and the reason for not doing so was that he feared lest the Germans would think our relations had been so intimate during the war that I could not have been an impartial judge of events, as far as they were concerned. I told him I was glad he had placed our relations just as he did and that I should have regretted it if he had stated them in any warmer terms.[45]

Grey's explanation to House that he hesitated to reveal the complete picture of his friendship and diplomacy with the Colonel in his autobiography because the Germans might think House was not an impartial judge of events during the war does not seem logical. The fact was that America, guided by its diplomats one supposes, had gone to war against Germany. Given such a result, how could House serving as an American diplomatic agent for the President have remained impartial? Possibly Grey had more to hide from the Americans than from the Germans.

House, of course, protested too much when he said he would not have wished Grey to have made a different presentation of the House-Grey diplomacy in his *Twenty-Five Years.* He must have been puzzled by Grey's failure to have mentioned the House missions of 1913, 1914, and 1915, about which he and Seymour wrote with such zest.

There may be two explanations for Grey's omission of the 1913 and 1914 journeys House made to England. First, Grey may not have considered House's contributions in either mission important. House did not properly inform Grey about Wilson's intentions toward Huerta; the ultimate settlement of the Mexican problem was due to Page and Tyrrell. Nor was House successful in his attempt to bring about a better understanding between Great Britain and Germany in June, 1914. Grey may have operated on the theory that it was better to say nothing than to point out that the missions were failures. Second, the friendship Grey developed with House during those two missions could have been as contrived as was House's original association with Wilson. To have written warmly about friendship developing in the years before the war (as House did in his *Intimate Papers*) would have called for a duplicity which Grey did not possess. A critic of Grey once said that it was always difficult to find a situation in which Grey had been utterly deceitful: "The most that could be said with truth about him was, [he] did not tell us all."[46] Refusing to write about the beginning of his friendship with House would have seemed infinitely more honest to Grey than to have mentioned it with enthusiasm.[47]

George Macaulay Trevelyan, however, who published a biography of Grey in 1937, did not hesitate to describe the basis for Grey's friendships with the Americans. In *Grey of Fallodon*, Trevelyan stated that in 1913 and 1914 Grey purposefully pursued friendship with the government and people of the United States. Sandwiching House's name between those of Theodore Roosevelt and Walter Hines Page, Trevelyan wrote that Grey had an affinity for the type of Americans with whom he had to deal: "the more easily did he make the conquest of their private affections, which proved of no small public importance."[48]

One might conclude that in the years before the war House's missions were of no real consequence to the government of Great Britain, other than to provide another tie with the United States. Grey had no impelling reason to mention them.

But the 1915 mission undertaken by House was of high meaning to the British government. One might wonder, as House probably did, why Grey chose to omit it from his memoirs. House went to Europe in 1915 to straighten out the controversy between England and the United States concerning the Royal Navy's infractions of neutral rights while enforcing the blockade of Germany, and to discuss the possibility of mediation by Wilson since there had been indications via Gerard and Bernstorff that Germany was interested in peace. In the second volume of *Twenty-Five Years* Grey wrote about problems of the blockade with what appeared to be the utmost candor, stating that "the object of diplomacy . . . was to secure the maximum of blockade without rupture with the United States."[49] Apparently he did not mind talking about the goal, but wished to avoid the means. One could understand. Grey charmed House into staying in England for about four months in 1915 during which House sent moderating letters to Wilson and the State Department concerning the blockade. This gave the Allies time to perfect their system, and each added day to House's sojourn increased the economic dependence of the United States on the Allies. Grey delayed House's visit to Germany until the desire for peace in that country had passed.[50] To have written that such tactics were used on the President's personal envoy to accomplish British purposes in the spring of 1915 when these tactics included the application of Grey's personal magnetism with emphasis on their common interests, among them the love of nature (there was a lot of talk about the beauty of Northumberland and Texas sunsets) would not have been helpful to Anglo-American relations of the 1920s. It would have alienated House, with whom Grey still maintained a friendship. And who could tell—perhaps House again would become an important public figure.

The 1915 mission with its theme of delay was ignored in Grey's writings. The 1916 mission, which culminated in the Memorandum, was not. Yet the Memorandum itself was a document of delay. A conservative estimate of time spent in development of the Memorandum and in correspondence between House and Grey concerning possible application of it would be about seven months. During this time—January to August, 1916—Grey was able to postpone a confrontation with the United States over neutral rights. House's faith in the Memorandum (which was, after all, faith in Grey) enabled him to moderate the Wilson-Lansing demands on the British. Naturally Grey did not write about the Memorandum in this way. In his memoirs he devoted eight or ten pages to the document, choosing this subject to introduce House for the first time as his friend.[51] There did not seem to be any hypocrisy in this account of the genuineness of friendship, and one feels that Grey as well as House by early 1916 felt the close relationship. It would have been hard not to have liked House after Grey had spent so much time with him through the years. House, after all, had his own way of inspiring friendship, and had displayed devotion to the British cause.

Grey's comments on the Memorandum masterfully played down any commitment made by the Allies, and insinuated that the Germans had missed an opportunity for peace by not agreeing to the conference called for in the Memorandum.[52] But because of Grey's delaying tactics in the spring and summer of 1916 the Memorandum was never invoked. Grey's entire account of this episode was evasive, to say the least. If his final memoir comment on the subject may have been idealistic (and lyrical) enough to have satisfied American diplomats, it revealed that he did not regard the Memorandum in the same light as had Wilson and House: "So disappointing have events been since 1919, so dark are the troubles still, that we are tempted to find some relief in building castles in the air, and if the future is clouded for this, we build them in the past."[53]

Grey's memoirs subtly attested to the fact that the British did not have to recede from any major position on neutral rights during the war, despite American opposition.[54] Neither did the Allies accede to the desire of President Wilson to mediate in 1915 and 1916 when a negotiated peace would have been unsatisfactory for them. Juxtaposing these facts with evidences of the influence Grey exerted over the President's special agent, one might come to the conclusion that Grey manipulated House during their wartime encounters in such a way that the British nation benefited. It is interesting that Colonel House, whose political career had been established through powers of persuasion which culminated in his deliberate friendship with President Wilson, should have been outmaneuvered by another professional, the British Foreign Secretary.

If the House missions resulted in a diplomatic victory for Grey and Great Britain, does this mean that they were defeats for House and American policy? In one special sense they were not. Grey and House shared a hope which extended beyond the circumference of the war. Their diplomacy, or one could say Anglo-American wartime diplomacy, proved an important point of origin of the idea of collective security, so much talked about in the 1930s, so idealistically sought after in the 1940s and even the '50s and '60s and '70s.[55] The idea of a league of nations to secure a lasting peace developed during the trialogue of House, Grey, and Wilson. Grey's ideas had always looked toward a concert of nations, albeit in the old nineteenth-century notion of a concert; he had used this concept as a basis for calling a conference of ambassadors in 1913 to resolve the Balkan crisis. He attempted to invoke the same kind of a conference in late July, 1914, to halt the beginning of the World War. His messages to House in 1915, particularly his letter of September 22 and cable on November 10, stressed the need for an international organization to maintain peace in which America would participate. House, too, believed that a peaceful pact among nations would be beneficial for all, and had discovered early in his association with Wilson that the President's ethical sense of diplomacy responded to such a concept.[56] Because of his own beliefs and association with both Grey and Wilson, House realized—in a way no other individual could—that the ideas of Grey matched the idealism of Wilson. Through the Colonel's constant remarking that Grey and Wilson desired permanent peace for the world, the President, who was improvising diplomacy from month to month, attempting to maintain the honor of his country, came gratefully to accept the idea of a league of nations. This object seemed the one reasonable ideal, the moral justification, the balm to Wilson's conscience for engaging the United States in the European conflict. So Walter Lippmann wrote in *Foreign Affairs*, in April, 1926, and it is a convincing insight. House's role as catalyst between Grey and Wilson, promoting and strengthening the League concept until it became a reality, cannot be over-emphasized. In this he did not fail.

The last diplomatic meeting between House and Grey had occurred in 1919 because the two men were working for this same cause—the League of Nations. The President's illness and the resulting complications destroyed the hopes of both men. House did not accomplish his goal. Neither did Grey, who had stretched his hand in a Canning-like gesture toward the United States.[57] Perhaps this shared failure underlay the friendship between House and Grey in their twilight years. After the memoirs of each man had been published and each had reacted in his own way to what the other had said or not said, a warmer tone appeared in their correspondence. In the late '20s Grey could no longer see to read (he described this handicap as a sort of death in life) but he sent painstakingly handwritten letters to House.[58] House, for his part, visited Grey and continued to give the admiration he always had displayed. He sometimes wrote to ask if Grey would write articles on international peace for American publications "as the statesman who could best represent Great Britain and the one whose influence in the United States is more potent than any other."[59] Grey seemed to appreciate this affection and esteem, and in one of his last letters to House, on January 1, 1933, sent warm wishes for the New Year, and ended: "I very much miss the discontinuance of your visits here. I long to have a talk with you."[60]

The friendship of Grey and House was fated to endure for twenty years, into a time altogether different from that of the presidency of Woodrow Wilson. Grey died in September, 1933. By then a new President was buoyantly confronting a troubled America. A leader had arisen in Germany to threaten the hegemony of Great Britain. It was a pity that Grey's longed-for conversation with House did not materialize. The two men would have much to talk about. Perhaps they would have talked of the novel problems facing their countries, or they might have returned to nostalgic problems such as the enigma of Wilson, whose shadow haunted House until his own death in 1938. In a speculated last conversation it is probable, however, that each of the old friends would have continued to do what he had done best in the past—carefully and courteously performed his minuet of manipulation.

Notes

1. Georgina Battiscombe, *Queen Alexandra* (Boston, 1969), p. 279.

2. J. M. Blum, *Joe Tumulty and the Wilson Era*, p. 214.

3. E. B. Wilson, *My Memoir*, p. 289.

4. Daniel F. Smith, "Lansing and the Wilson Interregnum, 1919-1920," *The Historian*, 21 (Fall, 1959), pp. 154-160.

5. Lansing's daily schedule during Wilson's illness described Dec. 6, 1919, in his Confidential Memorandum, Lansing Papers, Library of Congress.

6. Lansing Confidential Memorandum, Oct. 22, 1919, Lansing Papers, Library of Congress; also D. M. Smith, "Lansing and the Wilson Interregnum," p. 155.

7. Alan Cranston, *The Killing of the Peace* (New York, 1945), p. 209.

8. Selig Adler, *The Isolationist Impulse: Its Twentieth Century Reaction* (New York, 1957), pp. 54-59, 73-78.

9. Ibid., pp. 54-59, 73-78. Among those on the other side who attempted to defend the decision to allow Britain's Dominions to be represented in the League was William Gibbs McAdoo, Wilson's son-in-law and Secretary of Treasury. He tried to point out to those who might influence Senators (usually by letter) that while Britain might have six voices, she would have only one vote in the Assembly of the League. McAdoo to E. B. Craig, General Correspondence, Container 224, William G. McAdoo Papers, Library of Congress.

10. Grey to Curzon, Oct. 16, 1919, Woodward and Butler, eds., *British Documents*, V, pp. 1009-1010; also Lansing Desk Diary for month of October, Lansing Papers, Library of Congress.

11. Grey to Curzon, Nov. 6, 1919, Woodward and Butler, eds., *British Documents*, V, pp. 1017-1018. Grey's remark about Lansing's request: "I do not think I should shirk this responsibility though it is unwelcome . . . ."

12. Ibid. A second dispatch was sent to Curzon on the same day.

13. David F. Houston, *Eight Years with Wilson's Cabinet, 1913-1920* (2 vols., Garden City, New York, 1926), II, p. 49.

14. Grey to Curzon, Oct. 26, 1919, Woodward and Butler, eds., *British Documents*, V, p. 1012.

15. Ruhl Bartlett, *The League to Enforce Peace*, pp. 148-154.

16. Minutes of the Executive Committee of the League to Enforce Peace, which met on Thursday, November 13, 1919, were sent to W. G. McAdoo, a member of the group with this explanation: "The opinion of this committee is that we had better accept this treaty with such reservations as the majority pass rather than have it rejected by this present session of the Senate." W. G. McAdoo Papers, Library of Congress.

17.   Grey to House, May 16, 1930, Edward M. House Papers, Yale University Library.

18.   "Obsession" is a word which might best describe Lodge's commitment to his reservations, and in back of the obsession may not have been the desire to gain passage for a modified League, but an intense hatred for Wilson which made it necessary for Lodge to thwart him.

19.   F. O. 371/4251/1777, Nov. 8, 1919, Secretary of State to Governors General. The replies summarized later in a statement made by Henry Lambert, Assistant Under-Secretary of State, Colonial Office, to Curzon marked *Secret and Pressing* revealed that Canada and New Zealand agreed with Grey's stand while the Governments of the Commonwealth of Australia and the Union of South Africa did not. F. O. 371/4251/1777, Dec. 4, 1919, Under-Secretary of State, Colonial Office, to Secretary of State.

20.   F. O. 371/4251/1777, Grey to Curzon, Nov. 14, 1919.

21.   Grey to Curzon, Oct. 15, 1919, Woodward and Butler, eds., *British Documents,* V, p. 1009.

22.   Grey to Curzon, Nov. 17, 1919, Woodward and Butler, eds., *British Documents,* V, p. 1022.

23.   House Diary, Nov. 23, 1919, Edward M. House Papers, Yale University Library.

24.   Grey referred to the statement signed by Wilson, Lloyd George, and Clemenceau that assured each of the Dominions a vote, and according to a letter he sent Lansing on Nov. 19, his commitment extended to Lansing, Hitchcock, and possibly President Lowell and Members of the League to Enforce Peace with whom he had talked. F. O. 371/4251/1777; also F. O. 371/4251/1777/A504, Grey to Curzon, Nov. 26, 1919.

25.   Curzon to Grey, Nov. 27, 1919, Woodward and Butler, eds., *British Documents,* V, p. 1040.

26.   House Diary, Dec. 5, 1919, Edward M. House Papers, Yale University Library.

27.   Ibid.

28.   House Diary, Nov. 20, 1919, Edward M. House Papers, Yale University Library.

29.   Information in this paragraph is from a long statement made by Wilson's secretary, Edith Benham Helm, during February, 1920, concerning events in the autumn of 1919, including Secretary Lansing's resignation. The latter ostensibly occurred after the President learned of the Cabinet meetings, but Mrs. Helm felt that Mrs. Wilson had presented Lansing's efforts in a false light. Edith Benham Helm Papers, Library of Congress.

30.   F. O. 371/4251/1777, Grey to Foreign Office, Dec. 25, 1919.

31.   *New York Times,* Feb. 1, 1920.

32.   *New York Times,* Feb. 3, 1920.

33.   Bailey, *Woodrow Wilson and the Great Betrayal,* p. 238.

34.   Lloyd George quoted in a letter from Ambassador Davis to Secretary of State, Feb. 6, 1920, vol. 51, Lansing Papers, Library of Congress.

35.   Gene Smith, *When the Cheering Stopped,* pp. 141-142.

36.   Lansing Desk Diary, Dec. 10, 1919, Lansing Papers, Library of Congress.

37.   Harding's speech was the lead-off against the League before the vote was taken in the Senate in November, 1919. Francis, Russell, *The Shadow of Blooming Grove: Warren G. Harding in His Times* (New York, 1968), pp. 324-325.

38.   *New York Times,* Jan. 6, 1920.

39.   Confidential Memorandum, Dec. 27, 1919, Lansing Papers, Library of Congress. On this occasion, House told Lansing that he did not blame Dr. Greyson for keeping him from the President as some of his friends did, because Grayson had sent him a ham for Christmas.

40.   E. Buehrig, *Wilson's Foreign Policy on Perspective,* p. 13.

41.   *New York Tribune Book Section,* March 7, 1926, *The Intimate Papers of Colonel House,* reviewed by Stuart Sherman.

42.   House to Grey, April 25, 1926, Edward M. House Papers, Yale University Library.

43.   C. Seymour, *The Intimate Papers of Colonel House,* I, p. 195.

44.   Grey to House, Aug. 6, 1926, Edward M. House Papers, Yale University Library.

45.   House Supplement to Diary, Sept. 12, 1924., Edward M. House Papers, Yale University Library.

46.   H. Sidebotham, *Pillars of the State,* p. 38.

47.   Grey's only reference to these missions: "We had met pleasantly once or twice on his [House's] visits to London before the war." Grey, *Twenty-Five Years,* II, p. 119.

48.   Trevelyan, *Grey of Fallodon,* pp. 131, 232.

49.   Grey, *Twenty-Five Years,* II, p. 103.

50.   R. S. Baker, *Wilson,* V, pp. 261, 264.

51.   Grey, *Twenty-Five Years,* II, pp. 119-120.

52.   Ibid., pp. 123-131.

53.   Ibid., p. 132.

54.   Edwin Borchard and William P. Lage, *Neutrality for the United States* (New Haven, Conn., 1940), pp. 33-44.

55.   E. Buehrig, *Wilson's Foreign Policies in Perspective,* p. 50.

56.   Ibid., pp. 50-51. The initial discussion between House and Wilson of such an idea probably took place in 1914 when House proposed a Pan-American pact.

57.   A. Cecil, *British Foreign Secretaries,* p. 263.

58.   Grey to House, March 25, 1932, Edward M. House Papers, Yale University Library.

59.   Grey to House, March 25, 1932; House to Grey, May 20, 1928; House to Grey, June 28, 1929, Edward M. House Papers, Yale University Library.

60.   Grey to House, Jan. 1, 1933, Edward M. House Papers, Yale University Library.

Bibliographical Essay

I. Government Collections and Personal Papers

Sir Edward Grey held a position in the British Government; Colonel House was a private citizen, working for his government only as an executive agent, except for a brief time when Wilson appointed him a member of the Peace Commission. This difference is reflected in the sources of information about each man. Much material about Grey is in the Collections of the British Government, while data about House are more available in his personal papers and in the papers of those individuals with whom he had contact during his close association with the Wilson Administration.

I consulted the Public Record office originally located in London, but presently in Kew, Richmond, Surrey. Sir Edward Grey's papers are listed under the category Foreign Office 800 which is titled "Private Secretary Archives;" also under this category are the papers of other diplomatic officials such as undersecretaries in the Foreign Office, and the ambassadors. For a general view of the Anglo-American diplomatic relations prior to American entrance into the war the Grey papers and those of Sir Cecil Spring Rice, British Ambassador to the United States, are most helpful. Correspondence between the two men is literate, even witty (I do not agree with those who say Sir Edward had no sense of humor), full of opinions about Americans and their attitudes as this affected England's future. Other collections yielding important information about the blockade, and about the feeling of the British, French and Germans toward American attempts at mediation, are the papers of Sir Arthur Nicolson, Permanent Undersecretary of State from 1910 to 1916, and those of Sir Francis Bertie, Ambassador to France. Also consulted: the papers of Sir Eyre Crowe, and Sir Walter Langley, both Assistant Undersecretaries during the period 1912 to 1916. The A. J. Balfour Collection and the Lord Curzon Collection (both listed, as is Grey's, in the Private Secretary Archives) did not provide much help for this study. One file, that of Sir Eric Drummond, who served as a kind of floating secretary for the British Cabinet, first to Asquith, then to Grey, afterward to Balfour, was not available, and I was told that the Foreign Office was currently using it.

Naturally one gets an immense amount of general information from these documents, but on the subject of the House-Grey relationship these records proved somewhat sterile. In Grey's file, H through L, 1905 to 1916, I found no correspondence with House. Correspondence exists, as evidenced from the House Collection at Yale, but it is not in the records in London. There are letters about House, usually from Grey to Spring Rice, but not as many as one might expect, and they are usually in the Spring Rice rather than the Grey file. For such letters as there are about the House-Grey Memorandum, some can be found in Sir Arthur Nicolson's file or Lord Bertie's file. The Grey Papers seem glaringly empty of information about House.

Three other categories were examined: F. O. 371, the General Political file, F. O. 372, the Treaty Classification; and F. O. 899, Foreign Press Summaries, digests of American newspapers for use by the British Cabinet. Occasionally among card files of these categories I would find House's name with a numbr to look up, but in several instances this led only to a blank page stamped "Missing when volume bound in 1945."

The private papers of Arthur Balfour and Sir Robert Cecil at the British Museum contain several interesting personal letters between Grey and Balfour. The two were friends and confided in each other. Grey's handwritten letters are hard to read because of his partial blindness, but in a letter of February 7, 1916 (even allowing for some illegible words), Grey wrote Balfour that regarding "the American note" he saw a way "to turn the situation to good account." The House-Grey Memorandum, of course, followed shortly thereafter.

I also examined the Asquith Papers at Bodleian Library, Oxford. I found one important document showing British reaction to House: a lengthy, handwritten letter to Prime Minister Asquith from Edwin Montagu, Minister of Munitions.

A printed volume deserves to be in the category Government Collections and Personal Papers. F. H. Hinsley, president of St. John's College, Cambridge, had edited a book *British Foreign Policy under Sir Edward Grey* (Cambridge University Press, Cambridge, 1977). The book contains thirty-one chapters written by scholars who have used the archives of the British government department which were released in the 1950s continuing through the 1970s. Every aspect of Grey's diplomacy from 1905 through 1916 is thoroughly examined. This lengthy volume—702 pages—could be described as a primary source because of the primary nature of the sources used by authors of the chapters. *One could not make an adequate study of Sir Edward Grey without this volume.* The chapters most helpful for this study are Chapter Two, "The Foreign Office under Sir Edward Grey, 1905-1914," by Zara Steiner and Chapter Twenty-eight, "Anglo-American Relations: Mediation and Permanent Peace," written by C. M. Mason.

While searching in the British records and private papers I undertook a quest for Grey's private papers, which no one seemed to be able to locate. I approached this in two ways—by addressing a letter to Fallodon (I assumed one of Grey's relatives still lived there—his nephew Sir Cecil Graves had inherited the estate when Grey died) and by writing to Rohan Butler, the Secretary of State's Historical Advisor with Headquarters at the Foreign Office on Downing Street. Both letters brought answers.

One letter came from Fallodon. Grey's nephew had sold the estate in 1946 to a family which still lives there, the Bridgemans. Peter Bridgeman, the current resident, wrote to me several times giving general information about the size of and beauty of the estate, (over 2,000 acres in Northumberland) and describing Lord Grey's friendship with his parents—the elder Bridgemans—who had been Grey's neighbors from 1930-1933. In an unusually gracious gesture he invited me to visit the estate and in January 1972, I did.

I was served tea and spent several hours exploring the mansion and talking to Peter Bridgeman and his mother, a very vibrant woman in her late seventies, Joan Bridgeman.

The mansion seemed typical of Grey's personality, romantic in a way, and showing his desire for privacy. The study was the room most completely Grey's, and in order to insure absolute seclusion when he worked, Grey had had a hall built with another entrance so that people could not drive past this room.

A large central hall with a staircase leading to the bedrooms above was lined with portraits of Grey's ancestors. There was an especially fine one of Grey himself painted by Longsdale revealing an elegant and aristocratic face.

Grey had identified each of the bedrooms in an imaginative way and engaged a painter to put gold lettering above each door; the rooms had been given the names of trees: Beech (Grey's room), Lime, Maple, Silver Fir, Yew Hedge, and Deodar.

Outside Grey had two formal gardens maintained in memory of each of his wives, Dorothy, killed in 1906, and Pamela, whom he married in 1922.

The Bridgemans stressed his love of nature and pointed out that Grey had moved several trees from the middle of the forest surrounding the mansion so that he could have a view of the North Sea from his bedroom.

Joan Bridgeman said that she had been invited to lunch at Fallodon many times when Grey was alive in the early 1930s and that she found him full of charm, a marvelous host who gave himself completely to his guests.

Concerning Grey's private papers, Peter Bridgeman reported that Grey's nephew, Cecil Graves, had given most of them to George Macaulay Trevelyan who used them to write *Grey of Fallodon* in 1937. When Trevelyan completed his work the papers did not surface and it is thought possible that he [Trevelyan] burned them. The present owner of Fallodon said that it was known that Grey kept a "Green Book"—a complete diary—"more than the planting of trees," and that it had disappeared and may also have been burned.

Information concerning the whereabouts of Grey's private papers was further elucidated when I followed suggestions in a letter received from Rohan Butler, who thought the best approach would be through Cambridge where Trevelyan had lived many years and served as Master. I wrote to St. John's College, Cambridge, asking for information about Grey's papers, or Trevelyan's notes or papers about Grey, and received a fascinating letter from a librarian there, Mr. A. Halcrow, who wrote that wherever the papers were, they were not at Cambridge. He directed me to G. Kitson Clark, at Cambridge and suggested that if I wrote in a diplomatic tone he might answer.

Dr. Kitson Clark did answer in a helpful and friendly way, November 26, 1969, writing that the fate of the Grey papers "is rather mysterious." No Grey manuscripts were at Trevelyan's house in Cambridge, nor at Hallington, Trevelyan's house in Northumberland (he was a neighbor of Grey). Two or three scholars had attempted to track them down, going to Grey's nephew's solicitors in Scotland, and following other leads, with no result, and in Kitson Clark's opinion the papers were irretrievably lost.

It is speculative, of course, but it does not seem implausible that Trevelyan may indeed have destroyed the papers since they were last known to have been in his possession.

In reverse order, I began research about House through personal papers, the House Collection, in the Sterling Library at Yale, a massive archive containing a diary in several bound volumes—usually daily entries for the years 1912-1919, thereafter occasional entries identified as "Supplements to the Diary," House's letters to Wilson, correspondence with Cabinet members, many letters to and from Grey (so far as I know, the only locus of these letters). There are folders of newspaper clippings, magazine articles, most of which praise House (a critical one occasionally appears—such as "The Legend of Colonel House" by William MacDonald in *Current History,* June 1926, in which it was said that everything the Colonel did ended in failure), and two long autobiographical memoranda by House entitled "Reminiscences" and "Memories," the last of these written in 1929 indicating that House felt satisfied with what he had accomplished in life. Of considerable value and interest are transcripts of conversations with Charles Seymour during the '20s and of conversations with George S. Viereck during the early '30s, the latter listed as part of the Viereck Papers. These conversations seem less studied than House's diary, more relaxed and perhaps more revealing. House told Viereck on December 1, 1930, when asked why he stopped advising the President: *"Cherchez la femme!"* a remark of a sort he never would have permitted in his diaries.

In the George Sylvester Viereck Collection at the University of Iowa, Iowa City, Iowa, 89 typed letters from Colonel House to Viereck exist dated from August 18, 1929 to September 11, 1937. These very short notes are primarily about the publication of *The Strangest Friendship in History,* the story of the Wilson-House friendship. Viereck was the author but he had House's approval and the Colonel supplied him with information. House seemed pleased with the book, and there was some discussion of a collaboration on another book which had to be dropped due to House's ill health. Occasionally, House made suggestions about sources concerning the House-Wilson relationship. One such interesting paragraph reads: "If I were you I would see Grayson. [Dr. Cary T. Grayson, Wilson's physician]. He is a great talker and probably you would get something of value. In any event, see Joe Tumulty and David Lawrence."

The papers of Walter Hines Page at Houghton Library proved invaluable because Page as ambassador to Great Britain and a friend of Sir Edward as well as House knew many details about their diplomacy which no one else knew (it is true, however, that in 1916 Page was left out of the picture). What he knew about he wrote about, often flamboyantly, in his diary and in letters to friends and officials. These letters he sometimes labelled "Private and Dangerous;" if the information did not actually seem dangerous it often was indiscreet since he criticized the United States government freely for not entering the war earlier on the side of the Allies.

Among folders in the Page Papers are several with Sir Edward Grey's name. One contains Grey's published pamphet on the League of Nations—not readily available at the Public Record Office. Several British documents on the blockade are here, which I did not find in London.

Page received fifty-nine letters from Wilson and they are in his collection—elaborately boxed and ribbon-tied.

Another collection at the Houghton Library is that of David F. Houston, the Secretary of Agriculture, who was fond of Wilson and his letters attest to the fact that he considered him the finest of Presidents. Houston also seemed to like House. The Colonel wrote occasionally, once from Paris on January 24, 1919, telling that he intended to retire from public life as soon as Wilson left the Presidency. This would seem to refute the claim of some historians who maintain that a break occurred between House and Wilson because House at Paris became politically ambitious.

The Library of Congress contains the Wilson papers, and I attempted to limit my study to manuscripts about Grey and House (it is easy to become so fascinated with Wilson memorabilia that the original purpose is forgotten). Letters from House and Grey are usually in Series II, listed alphabetically and chronologically. Most of those usuable for this study can be seen at Yale. Mrs. Edith Bolling Wilson's papers are listed in the index of Wilson's Papers. These papers were released in 1976. I examined her scrapbooks, which contain clippings of her activities as wife of the President. In this collection her pictures abound.

Ray Stannard Baker, chosen by Wilson as his biographer, has a collection at the Library of Congress put together while he prepared for his eight-volume account of Wilson. Many letters between House and Wilson are in the Baker Collection, Series I, Contemporary Correspondence of Woodrow Wilson, 1911-1920. Baker reconstructed Wilson's days in sequence, using Wilson's papers, newspaper clippings, and source material from other individuals in touch with the President and made elaborate notes. I found these chronological notes helpful.

Other collections seen at the Library of Congress were the William Jennings Bryan Papers, the William G. McAdoo Papers, the Papers of John Bassett Moore and the Papers of Robert Lansing—in which there is a Desk Diary and his Confidential Memoranda. The latter are full of intellectual introspection. While it might be said that Lansing did not always act like a Secretary of State, he certainly thought like one, as his Memoranda reveal.

I examined the papers of Edith Benham Helm, personal secretary to Mrs. Edith Wilson; these papers have just been released this past decade. Her peace conference notes are fascinating, as is her analysis of Lansing's resignation.

Also in the Library of Congress are the papers of Irwin H. Hoover, Chief Usher of the White House during the Wilson period. Hoover accompanied the Wilsons to the Paris Peace Conference. Among the papers is a long handwritten note (seventeen pages) in which Hoover describes the last illness of Wilson as he saw it from his vantage point. It is chillingly frank when Hoover details the decline of Wilson's mental capabilities and one feels pity for the stricken President, as did Hoover.

Last, I went to the National Archives to check records of the government concerning the activities of House and Grey. General Records of the State Department, listed as Record Group 59, show business between the United States and Britain during the years 1910-1929. The records are listed chronlogically under two title filings—one under "British Embassy" and the other under "Great Britain." With thousands of cards it is often difficult to find reference to the diplomacy of House and Grey. Many cards deal with such subjects as fishing rights near the American-Canadian border, or passport requirements. There were several cards referring to Grey's ambassador-ship in the autumn of 1919; these led to a few documents concerning the Crauford-Stuart affair—specifically the Major's denial of slanderous gossip, and some newspaper clippings deploring Wilson's nonrecogni-tion of Grey.

One other source was checked at the Archives: the name-card index of U.S. and British business, 1910-1929. Under the name of E. M. House, I found about twelve cards referring to messages sent to or received from the State Department; some of the documents were on microfilm, but when checked out were not especially helpful as they often included House's name in the message and had no signi-ficance applicable to this study. I found no name file on Grey.

II. Printed Sources

Papers Relating to the Foreign Relations of the United States, Supple-ments, 1914-1917 (6 vols., Washington, D. C., 1928-29, 1931-32), to-gether with the Lansing Papers (2 vols., Washington, 1930-40), contain practically all diplomatic correspondence of value during Wilson's

Administration, including reports House sent back while in Europe on missions for the President. *Documents on British Foreign Policy: 1919-1939* (London, 1946-65), edited by Rohan Butler and E. L. Woodward, has in its First Series, Volume V, a section devoted to the Grey mission which uses documents from the Foreign Office and from the papers of Curzon.

III. Published Diaries and Letters

American

The Intimate Papers of Colonel House (4 vols., Boston, 1926-1928), edited by Charles Seymour, is a careful collection of House's diary and letters with a bridging narrative by Seymour. Seymour, a friend of the Colonel, displays prejudice in House's favor by his editing. Wilson for the most part is treated gently, and Grey emerges, if not *the* hero, at least *a* hero. Ray Stannard Baker's eight-volume *Woodrow Wilson, Life and Letters* (New York, 1927-39) is impressively put together, presenting Wilson's letters through a biographical approach. The middle volumes, V and VI, seem more critical than the beginning or ending volumes. Burton J. Hendrick, *The Life and Letters of Walter Hines Page* (3 vols., Garden City, N. Y., 1924-26), is a fine job of combining Page's erudite letters with diplomacy of the era. The background of the Mexican problem is handled especially well.

The Papers of Woodrow Wilson (Princeton University Press) edited by Arthur S. Link, David W. Hirst, John E. Little, Ann Dexter Gordon, Phyllis Marchand, Margaret D. Link, is the title of an impressive collection.

In 46 volumes to date, the editors publish all personal and public papers that are essential to understanding Wilson's thought and activity. Incoming letters or extracts from such letters are included, particularly when they provide the only information concerning Wilson's speeches. Additionally, a large portion of his manuscripts are published, all diaries, samples of his classroom and lecture notes, all of his important journal articles, many papers which were never before printed. Use is made of Wilson's books *Congressional Government* and *Constitutional Government in the United States.*

British

Stephen Gwynn has edited *The Life and Friendship of Sir Cecil Spring Rice* (2 vols., London, 1929). Spring Rice sensed the uncertainity of Wilson's policies and conveyed this to the Foreign Office. He once wrote Balfour: "We regard the White House rather as Vesuvius is regarded in Naples, that is as a mysterious source of unexpected explosions." *The Diary of Lord Bertie of Thame*, edited by Lady Algernon Gordon Lennox (2 vols., London, 1924) provides an interesting source for the French attitude toward House and his missions. The French, Bertie implied throughout his diary, were bored.

IV. Autobiographies and Memoirs

Wilson on November 18, 1920, a year after his stroke wrote a publisher that he had no intention of writing memoirs. "I have always acquiesced in the joke that there are three kinds of personal memoirs—biographies, autobiographies, and ought-not-to-be biographies." Because he felt this way, some parts of diplomacy between Great Britain and the United States are still in the shadow. There are memoirs of Cabinet members, most of whom felt compelled to tell their story of the administration. Autobiographies of the two Secretaries of State, Bryan and Lansing (each eager to explain his attitude toward the European war), are helpful: *The Memoirs of William Jennings Bryan* (Philadelphia, 1925) partly edited by his wife, and *War Memoirs of Robert Lansing* (Indianapolis, 1935).

Two other autobiographies by Cabinet members have value: Daniel F. Houston, *Eight Years with Wilson's Cabinet* (2 vol., Garden City, N. Y., 1926), and Josephus Daniels, *The Wilson Era, Years of War and After: 1917-23* (Chapel Hill, N. C., 1946); Daniels wrote sensitively of the feud between Wilson and Lodge.

Mrs. Edith Bolling Wilson's *My Memoir* (Indianapolis, 1938) seems to verify Colonel House's statement to Seymour in that the second Mrs. Wilson made the President happy and looked after him but was bad for Wilson politically because she encouraged his less admirable political traits.

From the British side Sir Edward Grey's *Twenty-Five Years* 1892-1916 (2 vols., London, 1925) seems cautiously put together albeit lyrically expressed. Grey kept the description of diplomacy with the United States at a minimum, as he did his relation with House. He could, of course, write well about anything, even people he disliked. He did not appreciate Lloyd George but recognized in him such qualities as great energy and enthusiasm. Grey wrote that "the intensity of his activity foamed at the obstruction." Lloyd George wrote less kindly of Grey. In *War Memoirs of David Lloyd George* (2 vols., London, 1938) he deplored what he felt was Grey's timidity. His description of the Cabinet members meeting with House during the sketching out of the House-Grey Memorandum is interesting. Although Grey in his book did not mention the insertion of the word "probably" by the President, Lloyd George wrote about it and implied that House credited Wilson with greater readiness to participate in the war than he, Wilson, felt. In *Memoirs of the Peace Conference* (2 vols., New Haven, 1939) the Prime Minister revealed how well he understood Wilson in a few telling paragraphs about the reasons for failure of the Peace Treaty in the Senate.

V. Secondary works

House-Grey diplomacy was conducted in the parlors of their personalities; it was affected by the surroundings and by the unfolding of events. Secondary works touching these three aspects are so numerous that one cannot name them; an attempt has been made to list only those most helpful.

James Froude, the nineteenth-century historian, has suggested that it is useful "to look wherever we can through the eyes of contemporaries, from whom the future was concealed." Perhaps for this reason many articles and books about House and Grey written in the '20s and '30s still seem fresh and valuable. Two of House's biographers, A. D. H. Smith and George S. Viereck often visited the Colonel at his apartment in New York. One might almost say that House assisted them in their writing. Smith published *The Real Colonel House* (New York, 1918) and *Mr. House of Texas* (New York, 1940), both thorough accounts of the Colonel's background and association with Wilson. Viereck's biography of House, *The Strangest Friendship in History* (New York, 1932), is almost as strange as its title, attempting a psychological interpretation of House's relation with Wilson, and interspersing conversations by Viereck with House—many of them real, some perhaps imaginery; Viereck also wrote a series of articles about House which appeared in *Liberty* in 1932.

A biography of House by Rupert Norval Richardson, *Colonel Edward M. House: The Texas Years, 1858-1912* (Hardin-Simmons University 1964) focuses upon the Texas politics in which House engaged before turning his attention to the national scene. One of the most valuable chapters analyzes House's book *Philip Dru: Administrator;* Richardson points out that although the book seemed radical at that time advocating projected reform such as old age pensions, laborer's insurance and public employment agencies, it indicates that

House, for all of his political maneuvering, was idealistic at heart, and wanted the best for American society.

The most recent book about House is *Colonel House in Paris* by Ingo Floto, first published in Denmark in 1973, and reprinted again in 1980 (Princeton University Press, Princeton, New Jersey) as a supplementary volume to *The Papers of Woodrow Wilson*, Arthur S. Link, Editor. It is an excellent book about the Pre-Armistice Negotiations and the Paris Peace Conference in 1919 and it shows impeccable documentation for those singular proceedings.

Floto, in her introduction, examines the House-Wilson relationship, and makes comments on other studies about the two men; she feels Charles Seymour (House's biographer) has taken House too seriously and while she lauds the Georges' book as being "epoch making" she writes that "the two authors have . . . precluded themselves from gaining the full benefit of their own analysis" when they accept the theory of the gradual break between the two men.* Floto herself feels that House betrayed Wilson at the Conference and that their break came abruptly because of this.

Articles about House appeared between 1926 and 1928 after the Colonel had published his *Intimate Papers*. Two of them, by L. J. Maxse in the March and May issues of *National Review*, 1926, and one by Walter Lippman in Foreign Affairs, April, 1926, give fine interpretations of House's European missions. "The Personal Diplomacy of Colonel House" in American *Journal of International Law*, XXI (1927), 706-715, gives a competent summary of House's activities. A characterization of House following his death appeared in a New York *Times* editorial on March 19, 1938.

A recent article, "A Texan in London: A British Editor Lunches with Colonel Edward M. House, February 15, 1916, "edited by Lewis L. Gould in the *Southwest Historical Quarterly*, 1980-81, 84 (4), contains a memorandum written by John St. Loe Strachey (editor of *The Spectator*) who comments about House's thinking after his visit to Germany in early 1916. Strachey wrote after lunching with House that the Colonel was convinced, and wanted to convince the British, that the German's were getting ready for offensive *very soon indeed* (the emphasis is Strachey's). Significantly the House-Grey Memorandum followed.

---

*See comment on *Woodrow Wilson and Colonel House* by Alexander and Juliete George, in this bibliography. See also the Georges' reaction to another assessment of their book in "Woodrow Wilson and Colonel House: A Reply to Weinstein, Anderson and Link," *Political Science Quarterly*, Volume 96, Number 4, Winter, 1981-82, pp. 641-665.

Another article describing House's activities is "Arthur Bullard and the Creation of the Committee on Public Information," by Stephen Vaughn, *New Jersey History*, 1979, 97 (1). Bullard, an American author, had an extensive correspondence with Colonel House in the months just before the United States entered the war. He was intensely interested in awakening the American public to the critical issues of war. House had the same goal and often quoted Bullard to President Wilson. The source used for documentation by Vaughn is the Bullard Mss, Mudd Library, Princeton University.

In *The Historical Journal* printed in Great Britain, 21, 4 (1978) pp. 885-911, George W. Egerton has authored "Britain and the Great Betrayal: Anglo-American Relations and the Struggle for United States Ratification of the Treaty of Versailles, 1919-1920." Lord Grey's futile mission to the U. S. in 1919 is examined at length, revealing also the futility of House's position after the President's illness.

Appraisals of Grey are in three books published in England which give fascinating sketches of statesmen of that era: *Contemporary Personalities* written by one of those statesmen, The Earl of Birkenhead (London, 1924); *British Foreign Secretaries* by Algernon Cecil (London, 1927); and Herbert Sidebotham, *Pillars of the State* (London, 1921). Sketches in the latter appeared serially in the London *Times*.

Grey of Fallodon (Boston, 1937), the first complete story of Grey's life, can be read in conjunction with the author's autobiography, *G. M. Treveylan: An Autobiography and Other Essays* (London, 1949), in which Trevelyan states that his book about his Northumberland neighbor, Grey, was "a labour of love." Other biographies of Grey by contemporaries are the anonymous *Sir Edward Grey, K.G.;* Herman Lutz, *Lord Grey and The World War* (London, 1928); and Count Max Montgelas, *British Foreign Policy Under Sir Edward Grey* (New York, 1928).

The latest biography of Grey is *Sir Edward Grey: A Biography of Lord Grey of Fallodon* by Keith Robbins (Cassell and Company Ltd., London, 1971). The author states in the introduction that Grey had his critics who felt he would have done well "to stick to fishing and his ducks;" this is not Robbins' position, however, and he handles the details of Grey's life with dignity. There are no surprises here, but the book is useful simply because of the completeness of the details.

For a look at the times see Henry May, *The End of American Innocence* (New York, 1959). Barbara Tuchman gives a portrait of the world before the war in *The Proud Tower* (New York, 1966). Also of interest is Virginia Cowles, 1913, *An End and A Beginnng* (New York, 1967). For understanding of the bond between Britain and

America read Bradford Perkins, *The Great Rapprochment* (New York, 1968). The latter book emphasizes the "sub-structures" of diplomacy, intellectual ties of literature, Anglo-American social values, the more material bond of trade.

It is necessary to examine some of the Wilson literature. One might begin with Richard L. Watson, Jr., "Woodrow Wilson and his Interpreters, 1947-1957," *Mississippi Valley Historical Review,* XLIV (Sept. 1957), 207-236. Arthur S. Link's multivolume (currently five) work on Wilson is scholarly and impressive, with two volumes especially pertinent for this study—*The Struggle for Neutrality,* 1914-1915, (Princeton, 1960), and *Confusion and Crisis, 1915-1916* (Princeton, 1964). Also useful and authored by Link, are *Woodrow Wilson and the Progressive Era* (New York, 1954), *Wilson the Diplomatist* (Baltimore, 1957), and *The Higher Realism of Woodrow Wilson* (Vanderbilt University Press, Nashville, 1971).

After a look at the Link volumes one could benefit greatly from reading a fine study written by Alexander L. George and Juliette L. George, *Woodrow Wilson and Colonel House* (New York, 1956), a work which examines historical data in the light of psychoanalytic theory. The Georges do much to explain the friendship between the two men and to illustrate House's considerable influence on Wilson through domestic and foreign issues. A recent study *Woodrow Wilson: A Medical and Psychology Biography,* by Edwin Weinstein, published as another supplementary volume to the *Papers of Woodrow Wilson* (Princeton University Press, Princeton, New Jersey, 1981), examines Wilson's friendship with House and sees it as a psychological necessity for the President in his first year in office. Weinstein also gives a detailed account of Wilson's major illnesses, linking them to his ability to govern.

Another valuable study for those who are interested in the working relationship between House and Wilson is *The Department of State on The Eve of The First World War* by Rachel West (University of Georgia Press, Athens, 1978). In a chapter entitled "Supervisors: Wilson and House" the author shows how much Wilson depended on House for the day-to-day business of the State Department. West puts it: "Nearly every diplomatic aspirant came to House, either to seek preferment or to ask advice."

Most historians writing about Wilson's foreign policy accept House's position as quasi-secretary of state and include him in their accounts.

Arthur Walworth's *America's Moment: 1918: American Diplomacy at the End of World War I* (W. W. Norton & Co., New York, 1977) is and interesting volume which covers a year not examined in this study.

Walworth treats House with respect devoting two chapters to him showing his extensive preparation for the Paris Peace talks. Grey was not in office, and House-Grey diplomacy is outside the scope of the book.

Substantial studies of the Wilson diplomacy with assistance by House include Harley Notter, *The Origins of the Foreign Policy of Woodrow Wilson* (Baltimore, 1937), Charles Seymour, *American Diplomacy During the World War* (Baltimore, 1934), and Ernest R. May, *The World War and American Isolation,* 1914-1917 (Cambridge, Mass., 1595), the latter using Russian material. See also Charles Tansill, *America Goes to War* (Boston, 1938), a large volume which emphasizes the effectiveness of Grey's charm on American policy. Edwin Borchard and William Lage, *Neutrality for the United States* (New Haven, 1940), and Kent Forster, *The Failures of Peace* (Washington, D. C., 1941), give accounts of the House missions.

Two volumes presenting Wilson's foreign policy from a viewpoint of national security as well as idealism are Edward H. Buehrig, *Woodrow Wilson and the Balance of Power* (Bloomington, Indiana, 1955), and Robert E. Osgood, *Ideals and Self-Interest in America's Foreign Relations* (Chicago, 1953). Buehrig's interesting volume devotes more space to House's part in American diplomacy than does Osgood.

British diplomacy applicable to this study can be assessed through autobiographies of Grey and Lloyd George, already mentioned. For a comprehensive survey one could read William Strang, *Great Britain in World Affairs* (New York, 1961). Earlier information about Grey's diplomacy can be obtained from Robert Rhodes James, *Rosebery* (London, 1963). The latter was considered to be Grey's political godfather. Also Harold Nicholson's fine book about his father, *Sir Arthur Nicolson, Lord Carnock* (London, 1930), fills in the gaps about British prewar diplomacy.

A biography of the Secretary of the War Committee under Asquith, Lord Maurice Hankey, entitled *Hankey, Man of Secrets* by Stephen Roskill (Collins, St. James' Place, London, 1970) contains excerpts from Hankey's diary which heretofore had been considered too frank to be published. Hankey does write very plainly, often critically about British officials and what he perceived to be a lack of foresight in foreign affairs; his impressions of Colonel House's abilities revealed by the diary, are distinctly unfavorable.

More recent studies of British diplomacy: *British War Aims and Peace Diplomacy 1914-1918* by V. H. Rothwell (Clarendon Press, Oxford, 1971) reveals why the British thought the military defeat of Germany was justified, and how they went about making peace with her smaller allies. Rothwell says the two have to be studied together, and he does a fine job of describing all efforts made by the British to this end, including some military history of the war. The first chapter is of great importance in an examination of the House-Grey relationship; Rothwell is one of the very few authors who says that House was treated with dishonesty by the British in 1914-1916. Zara S. Steiner, a Fellow in Modern History at Cambridge, has provided a fine overview of British policy prior to the war in *Britain and the Origins of the First World War* (The MacMillan Press, London and Basingstoke, 1977). Steiner has focused on motivations and reasoning of men (she calls these "unspoken assumptions") responsible for the pre-1914 situations rather than diplomatic documents. She devotes a chapter to Wilson and House concluding that the two were amateurs in foreign affairs and intimating that Sir Edward knew this quite well but recognized the value to England of the Colonel's friendship.

For Anglo-American diplomacy in general H. C. Allen, *Great Britain and the United States* (New York, 1955) gives an adequate survey. Encounters between the two countries are described by William S. Coker, "The Panama Canal Tolls Controversy: a Different Perspective," *Journal of American History* (December, 1968); Richard W. Van Alstyne, "The Policy of the United States Regarding the Declaration of London at the Outbreak of the Great War," *Journal of Modern History*, VII (December, 1935); and Thomas A. Bailey, "The United States and the Blacklist during the Great War," *Journal of Modern History*, VI (March, 1934). Other works dealing with the relationship between the English-speaking nations are Ross Gregory, *Walter Hines Page* (Lexington, Kentucky, 1970); Sir Arthur Willert, *The Road to Safety: a Study in Anglo-American Relations* (London, 1952);and W. B. Fowler, *British-American Relations, 1917-1918* (Princeton, 1959). Sir Evelyn Wrench, *Struggle, 1914-1920* (London, 1935), describes private efforts in Britain to strengthen Anglo-American ties. Armin Rappaport, in *The British Press and Wilsonian Neutrality* (Stanford, 1951), gives the reaction of British publications to American foreign policy, and has commentary on problems between the two countries.

Sources on the Paris Peace Conference include Sir Harold Nicolson, *Peacemaking* (Boston, 1933), and Seth P. Tillman, *Anglo-American Relations at the Paris Peace Conference of 1919* (Princeton, 1961). Edward M. House and Charles Seymour, eds., *What Really Happened at Paris* (New York, 1921), should be read not only because it contains essays on problems at Paris, but because House wrote the preface and final essay "The Versailles Peace in Retrospect," and in both he gives generous appraisals of Wilson.

The treaty fight can be examined through the prejudiced eyes of Henry Cabot Lodge, *The Senate and the League of Nations* (New York and London, 1925). See also Thomas A. Bailey, *Woodrow Wilson and the Great Betrayal* (New York, 1945). Bailey says that he tries to describe "what went wrong"; almost everything did. Another useful account is Alan Cranston, *The Killing of the Peace* (New York, 1945), which covers much of the same material but is related chronologically and possibly easier to follow. Gene Smith gives a sentimental account of Wilson's last struggle in *When the Cheering Stopped* (New York, 1964). Surprisingly, he gives a full account of the Grey mission but scarcely mentions House in 261 pages. Daniel M. Smith's fine article, "Robert Lansing and the Wilson Interregnum, 1919-1920," The Historian, XXI (Autumn, 1959), shows the complex situation in Washington during the period of Wilson's illness.

Daniel Smith's book, *The Aftermath of the War: Bainbridge Colby Wilsonian Diplomacy, 1920-1921* (Philadelphia, 1970), could provide an epilogue to this study. Smith points out ironically that Wilson in the last months of his presidency advocated limited internationalism because of his bitter personal reaction to the attitude of the Senators toward the League and also because of a suspicion of French and British purposes. Colby, who succeeded Lansing as Secretary of State, demonstrated a flattering loyalty toward the President and may have assumed the role vacated involuntarily by Colonel House.

Index